THE LAWYERS

THE GARRICK COLLECTION

THE LAWYERS

Robert Low

To David

In admiration

with my best wishes

Robert Low

18·vi·12

THE GARRICK CLUB

LONDON

First published in 2011 by The Garrick Club
15 Garrick Street, London, WC2E 9AY
Tel: +44 (0)20 7836 1737/ Fax: +44 (0)20 7379 5966
e-mail: office@garrickclub.co.uk
Web: www.garrickclub.co.uk

A catalogue record for this book is available from the British Library.

ISBN: 978-0-95674-361-9

All images from Garrick Club / Art Archive
and are from works in the Garrick Club collections

The Garrick Club / The Art Archive have made every effort to trace the
copyright holders of all images reprinted in this book. Acknowledgement
is made in all cases where the image source is available, but we would be
grateful for information about any images where sources could not be traced.

Cover Image: *The Bench*, by William Hogarth 1758
Garrick Club / Art Archive

Typeset and design by Oberon Books London
Printed and bound by CPI Group (UK) Ltd, Croydon, CR0 4YY

Acknowledgements

I wish to thank Marcus Risdell, Curator of the Garrick Club, and Samantha Wyndham for their meticulous research into the club's history and membership, without which I could not have written this book. Marcus also carried out the picture and photographic research with his usual energy and enthusiasm. He is a great asset to the club. Marcus would like to thank all those who assisted him in gaining access to portraits from outside the Garrick's own collections. Much of my own research was conducted in the British Library and the London Library, the help of whose staff I gratefully acknowledge. I thank Anthony Butcher QC, Stanley Prothero, Lord Falconer, Roma Ferguson, Robert Marshall-Andrews QC, the Hon Louis Taylor, Roderick Young, Brian Masters and Sir Alan Ward for their recollections. I owe a huge debt to Joshua Rozenberg, who read the entire manuscript and pointed out many errors and solecisms, and to Joseph Harper QC, who read the proofs. Any mistakes that remain are entirely my fault. I am very grateful to James Hogan and James Illman, of Oberon Books, for producing the book so efficiently. Above all, I must thank Dr Barry Turner, senior Trustee and former Chairman of the Garrick Club, Jonathan Acton Davis QC, the current Chairman, and Jonathan Holmes, Chairman of the House Committee, for proposing this book and nominating me to write it. I hope they and the members of the club enjoy the result.

Robert Low

CONTENTS

CONTENTS

INTRODUCTION

T he Garrick Club was founded in London in 1831 primarily to provide a place where actors would be welcome, which was not necessarily the case everywhere in that era. There they would be able to meet members of the world of arts and letters in congenial surroundings. It has fulfilled that role from its inception to the present day but it is equally well known as a club for lawyers as it is for the stage, the arts, letters and journalism.

Indeed, it was that way from the very beginning: nine of its 155 founding members were lawyers and a further nine lawyers were elected in its first year of existence. This should not be seen as surprising, for the worlds of the law and the arts are instinctively attracted to each other, as are the law and the press. Some of our most distinguished lawyers over the past century and a half have been actors at heart. It has been said of not a few barristers who were fine courtroom performers that they were actors *manqués*, and it is as true today as ever. Actors can appreciate this quality in lawyers, who usually have a good story to tell over dinner about their latest case, and I have often witnessed a polished barrister or judge performing at the Garrick members' table to an enthralled audience of journalists, writers, doctors—and actors. Memoirs written by nineteenth-century Garrick members describe the same thing.

What distinguishes lawyers from actors is that their dramas are based on real life: they may consist of civil cases involving the rich and famous with huge sums of money at stake, or reputations in the case of libel actions, or the most notorious criminal cases, commanding daily headlines in the popular (and serious) newspapers. The barristers who joust against each other in court and the judges who preside over their tournaments often go on to the Garrick in the evening to wind down, and those involved in celebrated cases are likely to be the centre of attention in the bar or at dinner. While a case is going on, they are usually the soul of discretion, although "Garrick rules"—which forbid members from divulging confidential information they have heard at the club to non-members off the premises—do in theory protect them. But once a case is finished, one may hear some fascinating insights from those most intimately involved.

Most journalists—who provide a sizeable and active proportion of the Garrick's members—have dealings with lawyers on a daily basis: they attend the High Court or criminal courts to report on cases being tried there, they talk to lawyers all the time on a confidential basis to be briefed on forthcoming cases or on their significance, they call lawyers to ask them to explain new laws, and of course they are in constant discussion with lawyers working for their own newspaper or magazine on matters of libel and privilege. Lawyers in turn are often fascinated by what they perceive as the more carefree worlds of entertainment, the arts and journalism and can even seem envious of their practitioners' less structured lifestyles, though probably not of their incomes. In looking into the lives of the Garrick's first lawyer members, it is interesting to see how many of them moved easily through the artistic and cultural world of nineteenth-century London, numbering the great writers and actors of the age as their personal friends and indeed often writing plays, novels and lengthy magazine and newspaper articles in addition to their legal practice. This custom of having a foot in each camp, so to speak, has virtually disappeared in the twenty-first century: the late John Mortimer, a much-loved member of the Garrick, was probably the last of the line, and more's the pity.

Some of the Garrick's lawyer members can appear sensitive to the fact that they are not involved in the worlds of the stage, the arts, letters or journalism, and fear that they will appear dull to the rest of the membership, whom they, probably wrongly, see as having more flamboyant and interesting lives. I have lost count of the times I have been introduced to a fellow member previously unknown to me and when I have asked him what he does for a living, he has replied, "I'm another lawyer, I'm afraid." He then turns out to be the Master of the Rolls or the country's leading criminal silk. You never hear an actor describe himself with such diffidence.

This book can only offer a selection of the Garrick's lawyer members since 1831 and with such an extraordinary range of men to choose from I know I will not please everyone. I hope to provide an informal guide to the development of the law since the middle of the nineteenth century through the stories of some of its most distinguished practitioners, and a series of portraits of men with a couple of things in common over the past one hundred and eighty years: a love both of the law and the Garrick Club.

1
THE ORIGINALS

The Garrick's lawyers come in all shapes and sizes: some are indeed quiet, retiring, even shy types, but then so are lots of journalists and writers. Others are eminent in their branch of the law but not particularly interested or involved in the cultural life of the nation (beyond going to the opera, as most of them seem to). Many are however keenly interested in culture and the arts, and often active in artistic charities. Others are involved in politics in one way or another. Interestingly, it has always been thus. Of the nine lawyers on the list of original members in 1831, four have left little or no trace: George Steer, Lewis A. Lowdham, solicitor, George Raymond, barrister, and another solicitor, George Bedford, who was a member for only two years. Of the remaining five, two were distinguished barristers and judges who largely confined themselves to the law: Sir Joseph Littledale (1767-1842) and Sir James Wigram (1793-1866). The other three, John Adolphus (1768-1845), Sir Thomas Noon Talfourd (1795-1854) and Edmund Phipps (1808-1857) achieved various degrees of distinction not only in the law but in the wider world of history and letters.

Sir Joseph Littledale (Garrick member 1831-1834) was born into a wealthy Cumberland family and was a star student at St John's College, Cambridge, a senior wrangler and Smith's prizeman. He entered Gray's Inn and was called to the bar in 1798, having previously practised as a special pleader, that is, a specialist in drafting pleadings, which were the way in which lawyers formulated their clients' case, and were often extremely complicated. He joined the northern circuit and in 1813 was appointed counsel to his old university. In 1824, he was elevated to a judgeship in the court of the King's Bench, something of a surprise promotion as he was not even a KC. The then Court of King's Bench (four judges including Littledale) was described as "one of the strongest ever constituted"; Lord Campbell, the Lord Chief Justice, described it as "the golden age of justice", and characterised Littledale as "one of the most acute, learned and simple-minded of men." He lived in Bedford Square where he died in 1842, leaving £250,000, a huge sum in today's money. He was something of a literary scholar: he edited the rackety Tudor court poet John Skelton's poem *Magnyfynce, an Interlude* for the Roxburghe Club in 1821. "He enjoyed the entire respect of the profession," his obituary in *The Times* respectfully noted. "An upright, laborious and impartial judge, he possesed the confidence of his brethren and the public; an amiable and kindhearted man, he was beloved by all who knew him, at the bar, on the bench, or in his private circle."

Sir James Wigram (Garrick 1831-1832), third son of Sir Robert Wigram Bt, was also a brilliant Cambridge scholar, graduating from Trinity College as fifth wrangler in 1815 and being awarded a fellowship of the college. He was called to the bar at Lincoln's Inn in 1819 and embarked on a successful career as a chancery lawyer. He became KC in

1834 and a bencher of Lincoln's Inn the following year. His sole excursion outside the law was to stand for Leominster in Herefordshire as a Tory in 1837, without success. He was however elected unopposed in 1841 but had no opportunity to distinguish himself in the Commons as he was raised to the bench a few months later as a second vice-chancellor. But he lost his sight and was obliged to retire in 1850 at the age of 57 on a pension of £3,500 a year.

Edmund Phipps was the third son of Henry Phipps, first Earl of Mulgrave, a soldier and diplomat who became William Pitt's Foreign Secretary in 1804, was subsequently First Lord of the Admiralty, and was a thoroughgoing old reactionary who opposed the abolition of slavery and the "abominable doctrines of equality associated with the French Revolution". Edmund Phipps graduated from Trinity College, Oxford, and was called to the bar at the Inner Temple. He practised on the northern circuit, and was Recorder of first Scarborough, then Doncaster. But he had many wider interests beyond the law: he wrote several works of fiction and non-fiction, and pamphlets on economic and currency matters. He was obviously both learned and imaginative. One pamphlet, in defence of the economic importance of the then nascent railways, was entitled *Adventures of a £1,000 Note; or Railway Ruin reviewed*, while he also rendered into English blank verse, via German translations, a Danish poem *King René's Daughter* by Henrik Hertz, which sounds tough going. He died prematurely at the age of 48 at his house in Wilton Crescent.

Reviewing the lives of educated men of the era, one is constantly struck by the range of their interests and the energy with which they approached them. Sir Thomas Noon Talfourd (Garrick 1831-1854), son of a Reading brewer, was not only a successful barrister and then a respected judge, but also a prolific author and lover of the theatre who wrote a number of dramatic works that were produced on the London stage. He numbered among his friends the leading artistic and literary figures of the 1830s and '40s. He hosted a notable salon, as a memoir published in 1854 just after his death made clear:

> Actors of merit were always welcomed to his friendship, and received manifold proofs of his estimation of their art. [William] Macready was among his most intimate friends; and actors of far less note were admitted to the lavish hospitalities of his house. Nor was his love of artists confined to those on the stage. His soirées were celebrated for the assemblage of men and women of eminence in every walk of letters and the fine arts; they were to the last, mélanges of celebrities: – Painters, poets, orators, lawyers, players, novelists, historians, sculptors, editors, and miscellaneous lions of every caste and class, met in the convivial musters which he so dearly loved to gather round him. And never was there a man better fitted to infuse into his motley and loving guests the social and mirthful spirit which glowed in his own kindly heart, and lit up all around him.

It is easy to see why he would have been a popular figure at the Garrick, of which he was a Trustee.

As well as developing a successful career at the bar, Talfourd wrote learned articles for legal journals, laboured at lengthy poetic dramas and poured out a stream of essays on a wide variety of topics for such periodicals as the *New Monthly Magazine* and the *London Magazine*. His pen took in anything from British novels to Fanny Kemble to accounts of his holidays. If he had lived today, he would have been snapped up by the *Daily Mail* for he could clearly turn his hand to anything.

But he was not content with mere journalistic trifles. His poetic tragedy *Ion* was produced at Covent Garden in 1835. On the first night, Talfourd's fellow lawyers turned out in force to support him, and gave him a rousing ovation as he came forward rather hesitantly to the front of his box. Two more verse dramas followed, *The Athenian Captive* and *Glencoe*, both written for Talfourd's colourful friend Macready, then one of London's leading actors, and produced by him at the Haymarket theatre.

Indeed, it is hard to escape the conclusion that Talfourd might have made a better actor than advocate. His anonymous memoirist, who clearly knew him well, wrote:

> It is sufficiently obvious that Talfourd pursued his profession from no natural love for its avocations, or from any notion that it could afford him a fitting means of gratifying the aspirations of his soul, or giving scope to the exercise and of the high and peculiar powers of his mind. It is no derogation of the man to affirm *that it never did so* [original italics]. The whole calibre of his moral being was ill attuned for the work. A few great occasions were presented – ten or a dozen in his lifetime – when the bar gave full scope to his genius, and into which his whole soul could rise.

Talfourd was "a sound rather than a first-rate lawyer" who worked diligently to establish a decent practice on the Oxford circuit. Where he excelled was in courtroom oratory. "His eloquence was innate," his obituarist recorded. "He spoke from the heart and he had no ordinary command of language... As an advocate at the bar his powers were far more suited to appeals on behalf of noble impulses and great principles than to the ordinary duties of advocacy." He was not interested in, or very good at, pleading cases which involved "the disentanglement and lucid statement of involved and complicated matters of fact, in which no principle was concerned". But given a cause he could believe in, "he got good verdicts from the densest jurymen", much as an actor can get a round of applause from the most ignorant audience. He wasn't very good at cross-examination but "wherever justice was in peril from force, falsehood, or intrigue ... the fervour of his soul found utterance, and his great heart spoke out in the glowing words in which his rich imagination so gorgeously clothed his thoughts. A more impassioned or a more impressive speaker, on these occasions, rarely moved an English audience with such effect."

He could get carried away in the most minor cases. Defending a client at Hereford who was being sued for libel for rashly (and mistakenly) accusing a man of cruelty to a horse, he ended up eloquently denouncing slavery and was allowed to get away with digressing so widely from the core of the case by a benevolent judge who clearly enjoyed his speech. Defending a Mr Tait, from Edinburgh, on another charge of libel, Talfourd embarked on "one of the most powerful diatribes ever heard at the bar", culminating in such a rousing climax that it drew a roar of approval from the public gallery in which some of the jurymen joined. The plaintiff slunk away from the court, a beaten man.

Talfourd was not merely interested in the law and the theatre. He stood for Parliament in his home town of Reading in 1835 in the first general election since the Great Reform Act of 1832 and came top of the poll. He found a new audience for his oratory in the House of

Commons but already his rhetorical style was looking a little old-fashioned. However, before long he had piloted a Copyright Bill through the House which extended the protection given to authors, with the ringing declaration, "The community have no right to be enriched at the expense of individuals, nor is the liberty of the press … the liberty to smuggle and to steal," words which still ring true today. He lost his seat in 1841 but was re-elected in 1847. Two years later, in his last speech to Parliament before he became a judge and therefore had to resign his seat, he stood up for the right of Jewish MPs to swear the oath of allegiance on the Old Testament rather than the New.

He did not distinguish himself as a judge, although he was much liked by all concerned for his courteous behaviour. "To say that Mr Justice Talfourd was a first-rate judge, or a first-rate lawyer, would be an error," wrote his memoirist. "But persevering labour, and perfect love of justice and great practice, made him more than respectable in both vocations."

Unlike many early members of the Garrick, Talfourd was no political radical. But he was acutely conscious of the class divisions that afflicted British society as he made clear in his last speech from the bench, at Stafford in 1854. He sought explanations for a steep rise in crime in terms which seem equally valid today, musing on the paradox that increasing prosperity had led to increased criminal activity, while education standards had also improved. He went on: "I cannot help thinking that it [the rise in crime] may, in no small degree, be attributed to that separation between class and class which is the great curse of British society, and for which we all, in our respective spheres, are in some degree, more or less, responsible." A few seconds later, Mr Justice Talfourd slumped forward and died. It was thought to be the first time a judge had passed away on the bench, and constituted a suitably dramatic ending to the life of a man who loved the theatre above all things.

The final notable member of the Garrick's original lawyer members was another man whose vigour and range of interests can leave the modern observer feeling rather breathless. John Adolphus (Garrick 1831-1834) was of German Jewish extraction, and was sent away to the West Indian island of St Kitts at the age of fifteen to work in a wealthy uncle's agent's office. He spent a year there, most of it attending the island's only court, which may have sparked an interest in the law. His other great love was history, in which he seems to have been largely self-taught. Returning to London, he was admitted as an attorney in 1790 but soon quit the law for the life of a writer and historian. After writing a couple of hack works, he published in 1802 the work which made his name, *The History of England from the Accession of George III to the Conclusion of Peace in 1783*, which was admired by the monarch himself. It also brought Adolphus to the attention of the Prime Minister, Henry Addington, who employed him as a sort of early spin-doctor, writing pamphlets and electioneering for him. A history of modern France followed but meanwhile Adolphus had taken up the law again, being called to the bar at the Inner Temple in 1807. His practice was almost exclusively criminal and he eventually rose to be the leading counsel at the Old Bailey, taking a leading role in such celebrated trials as that of the Cato Street conspirators.

Adolphus was clearly a brilliant but prickly man. The lawyer Mr Serjeant Benjamin Robinson wrote in his memoirs: "Adolphus was a very clever and astute old man, but somewhat sour and crabbed in his manner." Robinson ascribed his bitterness in old age to a feeling that he had been "shouldered out of a lucrative practice by younger men", in particular one Charles Phillips whom Adolphus was heard to describe as "that Irish blackguard, with his plausible brogue and slimy manner".

His feud with Phillips was confirmed by William Ballantine, another notable Garrick lawyer, whose own rich life is detailed in the next chapter. He recorded: "I remember on one occasion, in the robing room, when poor Adolphus in a state of irritation, and when his business had nearly all fallen into the hands of Phillips, said to that gentleman, 'You remind me of three B's – Blarney, Bully, and Bluster'; 'Ah!' said Phillips, 'you never complained of my B's until they began to suck your honey.'"

In his notorious collection of pen portraits of Garrick members, the Rev R.H. Barham wrote of Adolphus: "He was a man full of anecdote, but occasionally very rude, which made him, although a very eloquent, also a very unpopular member of the bar, and unquestionably prevented his rising to the highest rank in his profession."

Adolphus's temper was fiery enough to provoke him into fighting a famous duel with a leading criminal lawyer at the Old Bailey, Peter Alley, another Irishman who was something of a rough diamond. Both men are described in Ballantine's memoirs, an invaluable record of a lawyer's life in the early nineteenth century which also provides fascinating insights into the characters of many of his most distinguished contemporaries and Garrick friends. He relates how Alley and Adolphus "had numerous quarrels", one of which ended in a duel on Calais Sands, presumably because duelling had by then been outlawed in Britain. As Ballantine tells it, after one of their rows Adolphus sent a highly insulting letter to Alley at his home. The matter might have ended there had not Alley left the open letter on a table where his wife, a feisty Irishwoman, read it and insisted that her husband could not let the matter rest there. So instead of settling the affair over a drink at the Garrick, the pair decamped to France with their pistols. The result was that one of them (Ballantine does not say who) had part of his ear shot off. "They were both very proud of the exploit," wrote Ballantine, "and, with a few growls, remained afterwards tolerable friends."

Ballantine's considered judgment of Adolphus was as follows: "He was nearly a great man, and but for an unfortunate temper would probably have risen to the highest honours of the profession. He was a lucid and impressive speaker, and possessed a singularly logical mind."

Adolphus's sharp tongue spared no one, not even the most august of the judges before whom he appeared, which was probably another reason he did not rise further. In a civil case in which Adolphus was appearing, Mr Justice Tenterden, Chief Justice of the King's Bench – "a morose judge", according to Ballantine – remarked sourly, "Mr Adolphus, we are not at the Old Bailey."

"No," retorted Adolphus, "for there the judge presides and not the counsel."

Ballantine went on to say that he only knew Adolphus towards the end of his life when "it was sad to witnesss the wreck he had become; sad to think of a life so wasted, of great abilities so cast away." But Adolphus did not vent his temper on his juniors: "To them he was unvaryingly considerate and kind."

What Ballantine did not perhaps take into account was how much Adolphus might have been affected by his awareness of prejudice against him because he was a Jew, although he was apparently not very devout. He was much praised for his performance in the trial of the Cato Street conspirators in 1820. But when the following year he defended the Life Guard officers charged with killing two men in a riot during Queen Caroline's funeral, a caricaturist portrayed him carrying a brief saying "Jew v. Jury".

Adolphus carried on writing, producing in 1818 a four-volume study of the British Empire. However, like Talfourd, his range was wide: he also wrote the memoirs of a comedian friend, John Banister, as well as revising and updating his book on George III, which went into several editions. He was working on the eighth volume when he died at the age of 77.

To this day, Garrick members have cause to be grateful to Adolphus, for it is thanks to him that the club's splendid library came into being. As Barham related: "I first became acquainted with Mr Adolphus at the Literary Fund Club, where he afterwards dined as a visitor and was elected a member on my nomination, but owing to ill-health he withdrew the following year; the same cause prevented his coming much to the Garrick, in the formation of which, however, he took a part, and originated the library, by proposing that every member should be requested to give his duplicate dramatic books."

Of the other nine lawyers elected to the Garrick in its inaugural year, few left much of a mark. Sir William Goodenough Hayter QC MP (1792-1878) was more of a politician than a lawyer. But the extraordinary life of Robert Cutlar Fergusson (1768-1838) more than makes up for the obscurity of his Garrick contemporaries. He was a Scotsman and a radical who even before he headed for London to study law at Lincoln's Inn had already published a tract urging a widening of the franchise in Scotland. Called to the bar in 1797, he was within a year involved in a controversial and dramatic trial that would end with him, one of the defence counsel, imprisoned for a year.

It was because he was regarded as a reformer that he was retained as defence counsel for a personal friend, James Allen, who was one of four United Irishmen charged with high treason in 1798, the year of the Irish uprising led by Wolfe Tone. The men, headed by the leading Irish radical Arthur O'Connor, were accused of planning to sail to France from Kent bearing a letter from the United Irishmen asking the French revolutionary government to invade Britain in support of the Irish cause. In the febrile atmosphere of the period, the case, heard over two days in May at Maidstone, attracted enormous publicity and many of the leading Whigs of the day, including Charles James Fox, Lord John Russell, the Duke of Norfolk and Richard Brinsley Sheridan, the playwright, appeared as character witnesses on behalf of O'Connor. Allen and O'Connor were found not guilty by the jury, who however convicted another defendant, James O'Coigly, a 36-year-old Catholic priest better known in his native Ireland as Father Quigley. They returned their verdict at 1.25 a.m. However, Bow Street Runners arrived with a warrant for the rearrest of O'Connor on another charge of high treason should he be acquitted, as he was. After O'Coigly had been sentenced to death, and before O'Connor had been officially freed, O'Connor made a run for it. Chaos ensued, with O'Connor's friends trying to protect him from the Runners and aid his escape. In this they were eventually unsuccessful. The upshot was that Fergusson was arrested, among others who included the Earl of Thanet, charged with his alleged part in the affray and rescue attempt, and tried before the King's Bench. Although the evidence against him was said to be weak, he was found guilty and sentenced to a year's imprisonment, plus a £100 fine. (Poor O'Coigly was hanged in June, although the evidence against him was slim indeed. He protested his innocence to the last and his speech from the scaffold moved many in the large crowd to applaud.)

Fergusson's detention was a severe blow for a rising young barrister but he was a determined young man. Perhaps realising that with that sort of stain on his character he would stand little chance of progressing at the English bar, he left Britain for India and set up as a barrister in Calcutta, where presumably his setback would not be held against him. He eventually became standing counsel to the government and then king's advocate. After an exile of twenty years he returned to Britain a wealthy man and was elected as MP in the Liberal interest for Kircudbright in his native Scotland. He remained a notable proponent of radical causes, but this did not hinder his elevation to the office of judge advocate-general in 1834, three years after he was elected to the Garrick. He was also sworn of the Privy Council, which must have given particular satisfaction to the former guest of His Majesty.

At the age of 64 he married a French lady, who bore him two children, and he died in Paris in 1838.

2

WILLIAM BALLANTINE,
A NINETEENTH-CENTURY RUMPOLE.

A vivid portrait of legal life in the mid-nineteenth century and also of the Garrick Club at that time is painted by William Ballantine (1812-87, Garrick 1850-81), a successful barrister who was well connected in literary and artistic circles: largely through the Garrick, he was a friend or acquaintance of Dickens, Thackeray, Trollope, Bulwer-Lytton, Charles Reade and many other leading literary and theatrical figures of the age. He himself was also quite a character, whom John Mortimer likened to the Rumpole of his era, and who is said to be the model for the colourful barrister Mr Chaffanbrass in *Orley Farm* by Anthony Trollope, a fellow member of the Garrick Club. Trollope's initial description of Chaffanbrass is not at all flattering: "an elderly man, small, with sharp eyes and bushy eyebrows, dirty in his attire and poor in his general appearance...This was Mr Chaffanbrass, great at the Old Bailey, a man well able to hold his own in spite of the meanness of his appearance." Later on in the novel, Trollope expands on the lawyer's abilities:

> All the world knows Mr Chaffanbrass—either by sight or by reputation. Those who have been happy enough to see the face and gait of the man as, in years now gone, he used to lord it at the Old Bailey, may not have thought much of

the privilege which was theirs. But to those who have only read of him, and know his deeds simply by their triumphs, he was a man very famous and worthy to be seen. "Look; that's Chaffanbrass. It was he who cross-examined—at the Old Bailey, and sent him howling out of London, banished for ever into the wilderness." "Where, where? Is that Chaffanbrass? What a dirty little man!"

In 1856 Ballantine became a Serjeant-at-Law, a proud title borne by an elite group of barristers who for centuries had the exclusive right to appear as advocates in the Court of Common Pleas. Since the sixteenth century their primacy had been at first challenged and then overtaken by King's and Queen's Counsel, and by Ballantine's era the rank had almost run its course. No more were created after the Judicature Act of 1873 but Ballantine and his fellow Serjeants held jealously to the title: the author's name on Ballantine's memoirs, for instance, is Mr Serjeant Ballantine.

His fellow Garrick member Sir Edward Clarke, who was frequently Ballantine's junior before he rose to similar eminence himself, described him thus:

> William Ballantine, "the Serjeant," was a man of remarkable power. Rather over middle height, lean and hard, with the eye of a hawk. A voice capable of many tones, but with a curious drawl, half infirmity and half affectation. A man of slight legal knowledge, of idle and leisure-loving habits, but an advocate of quite extraordinary skill. He could rise to great eloquence, but his great power was in his cross-examination, which was the most subtle and deadly that I ever heard. There was a great fascination about him; whenever he was in Court he was the most conspicuous person there, and seemed by instinct to lead or coerce or dominate judge and witness and jury. His temper was violent, his humour bitter and sarcastic, but he was the

most generous of leaders. Once at Kingston, before Sir Alexander Cockburn, in a South Eastern Railway case which he had not read I was rather importunate in my questions, and he turned on me in Court with "Damn you, sir, am I conducting this case or are you?" But before the trial was over he explained to the Jury that I had been right, and had only been reminding him of facts which he ought to have known...I have often heard him when quoting cases mention his junior's name, and say he was indebted to his diligence.

One of his most regular juniors also joined him in the Garrick: Montagu Williams, who left a vivid portrait of him in his own memoirs:

> The Serjeant was a very extraordinary man. He was the best cross-examiner of his kind that I have ever heard, and the quickest at swallowing facts. It was not necessary for him to read his brief: he had a marvellous facility for picking up a case as it went along, or learning all the essentials in a hurried colloquy with his junior. There is no point that the Serjeant might not have attained in his profession, had he only possessed more ballast. He was, however, utterly reckless, generous to a fault, and heedless of the future. His opinion of men could never be relied upon, for he praised or blamed them from day to day, just as they happened to please or annoy him. He often said bitter things, but never, I think, ill-naturedly. His fault was probably that he did not give himself time to think before he spoke.

> Ballantine's manner of addressing a jury was somewhat drawling and hesitating. Nevertheless it was a manner that possessed a considerable charm, and he had a way of introducing jokes and anecdotes into his speech that was very effective. He was a great verdict-getter, sometimes being successful in the most desperate cases. He never funked what we lawyers call a "dead" case, and was always cheery and bright.

Ballantine recorded his memories in his book *Some Experiences of a Barrister's Life*, which was first published in 1882 and was popular enough to have gone into several further editions. It is a chaotic jumble of a book, for Ballantine admitted that he was thoroughly disorganised, but it still contains some marvellous vignettes of his life, both legal and social, and some penetrating observations about the law.

Ballantine was a great clubman, being a member of the Reform, the Clarence and the Union Club as well as the Garrick, to which he devotes a chapter in his book; he described it as "a labour of love". He wrote of the club when it occupied its first premises, "a small unpretending-looking house in King Street, Covent Garden". It is a valuable insight into what the club was like in the first thirty years of its life, before it moved to the much grander, purpose-built building in Garrick Street which it occupies to the present day. Despite its modest first premises, wrote Ballantine, "there was, however, no resort in London that could boast of attracting so much of brilliancy and wit".

> Named after Garrick, it was naturally sought by actors, poets, artists, and novelists, and members of the graver professions were only too glad to relieve the labours of the day by the society of all that was distinguished in literature and art.

He writes of the club's first years, before he was a member, and in doing so illustrates how the reputations of the most celebrated figures of a particular era do not necessarily stand the test of time:

> Although I joined it early in my career, I was not an original member, and missed those convivial meetings that I have heard described, in which Theodore Hook, Barham,

and the brothers [Albert and Arthur] Smith, shone and sparkled with so brilliant a light; and when the memory dwells upon "Gilbert Gurney," the "Ingoldsby Legends," and "Rejected Addresses" [by the Smiths], I can imagine at times, when their authors met in the social smoking-room, there must have been an absolute surfeit of fun.

The next generation of Garrick writers have lasted rather better.

Although a new generation had sprung up when I joined the club, it was by no means an undistinguished one. Dickens and Thackeray had made their marks, and they were broad and lasting ones...

Of the Garrick's two finest artists of that time, Clarkson Stanfield, an original member, and his great friend David Roberts, elected in 1835, Ballantine recorded:

Stanfield and David Roberts were noble representatives of art. The former, the great painter of ocean beauty and grandeur, was not often at the club, and I can scarcely recall his appearance. But David was there constantly, when his kindly, good-humoured face, reminding me of a country farmer upon market day, would often expand itself at our pleasant gatherings. I do not think that a greater favourite existed in the club.

Both artists' presences live on at the club. Roberts's magnificent painting *Remains of the Temple of the Sun at Baalbec* (1846/7) occupies most of one wall in the Irving Room, while Stanfield's *A Dutch Blazer Coming Out of Monnickendam, Zuyder Zee* (1856), hangs in the Milne Room.

Some things never change in clubland. Ballantine often saw the actor Charles Kemble at the Garrick but he was only a shadow of the man who had once been the toast of the London stage.

He was then the embodiment of life, but the light of those days had departed, he had become very deaf, and, like many people suffering from that infirmity, used every endeavour to make himself heard. This was impossible, but others were fully informed of his thoughts; and as these were far from complimentary to the hearer, his presence latterly in the club was looked upon with some apprehension.

Another great actor and Garrick member, Charles Kean, "was the most sensitive man I ever knew in my life", wrote Ballantine. He witnessed an example of this in the club's coffee room.

A great feud existed between him and Albert Smith. The original cause I forget, but he had offended Albert, who put into some penny paper that a patient audience had endured the infliction of Charles Kean in *Hamlet* in the expectation of seeing the Keeleys in the after-piece. One night I and a member named Arabin ... were talking with Albert Smith in the coffee-room. At the opposite side stood Charles Kean, scowling. Presently Albert departed. In about three strides Charles Kean reached us. "Richard," he said in the most tragic of voices, "I never thought that you, my old school-fellow, would have consorted with that viper." Poor good-natured Dick had heard nothing of the quarrel.

There was, said Ballantine, "one celebrity, by no means the least valued or appreciated", the steward of the club, Mr Hamblet.

He was its dictator, and reigned supreme. The sense of his position sat in placid dignity upon his countenance, as he moved about extending an occasional recognition to a favourite member. Sometimes, if he discovered any breach of the rules, a single frown upon his face made the culprit shrink abashed. For many years he ruled, and there were no rebels to his authority; but at last he also yielded to the decrees of fate, and his like will ne'er be seen again.

Ballantine had mixed feelings about the Garrick's fine new premises. "Some of its rooms are very good, the drawing-room and smoking-room particularly so…I doubt, however, whether the club is so cosy as it was."

He had decidedly mixed feelings too about some of his more celebrated Garrick acquaintances. He first met Thackeray at the Shakespeare Club, which met every evening at the Piazza tavern in the Covent Garden colonnade.

> I never thought him an agreeable companion. He was very egotistical, greedy of flattery, and sensitive of criticism to a ridiculous extent. He may have possessed great powers of conversation, but did not exhibit them upon the occasions when I had an opportunity of judging.

Ballantine was no fan of Thackeray's work either, apart from his lighter journalism, and deplored his habit of basing characters in his novels on people he knew personally, including fellow Garrick members. It is a very lawyerly attitude to fiction.

> He did not hesitate to introduce his associates and the members of his club into his novels, and one of these latter, a curious compound of drollery and simplicity, named Archdeckne, figures in *Pendennis*, under the name of 'Foker'.

But Ballantine adds a footnote:

> I am told that this gentleman was by no means offended by the celebrity he obtained through figuring in Thackeray's novel.

If Archdeckne really was anything like Foker, this would be entirely plausible. In *Pendennis*, Foker is an amiable, wealthy and rather ludicrous young fop, with no illusions about his intellectual ability – "I was always a stupid chap,

I was…I'm not good at the books" – a school friend of Arthur Pendennis who leads him into mischief when they chance to meet again as young men.

For all his dislike of Thackeray, Ballantine was anxious to be seen as fair towards him.

> I ought to mention…that he suffered from a most painful and irritating disease, and also that among those who knew him well and to whom he extended his confidence and friendship, he was most enthusiastically beloved.

For Dickens, however, Ballantine had nothing but praise.

> I was very much attached to Charles Dickens; there was a brightness and geniality about him that greatly fascinated his companions. His laugh was so cheery, and he seemed so thoroughly to enter into the feelings of those around him. He told a story well and never prosily; he was a capital listener, and in conversation was not in the slightest degree dictatorial…No man possessed more sincere friends, or deserved them better. He was the best after-dinner speaker I ever heard.

Of Trollope, he wrote:

> His appearance…presented the idea of a gentleman from the country, his manner was energetic, and he was a vehement politician. He was fond of hunting, and indulged in some ideas on the subject which certainly would not have been participated in by the objects of his sport. He declared that the fox ought to be deeply obliged to the sportsman, as through his instrumentality it led a comfortable life during a great portion of the year, living in luxury upon the poultry of the surrounding farmers.

The author Charles Reade "also was a man well worthy of remembrance". Ballantine, who had advised him on his will, applauded "his chivalrous advocacy of those he deemed to be oppressed and persecuted."

Ballantine recorded in 1884 that the last time he had seen Trollope and Reade was three or four years previously at the Garrick when "they, the late Marquis of Anglesey, and myself made up a party of cribbage. It is a melancholy thought that I alone of the party am left to record the fact."

Ballantine's own life was rich in incident, many of them worthy of a Dickens novel. His rambling memoir does not shy away from criticism of the state of the legal system when he first entered it. It was manifestly inefficient, slow and out of date, and many of its practitioners were lazy, stupid or plain corrupt. It all amounted to a system in which injustice could and did flourish. Ballantine loved the law and all its traditions but recognised its inadequacies. Half a century later, he would write: "The present generation would scarcely credit the amount of villainy, fraud and oppression which ... flourished under its [the law's] auspices. The gaols filled with victims, officers of the sheriffs robbing both creditors and debtors; small courts, the offices of which were put up for sale, and the costs incurred by the suitors brought ruin to both parties... Immense taxes were imposed upon legal proceedings by numerous sinecure offices paid out of suitors' pockets." It is a world that readers of Dickens, in particular, but also of Trollope and Thackeray will readily recognise.

Ballantine was born in Howland Street, off Tottenham Court Road, the son of a barrister, and sent to St Paul's School, then situated in the cathedral yard, and by Ballantine's account a nest of ignorant, tyrannical teachers and stupid, bullying boys. He loathed it and was delighted to be removed first to a school in Blackheath, then Hampstead, where his family had moved. On leaving school, he followed in his father's footsteps and studied law at the Inner Temple, in the chambers of William Watson. The study of law was neither organised nor arduous:

> I have little to record of the two years I passed in these chambers amongst a mass of papers, copying precedents of pleading which were a disgrace to common sense, and in gossip with my brother students, most of them as idle as myself.

Having been called to the bar, he started professional life in "grimy old buildings" at 5 Inner Temple Lane— "the same lane in which Dr Johnson had flourished". As he wryly put it, "Dirt seemed at that time an attribute of the law." For the first three years of his legal career, he earned very little, scratching meagre fees for a variety of mundane jobs, such as poor-law appeals and licensing applications, and supplementing his meagre income with occasional forays into the gambling dens that then flourished in central London.

He practised first at the Middlesex Sessions, then the Central Criminal Court and went on the Home Circuit, getting a lucky break when he was granted a revising barristership, reviewing the lists of parliamentary voters. A reviewing vacancy having arisen, Ballantine applied but another man was appointed. However, he had recently made a successful appearance before the Lord Chief Justice, Lord Denman, and his client was acquitted. Denman knew how much he wanted (and needed) the job, so he summoned another revising barrister, Montague Chambers, and suggested that as he was now doing well at the bar he might see his way to relinquishing his revising post. Chambers immediately agreed (not that he had much choice when the LCJ wanted something) and Ballantine was appointed in his place, which provided him with a measure of financial security. Chambers went on to lead the Home Circuit and to become a friend of Ballantine at the Garrick where, as Ballantine put it, he was "not altogether unwilling to furnish his numerous friends with some of the anecdotes of his career".

Ballantine built up a rich and varied practice, prosecuting or defending in some of the biggest trials of the period, all the while maintaining a vigorous social life, though he had bittersweet memories too of the years of the Crimean War and of young military men he had known at the Garrick and other clubs "who soon afterwards found their graves in a foreign land". He had a low view of the police in the Regent Street and Piccadilly areas, then full of gambling dens and brothels, regarding many officers as corrupt and venal. One night in Piccadilly he saw a policeman wrestling with a drunken woman and remonstrated with him. The officer seized Ballantine by the collar and arrested him for obstruction. A second policeman arrived and grabbed the woman, upon which another passer-by, like Ballantine, took exception to the way the policeman was handling her. It turned out to be Sir Alexander (later Lord) Cockburn, the Attorney-General, returning home from the Commons. The first policeman then arrested him too. Ballantine related what happened next.

> "Arrest me?" exclaimed the astonished Attorney-General; "what for?" "Oh," said my captor, "for many things. You are well known to the police."

The distinguished lawyers were only allowed to go when members of the public recognised them.

In court, Ballantine could be brilliant on his feet, capable of turning a case to his advantage in the blink of an eye. Montagu Williams described one such case, involving a number of Jewish witnesses, which he personally witnessed as Ballantine's junior. Ballantine did not, to be blunt, like Jews, but, said Williams, "they were very fond of him, and eagerly sought his services." In this case, an important witness was Jewish, and Ballantine needed to undermine him to have any chance of winning the case. He had no success with his cross-examination and was about to conclude it when an obviously Jewish gentleman sitting nearby whispered that he should not give up just yet. "Ask him, Serjeant—ask him if he ever had a fire." Williams described how "quick as lightning, Ballantine took the hint" and, prompted by the stranger, dragged from the witness the admission that he had been convicted of arson and sent to prison. Well pleased, Ballantine was again about to sit down when the man next to him murmured, "Watch robbery—Bow Street." Again, under Ballantine's improvised questioning, the witness admitted another prison sentence, this time passed at Bow Street Police Court for robbery. Next, his mysterious prompter suggested he ask the witness about a fraudulent bankruptcy, which, however, he vigorously denied. Ballantine remonstrated with his helper and asked him why he had provided false information. "It's true, Serjeant, it's true," the man replied. "I swear it, and I ought to know. I'm his cussed old father."

On a hot day at the Suffolk summer assizes in Bury St Edmunds, with the courtroom windows wide open, Ballantine was on his feet when a donkey started braying loud and long just outside. The judge, seeing an opportunity for laboured judicial wit, interrupted him: "Stop, brother, stop. One at a time, if you please." Ballantine was not put off his stride for a second. "I beg your lordship's pardon," he replied. "I was not aware that your lordship was giving judgment."

The most dramatic and colourful case in which Ballantine was involved was that of the Tichborne Claimant, which captured the public imagination at the time and has continued to do so ever since (it has even featured in an episode of *The Simpsons*). He represented the Claimant, who had arrived from Australia in 1866 purporting to be Roger Tichborne, heir to the Tichborne baronetcy, who was presumed dead in 1855 when the ship in which he was sailing from Brazil to New York disappeared. He did not speak French (the real Roger had been brought up in France) and bore little or no resemblance to the missing man but Roger's mother, Lady Tichborne, never believed her son was dead and proclaimed that she recognised him when the Claimant was presented to her. Ballantine does not mention his name in his memoir but he was really Arthur Orton, who was born in London and was working as a butcher in Wagga Wagga, New South Wales, when he read that Lady Tichborne was still searching for her son. Orton's claim to the baronetcy, which by then had passed to Roger's baby nephew, was heard in London in 1871 and lasted 102 days. Ballantine had persuaded himself that the Claimant had a reasonable case, particularly after he had interviewed Lady Tichborne. Ballantine's team included another Garrick man, Hardinge Giffard (later Lord Halsbury), while the Solicitor-General, Sir John Coleridge, led for the Tichborne estate. Orton, uneducated and overweight, cut a poor figure in the witness box under questioning by his own lawyer, Giffard. As Ballantine ruefully noted, "It was impossible to say that the effect produced diminished the unfavourable impression which, in the court at all events, had been produced by his appearance." Coleridge followed up with a devastating cross-examination which must have been like shooting fish in a barrel. "Certainly no cross-examination was ever heard in a Court of Justice which exhibited more labour and industry, or was more completely successful," Ballantine conceded. If, when he had concluded, the judge had asked Ballantine if he wished to continue, he admitted he would have happily thrown in the towel, but he did not, and an interminable parade of witnesses followed, each banging another nail in the Claimant's coffin. Ballantine eventually withdrew his client's case before it reached the jury, and Orton was promptly arrested and indicted for perjury. Ballantine took no further part on his behalf. Orton stood trial in 1873 (it lasted a barely credible 188 days), was found guilty and sentenced to fourteen years' hard labour, of which he served ten.

The last big case Ballantine featured in was in a very different jurisdiction: India, where he had never been before; indeed, the furthest he had ever previously travelled was Germany. But his fame as a tenacious defence counsel attracted the Gaekwar (monarch) of the populous and wealthy state of Baroda to hire him to defend him on a charge of the attempted poisoning of the British Resident, Colonel Robert Phayre, whom Ballantine described as "fussy, meddlesome and thoroughly injudicious". The British administration of India appears to have agreed, for the Governor of Bombay ordered him to resign, and the Governor-General sacked him. Then came the so-called poisoning incident: Phayre claimed that his morning tumbler of sherbet caused him to feel ill, and he threw the contents of the glass away in disgust. Two medical men examined the remains at the bottom of the glass and agreed it was poison: oddly, Phayre pressed them to say it included finely powdered diamond dust, which was believed locally to be poisonous.

The Gaekwar went on trial in 1875 before a commission composed of six judges, three Indian (including two Maharajahs) and three British. Ballantine had endured a long and at times gruelling journey to reach his destination, for the biggest fee of his long career, reputed to be ten thousand guineas, and he provided value for money. He believed the evidence against the Gaekwar was trumped up by Phayre's associates to enable him to keep his job, and the verdict was a hung jury, the English Commissioners finding the Gaekwar guilty, the Indians voting to acquit. This embarrassing verdict was swiftly rendered irrelevant by the Government deposing the monarch anyway and installing a more pliable successor.

Although he was ultimately unsuccessful, Ballantine's efforts on behalf of his client were greatly appreciated by the people of India. The route from the house in Bombay where he spent his last night in India and whence he travelled by carriage to the port to board the ship home was lined with thousands of people who wished to say goodbye, and he was presented with a shawl and a parchment signed by 1,500 Indians thanking him for his exertions on behalf of the Gaekwar, who also sent a portrait of himself as a mark of gratitude. Ballantine celebrated his return to London by entertaining the Prince of Wales to dinner at the Garrick along with Sir Lewis Pelly, who had temporarily taken over from Phayre as Resident of Baroda and had been Ballantine's host throughout his stay.

Alas, Ballantine invested his enormous fee on the stock market and lost most of it. "From that time he seemed to attend to business less and less and gradually became an altered man," remembered Montagu Williams. A judge's clerk, F.W. Ashley, wrote: "We were all aware that his practice was leaving him, but he maintained a pose of nonchalance easy enough for one who temperamentally was incapable of taking any thought for the morrow or troubling to notice the difference between a debit and a credit account."

An opportunity to replenish his coffers seemed to present itself when Ballantine was briefed, along with his son Walter, to represent the beautiful young widow of a wealthy MP whose family contested his will, from which she had benefited. "From his first meeting with his pretty client," remembered Ashley, "the serjeant, who always had a keen eye for beauty, took a deep interest in her. To one who had been struggling with debts and creditors for years it may have been soothing to come into close association with solvency and wealth in such attractive guise." Ballantine worked hard for his client and a compromise was agreed which left her with a healthy lump sum. Ballantine now apparently planned to win his client's heart as well but decided not to rush things. One morning, however, he opened his newspaper to read that the young widow had indeed married a Ballantine—his son Walter.

The serjeant may have recouped some money from the successful publication of his memoirs, which went into several editions, and he then had the idea of trying to emulate his friend and hero Dickens by sailing to America to give a series of readings based on the book. The venture was financed by the impresario Richard D'Oyly Carte, but the American public, which had flocked to hear Dickens, had little appetite for the reminiscences of an obscure English lawyer and the trip was not a success, financially at least. Ballantine published an account of his stay in the United States in 1884 and clearly had a wonderful time, going from club to club furnished with introductions from London that opened many doors. He delivered his first reading in the Chickering Hall, New York, the premier venue for such occasions, to a polite reception, but Ballantine wrote afterwards: "My venture proved the old adage *ne sutor ultra crepidam* [cobbler, stick to thy last]. The critics treated my attempt with much more humanity than I felt it to deserve."

His second public reading was in Boston. "I was listened to by an audience rather select than numerous, with attention and kindness," he recorded. The third and final show took place in the Association Hall, Philadelphia. "I was received very kindly," he noted, "but I believe, if natural politeness and a sense of hospitality had not largely prevailed, I might have been addressed in the not very complimentary quotation 'It's not your vocation, Hal'."

It was clear that the voice that had persuaded many an English jury left American audiences cold. "Somehow or other, his brain was no longer as strong as it had been," noted Montagu Williams. "One of the literary lights of New York afterwards described his entertainments as the 'Reminiscences of a Serjeant Who had Lost His Memory'."

"As a matter of business ... my adventure was a comparative failure," Ballantine wrote, and he asked D'Oyly Carte to be released from his agreement. The offer was received with alacrity, which freed Ballantine to embark on the long journey West to investigate the lifestyle of the Mormons in Salt Lake City.

It is no surprise, given his lifestyle, to learn that Ballantine had made little or no provision for his retirement. He spent much of it in Boulogne, a town which he loved and where he used to meet Dickens, who had a house there. His son and four Garrick lawyer friends—Hardinge Giffard, Harry Poland, Henry James and Montagu Williams—came to the rescue by subscribing to provide him with a regular allowance. True to form, he was always trying to obtain advance payments, calling at his friends' chambers and clubs to lobby them. And he did eventually find a second wife, who was even younger than his son's though not, unfortunately, as wealthy.

His health declined and he returned from France to Margate, where he cheerfully described to Williams, a constant visitor, an out-of-body experience. In January 1887, as he lay dying, he asked Williams to contact his son, from whom he had been estranged since Walter's marriage (and despite his generosity to his father). "I am bound to say," opined Williams, who had tried to mediate between them, "that the fault lay almost entirely with the poor Serjeant. He could not control his tongue, and the things he had said of his son were very disgraceful." He telegraphed Walter, who was recovering from scarlet fever in Monte Carlo, and he managed to get back to England in time to be reconciled with his father and to be with him at the end.

Although a prickly and difficult character, particularly in old age, Ballantine was regarded with great affection by the legal fraternity. "He had something of the airy fecklessness of Micawber [and] the humour of Rabelais," wrote Ashley. The Rumpole of his era indeed.

3
THE FOUR MUSKETEERS

In the mid-nineteenth century, a small group of barristers dominated the criminal bar, alongside William Ballantine, and like him they were all Garrick Club members. Their names crop up again and again opposing or supporting one another in many of the big cases that gripped the public imagination: Serjeant Parry, Henry Hawkins, Montagu Williams, Harry Poland and Charles "Willie" Mathews. Like Ballantine, Hawkins and Williams wrote lengthy (and, it must be said, to the modern taste long-winded) memoirs, providing portraits of their colleagues, extensive retelling of their biggest cases and plenty of the laboured humour which can be characteristic of the lawyer, in court at least. Tellingly, only Hawkins became a judge: the others preferred the cut and thrust of advocacy to the security of the bench, although Williams eventually became a stipendiary magistrate for health reasons.

John Humffreys Parry (1816-1880, Garrick Club 1853-1880) had much in common with William Ballantine. He too was a Serjeant-at-Law, and they appeared opposite each other in court on innumerable occasions. They were known to everyone as "the two Serjeants". Parry was, according to Ballantine, "a man of great knowledge, power, and ability".

"He was exceedingly popular at the Bar," noted Montagu Williams. He enjoyed the company of his fellow-men as much as Ballantine, but he was much more interested and involved in politics than his friend and opponent. He inherited a radical streak from his father, a Welsh antiquary and biographer who was killed by a bricklayer in a fight in a London street after a disagreement in a nearby public house. He was only forty-nine and left five children, who were provided for by a fund of more than a thousand pounds raised by his friends. His son John was educated at the Philological School, Marylebone, and worked first in an office and then in the printed books department of the British Museum, before studying law. He was called to the bar in 1843 by the Middle Temple, built up a good criminal practice in London and at the Middlesex Sessions, and went on to lead the Home Circuit. He was a supporter of the Chartists, though not of their more extreme members, a founder of the Complete Suffrage Movement in 1842, and he twice stood unsuccessfully for Parliament.

He differed in every respect from the wiry, nervous, bustling and spontaneous Ballantine. "Remarkably solid in appearance, his countenance was broad and expansive, beaming with honesty and frankness," recorded Williams. He went on:

> His cross-examination was of a quieter kind than Serjeant Ballantine's. It was, however, almost as effective. He drew the witness on, in a smooth, good-humoured, artful, and apparently magnetic fashion. His attitude towards his adversary also was peculiar. He never indulged in bickering, was always perfectly polite, and was most to be feared when he seemed to be making a concession. If in the course of a trial he, without being asked, handed his adversary a paper with the words: "Wouldn't you like to

see this?" or some kindred observation, let that adversary
beware, for there was something deadly underneath.

Another observer, F.W. Ashley, left a rather different
description: "Parry was round and definitely unquiet . . .
when aroused to those heights of passion which can pass
for eloquence with the witlings his voice could be heard
outside Westminster Hall."

Williams also provided a portrait of Parry at ease.

> He was a wonderful teller of anecdotes, fond of a good
> dinner, and a great judge of port wine. For many years he
> was a member of the Garrick Club, and numerous were
> the pleasant dinners given by him there.

Parry appeared in many of the most sensational cases
of the era, such as that of the Tichborne Claimant and
Whistler's libel action against Ruskin in 1878, in which
he represented the artist against the critic, who famously
accused Whistler of "flinging a pot of paint in the public's
face". In the event, only the lawyers benefited: the jury
found for Whistler but awarded him a mere farthing in
damages. Parry died within a few hours of his wife, when
still at the peak of his powers; they shared the same funeral
and grave.

After Eton, Montagu Williams (1835-1892, Garrick
1873-1892) first wanted to be a soldier, with the aim of
being sent out to the Crimea, where war had just broken
out. He then briefly became an actor. He was born in
Somerset to a family "steeped in law for generations," as
he put it in the first volume of his memoirs, *Leaves of a
Life*, published in 1890. He first got a taste for treading the
boards by taking part in amateur theatricals in the Army,
and continued after he quit, his regiment having been

posted to the West Indies, where he was unlikely to see the sort of action he craved. His amateur work went well enough for him to help to found a professional troupe which toured the provinces and Scotland. In Edinburgh he met Louise, actress daughter of the celebrated actor-manager Robert Keeley, who with his wife was then proprietor of the Theatre Royal, and the relationship deepened when they played opposite each other in *London Assurance*, Dion Boucicault's immortal farce. Smitten, Williams pursued her to Dublin, proposed, was accepted and the impetuous young couple married without the consent of either set of parents, although both came round to accepting the union eventually. They continued with the life of touring actors for a little while longer but it was Williams's actor-manager father-in-law who persuaded him that he would provide better for his daughter if he forsook the theatre for the law. He studied at the Inner Temple for three years and was called to the bar in 1862, specialising in criminal work. "I think I may safely say that I have defended more prisoners than any other living man," he reflected after he had retired in 1886 for health reasons.

He did not sever his connections with the theatre completely, however. He wrote, co-wrote or adapted several plays and farces which were performed professionally, in addition to writing for newspapers and owning a half-share in a magazine. Oddly enough, given his theatrical experience, he suffered severe stage-fright before his first prosecution brief at the Old Bailey, a simple case of horse theft, and did so badly that he was convinced he had chosen the wrong profession. But the criminal bar was composed of a relatively small group of men, headed by Ballantine and Parry, and before long Williams had become an established, popular and successful member of the fraternity. He was a short man, equally quick to lose his temper and to make friends. "His great vitality and vigour, his striking, if irregular features, his self-possession, and his knowledge of men and of all sides of life, led him quickly to a large practice, especially as a defender of prisoners," was the *Dictionary of National Biography's* verdict.

Williams's memoirs contain some interesting vignettes, lively portraits of his contemporaries, and valuable descriptions of the hectic life of a leading Old Bailey barrister of the mid-Victorian era:

> No one who is not in the swim can have any conception of the amount of work and worry that devolves upon a counsel in leading practice at the criminal Bar. He has to be at chambers at nine o'clock in the morning, and, an hour later, he has to be at his post. Several Courts sit simultaneously, and possibly he has a case going on in each of them at the same time. He has to do the best he can, with the assistance of juniors and "devils". In one Court, perhaps, he will open the case, in the next, cross-examine the principal witness, in the third, make the speech for the defence; and all this while he has to keep in touch with the various cases, and from time to time make himself acquainted with the course they are taking. When the Courts adjourn at five, he returns to chambers for consultations etc, which occupy him probably until half-past seven o'clock, when he rushes home to snatch a hasty dinner, after which he reads the briefs for the following day. Sometimes he has to keep up half the night perusing his papers, and, not unfrequently, when he gets to bed, his brain is too much occupied to allow him to sleep.

It's a wonder he ever had any time for the Garrick, to which he was elected in 1873, but he swiftly became a valued member. "The Garrick has always been, and still is, the cheeriest of clubs," he wrote. Before he became a member, he was often invited to visit the Club's original home:

> I remember the days of the old building, when Thackeray, Dickens, Albert Smith, Arcedeckne, "Assassin Smith," and Benjamin Webster, were members; and a very jovial place it was. The new premises were designed by one of the members, Nelson; and a curious circumstance was that, when the structure was nearly completed, it was discovered that the architect had forgotten all about the kitchens. When I joined the principal man in the club was Sir Charles Taylor. I am bound to say that he had done a great deal for the institution, by giving it financial assistance before debentures were raised and issued; and in point of fact, he rather ruled the establishment... His appearance was peculiar, being suggestive of one of the parrot tribe. He was rather overbearing in his manner, especially to those whom he considered beneath him socially.
>
> One day, on entering the club, he came across Dallas— then a well-known man on *The Times*—eating his lunch.
>
> "Well, my penny-a-liner," said Sir Charles, "and how are you?"
>
> Quick as lightning Dallas replied:
>
> "Quite well, thank you, you one-eyed macaw."
>
> Every one who remembers Sir Charles Taylor will understand the allusion.

Williams appeared in so many famous trials that it would be impossible to list them all but he was forced to retire as an advocate at the height of his career because of a malignant growth on his vocal cords. His life was saved by a team of top surgeons from Berlin who travelled to London specifically for the operation and stayed for a month afterwards to supervise his recovery. After a long convalescence he was advised that his voice could not stand the strain of court work and in 1886 he was appointed a metropolitan stipendiary magistrate, sitting first at Greenwich and Woolwich. For all his comfortable circumstances and clubman's life, Williams had always had a keen social conscience, and he was appalled to see at first hand the terrible living and working conditions of the citizens of the area of south-east London where he was now the law's principal representative. It contained some 600,000 people and was the poorest sector of the city. The metropolitan magistrates had at their disposal the funds of the poor box, from which they would dispense small sums to needy people who happened to appear before them for one reason or another. Being a generous, impulsive and warm-hearted soul, Williams soon exhausted the meagre funds available to him, and recalled, "I was at my wits' end to know what to do. To stand quietly by and see, morning after morning, those heartrending scenes—men and women, with gaunt cheeks and sunken eyes imploring my assistance—was impossible." Then a solution occurred to him: to appeal to the public for help. He did so by a letter to *The Times*, headlined "Distress in Greenwich", addressed to the "many who are blessed with a superabundance of the good things of this life." The response was immediate and gratifying: in little more than a month more than £1,500 was donated and disbursed, about ten times the normal amount distributed annually. Williams's initiative also sparked a lively public debate which prodded various bodies into speeding up public works that were planned for the area, providing work for many. By the time he moved on, first to Wandsworth, then to Worship Street in the East End, things had improved considerably. But Williams found the situation in the East End even worse than anything he had encountered in Greenwich and Woolwich, and once more set about trying to do what he could to improve the lot of the most desperately poor. He recorded what he found in some detail in his third and last volume of memoirs, *Late Leaves*, and the concluding chapters are a devastating indictment of the poverty, overcrowding and deprivation he witnessed, almost on a par with Mayhew's reports of three decades earlier. He despaired at the effects of drink on the working-class, which he saw for himself every day he sat in judgment on poor people charged with all manner of alcohol-related petty crimes. He invariably let them off with a caution, reasoning that to fine such offenders would only compound their difficulties: "I am convinced that—except with habitual criminals—leniency is a more powerful instrument of good than severity." He had few illusions about the ability of well-meaning individuals such as himself to effect radical reform and was scornful at the reluctance of wealthy men to give any money at all to charities for the poor, coming round to the necessity for a graduated scale of income tax instead. He died at the age of 57, and was affectionately, and justly, remembered as "the poor man's magistrate".

Sir Harry Bodkin Poland (1829-1928, Garrick 1867-1928), was a slightly eccentric workaholic and something of a legend at the criminal bar. "Perhaps no one has ever had such a reputation as a criminal lawyer as Poland," wrote F.W. Ashley, who began his long career as a junior clerk in Poland's chambers. The son of a Highgate furrier, Poland was educated at St Paul's School and called to the bar at the Inner Temple in 1851. He was the nephew by marriage of Sir William Henry Bodkin, a leading criminal silk, and shared chambers for three decades with Hardinge Giffard, later Lord Halsbury. Their working methods, and indeed their physiques, were somewhat different. Poland would devour his briefs until he had virtually memorised them; Giffard took a rather more expansive view. Giffard had a large head, the cadaverous Poland "the smallest I have ever seen", according to Ashley. When they accidentally put on each other's hats, Poland's "rolled off the massive head of Sir Hardinge, while Sir Hardinge's hat came down to Mr Poland's shoulders and completely enveloped his features."

In 1865 Poland was appointed Treasury Counsel at the Central Criminal Court and adviser to the Home Office on criminal matters, posts he held for nearly a quarter of a century, and he appeared for the Crown in many important criminal prosecutions. He took silk in 1888, gave up his post as Treasury Counsel and was able to switch his talents from prosecutor to defender, in which his quiet, judicious and scrupulously fair style was as successful as it had been previously.

> His capacity for work was enormous (wrote Ashley). I never knew him to take a real holiday, and Saturday and Sunday were full working days with him. Every year he went for three weeks to Folkestone, but always had enough work with him to keep him occupied. He would sit on the beach under the shade of a large white umbrella which had been his companion for more years than anyone could remember, and read legal documents as assiduously as if in his chambers in the Temple. He had some few minutes of relaxation daily which he never missed. That was to watch the arrival of the Channel boat, and, if it had been a rough passage, to enjoy gazing at the pale faces of the

passengers and congratulate himself that England was
good enough for him.

Long after his retirement, when he received a
knighthood, the elderly bachelor could be seen in the Inner
Temple library where "he was a familiar and picturesque
figure, in his black skull cap and slightly old-fashioned garb
... There he was wont to converse in sonorous tones which
aroused the affectionate interest of the other readers and
which his deafness doubtless caused him to suppose were
no louder than the customary discreet whisper."

It is a pity that Charles Willie Mathews (1850-1920,
Garrick 1877-1920) did not write his memoirs: they might
have been the wittiest of them all. He was the stepson
of the actor, dramatist and Garrick member Charles
Mathews, who had married (as her third husband) the
American actress Elizabeth West, whose stage name was
Lizzie Weston. She brought to the marriage with Mathews
her son Charles by her first marriage and he took his
stepfather's name, though he was known to one and all
as Willie. He was educated at Eton and then decided to
study for the law, becoming Montagu Williams's pupil.
Doubtless the Garrick connection did no harm in setting
up the pupillage but Mathews had no need of nepotism:
Williams called him the best pupil he ever had and he
acquired a thriving practice at the criminal bar, although
he appeared in many high-profile civil cases too. He was
small, dapper, able, hard-working and eloquent, although
hampered by "a weak and unpleasing voice".

Edward Marjoribanks, a young barrister who was also
a talented writer and briefly a Conservative MP before
committing suicide at the age of thirty-two after being

jilted for the second time, left an evocative description of Mathews. He was, he wrote, "one of the last advocates who were not afraid to use real eloquence at the Bar." He went on:

> His voice was high and thin, and his face somewhat feminine in appearance; but a jury soon became accustomed to these peculiarities, and, indeed, they increased the effectiveness of his questions and speeches. It was impossible not to listen to him...He had a great gift of moving the sympathy of the Court from the prisoner to the prosecution, and would sweep juries off their feet by the pathos he could put into a single sentence.

Another who was an up-and-coming junior when Mathews was at his peak, Travers Humphreys, wrote:

> He was a "character" indeed. Intensely dramatic, child of the stage as he was, he had a flow of language combined with a passionate earnestness that was irresistible. His English was as unorthodox as was compatible with eloquence. His habit of beginning a sentence with an accusative and ending on a preposition would have sounded ridiculous from any other man, but Willie could triumph in spite of solecisms.

Humpreys related how Mathews could reduce jurymen to tears and once did the same, with his unique grammatical cadences, to as tough a judge as Sir Henry Hawkins with the conclusion to his opening speech when prosecuting a labourer for the "mercy killing" of his baby son, blind through inherited syphilis: "Murder is the charge. Death, a dishonoured death, may be his fate. But the law is not and dare not be devoid of compassion for such an act, and I say to you, if My Lord will so permit—Act of manslaughter only, he pleading guilty to, act of manslaughter only shall he be found guilty of."

The writer Edgar Lustgarten, who specialised in re-creating historic trials, also picked up on Mathews's histrionic talents:

> The crouch which gave him a semblance of the dwarfish; the draping of the black gown upon the spindly form; the skilful use of that diabolical voice so that it rose on words like "kill" and "death" to a bloodcurdling shriek—these were not to be despised among the attributes that had made Charles Mathews leader of the Old Bailey Bar.

Mathews's first case as Recorder of Winchester went into bar legend. He eloquently summed up the prosecution case, whereupon the foreman of the jury stood up, about to announce a guilty verdict. "Wait gentlemen," said Mathews, "what say the defence?" He proceeded to outline the defence case just as fluently, and the bewildered jury split down the middle, six-six.

He was also an enthusiastic devotee of horse racing and a great clubman, a member of the Turf and the Beefsteak as well as the Garrick, of which he was a member for forty-three years. Clearly, he inherited his mother's (and perhaps by osmosis his stepfather's) dramatic talents. "He was an animated talker, always ready with some anecdote," recorded the *DNB*, "in telling which he could act, as well as narrate." In 1908 he was appointed Director of Public Prosecutions, a post he held until his death in 1920, when he was succeeded by another Garrick man, Archibald Bodkin.

4
ANYTHING BUT THE LAW

Among the ranks of the lawyers elected to the Garrick over the twenty years after the first tranche in 1831 were many more who, while attaining eminence in the legal sphere, led lives that were rich in interest outside it. Some sampled the law only briefly, before choosing a life of letters instead. One such was William Harrison Ainsworth (1805-1882, Garrick 1842-1869), who was articled to a solictor in his home city of Manchester at the age of 16 and moved to London three years later to further his legal education at the Inner Temple. But "his enthusiasms were wholly literary", recorded the *DNB*, adding: "Whatever intentions he may have formed of humdrum study and determined attention to the details of a profession in which he had no interest, were dissipated by contact with the literary world of the metropolis." Ainsworth went on to be a successful writer and novelist, producing a long series of potboilers which have not survived the test of time, many featuring the exploits of one Jack Sheppard.

Ainsworth formed friendships with Thackeray, Dickens, Landseer and other great contemporaries whom he would have met at the Garrick. He lived in an elegant house in Kilburn, moving later to Kemp Town, Brighton, and was described in middle age by William Ballantine as "still strikingly handsome; there is something artistic about his dress, and there be a little affectation in his manners, but even this may in some people be a not unpleasing element... No one was more genial, no one more popular."

A similar trajectory was taken by Tom Taylor (1817-80, Garrick 1850-1880), like Mr Justice Talfourd before him the son of a brewer. He was a brilliant student who won three gold medals at Glasgow University before going on to Trinity College, Cambridge, where he took a first in maths and classics and was elected a Fellow of the college at the age of 25. Pausing only to be Professor of English Literature and Language at London University for two years, he proceeded to study law and was called to the Bar at Inner Temple in 1846. He worked on the northern circuit for four years but his legal career ended when he became assistant secretary to the new Board of Health in 1850, the same year he was elected to the Garrick. He was promoted to secretary of the board four years later on £1,000 a year but maintained simultaneously a busy career as a journalist, author and playwright. After retiring from the board on the comfortable pension of £650 a year he became Editor of *Punch* in 1874, in which influential post he remained for six years. He was also active in artistic circles, a friend of the artist William Frith and art critic for *The Times* and *The Graphic*.

Francis Stack Murphy (1807-60, Garrick 1833-53; 1853-60) was another clever young man who was a well-regarded lawyer but preferred to devote more of his time to politics and journalism. A native of Cork, he went to Trinity College, Dublin, before moving to London to study law. At the same time he became involved in *Fraser's Magazine*, a staunchly Tory political and literary publication which was co-founded in 1830 by another Irishman William Maginn. Murphy assisted his former teacher Father Francis Mahony, a remarkable Catholic priest and a brilliant classicist and scholar who had swapped the daily practice of the priesthood to lead what was described as a Bohemian lifestyle, although he remained a devout Catholic. Mahoney wrote a celebrated column for the magazine, The Prout Papers, under the pseudonym Father Prout. Indeed, Murphy appears in The Prout Papers as "Frank Cresswell of Furnival's Inn". He was called to the bar at Lincoln's Inn in 1833, but left the law when he was elected MP for Cork in 1841, representing the constituency until he resigned in 1846. He was re-elected in 1851 but stood down again in 1853 to become a commissioner in bankruptcy in Dublin. He was a clever lawyer noted for his wit, some examples of which were recorded by Benjamin Robinson. "He was a gay, lively, rollicking person who could say smart things upon occasion," wrote Robinson. "It may be said of Murphy that, in speech and accent, he was much more Hibernian than his countrymen themselves. But this qualification only gave a more racy tone to his occasional impromptus."

Far from uniquely among wits, Murphy did not like to be among men who were as clever and amusing as himself. "He could never bear a rival near his throne," commented Robinson. "He was like a body charged with electricity, which, when it comes in contact with another saturated with electric fluid of the same kind, produces no action, and makes no sign. Murphy, in the presence of another jester, was always silent and dull; no sparks nor flashes of merriment were emitted from his lips, but he was in a thoroughly negative condition." Among such men, "Murphy always sat moody and subdued, and seemed to be indignant at his privileges being unfairly interfered with."

Murphy was also a member of the Reform Club, where he "could always find a fitting auditory to listen to his well-assorted *bon-mots*". The club's French chef, Soyer, was highly regarded, but his wife was said to have been a difficult woman who gave him a hard time at home. When she died, the chef asked Murphy for a suitable epitaph on her gravestone. Said Murphy, "You cannot do better than to inscribe upon it, 'Soyer tranquille'."

A doctor friend asked Murphy for advice about a man who had insulted him: should he challenge him to a duel? "Take my advice," said Murphy, "and instead of calling him out, get him to call you in, and have your revenge that way, it will be much more secure and certain."

Robinson's final verdict on Murphy was harsh. "What I did see of Murphy personally – and I saw him often – satisfied me that he was cold and heartless. His jokes often verged upon the indelicate, and, although not very objectionable, rendered some of my notes respecting him unadapted for general circulation."

His countryman Sir Charles Gavan Duffy was equally scathing. "Serjeant Murphy," he wrote, "was the type of Irish member loved by political clubs in London. He never embarrassed them by inconvenient proposals or alarming theories, and was ready to jest upon all subjects, his own nation being no exception; and nothing is pleasanter to Cockney ears than an Irishman who is ready to banter Irish patriotism or mock at Irish misery. The Serjeant was a Bohemian—a jolly good fellow, which nobody could deny, pleasant in smoking-rooms, and irresistible over a boiled bone at midnight ... It would be injustice not to note that he was neither a hypocrite nor an imposter; he made no pretence of using his political position for any other purpose than his own advancement."

Duffy recorded another example of Murphy's wit. An English MP asked him how he distinguished between two Irish MPs, who were brothers: Vincent Scully, who was eccentric and spoke with a pronounced lisp; and Francis Scully, who was not very bright. "Oh easily," replied Murphy. "We call Vincent 'Rum-Scully' and Francis 'Num-Skully'."

Another attractive Irishman was Sir John Walter Huddleston (1815-1890, Garrick 1850-1877), who featured as defence counsel in many celebrated trials. He defended the black Chartist leader William Cuffay in 1848, a year of revolutionary turmoil at home and abroad, represented (with Edwin James) William Palmer, the Rugeley poisoner, in 1856, and secured the acquittal of Mercy Catherine Newton at the end of her third trial for matricide in 1859. He was also successively MP for Canterbury and Norwich and judge-advocate of the fleet for ten years until 1875. He was a popular figure at the Garrick, being described as "a brilliant conversationalist, lover of the theatre, and an authority on turf matters," an attribute claimed with little or no foundation by succeeding generations of Garrick men to the present day.

Walter Coulson QC (1795-1860, Garrick 1832-1833, 1844-1860) also contrived to move smoothly between the law and journalism, achieving success in both fields. As a young man, he was an amanuensis to Jeremy Bentham and a parliamentary reporter for the *Morning Chronicle*, numbering James Mill and Francis Place among his friends. He was called to the bar at Gray's Inn in 1828, took silk in 1851 and was parliamentary draftsman at the Home Office. But his heart seems to have been in journalism: he was editor of *The Globe* magazine for many years until he fell out with its owners. He was offered a legal post in India but preferred to stay in London, apparently for its social life. He was said to be "a prodigy of knowledge" and "a walking encyclopedia" and was also renowned for his comic imitations. His later friends included Charles Lamb, Leigh Hunt and William Hazlitt, to whose first child he was a godfather.

Effortless brilliance was the hallmark of Sir Edward Shepherd Creasy (1812-78, Garrick 1837-1838), an Eton scholar and Fellow of King's College, Cambridge, who then decided to read for the bar at Lincoln's Inn. He was briefly a barrister on the Home Circuit and became a youthful judge at Westminster Sessions Court before returning to academe at the age of 28 as professor of modern and ancient history at the University of London. He produced a string of popular works of history beginning with *Fifteen Decisive Battles of the World* in 1852, then switched back to the law as Chief Justice of Ceylon in 1860. He held the post for ten years but the tropical climate ruined his health.

Even the more conventional Garrick lawyers of the era had unexpected talents. Sir James Bacon (1798-1895, Garrick 1834-1870) had an impeccable legal career of remarkable longevity, retiring from the bench at the age of 88. Shortly afterwards he ruefully remarked to a former colleague that had he known how pleasant a life of leisure was he would have retired sooner. He was spared to enjoy his retirement for a further nine years until his death at 97. He was said to have been a sub-editor on *The Times* at one stage. He was a specialist in conveyancing, chancery law and bankruptcy, and became commissioner in bankruptcy for the London district in 1868 and chief judge under the Bankruptcy Act of 1869 until its repeal in 1883 when bankruptcy jurisdiction passed to the Queen's Bench. He became a vice-chancellor in 1870 and was knighted in 1871. The post of vice-chancellor had been created in 1813 but was abolished during Bacon's tenure. However, those holding the title were allowed to retain it until their retirement. Bacon outlived the other three surviving vice-chancellors and so became the last holder of the title in the nineteenth century, a fact which gave him great satisfaction. It was re-established from 1971 to 2005. He was an old-fashioned judge, courteous and kindly, who tried to jolly proceedings along with a dash of humour. Most notably, he was an adept cartoonist who liked to adorn his trial notes with drawings of those before him in court. These notes were said to be much appreciated by the lords justice of appeal when they had to review his judgments.

Sir John Rolt (1804-71, Garrick 1845-1871) overcame the handicaps of poverty and deprivation to became a QC, an MP, Attorney-General and an Appeal Court judge, though the sheer hard work he took on to achieve his goals curtailed his life. Rolt was born in India and brought to England by his mother when he was about six. By the age of ten he was an orphan and at fourteen had to leave school to be apprenticed to a firm of woollen drapers in London. He was an exemplary case of the self-educated man: he used to read as he walked to work. He variously went to work in a warehouse and as an office clerk, and after that as secretary first to a school for orphans and then to the dissenters' school in Mill Hill, which later became Mill Hill School.

But Rolt had conceived the notion of becoming a lawyer, and entered the Inner Temple in 1833. He was called to the bar four years later, by which time he was thirty-three years old, but as if anxious to make up for lost time he rapidly built up a busy Chancery practice and took silk only nine years later. In 1857 he was elected Conservative MP for West Gloucestershire. He was a loyal party man and did not distinguish himself greatly in the Commons, but he did have one solid achievement to his name: in 1862 he shepherded through Parliament the Chancery Regulation Act which was an important step in fusing law and equity. In 1866 he became Attorney-General and was knighted but he held the post for less than a year before becoming a Lord Justice of Appeal. Struck down by illness within a few months, he was obliged to resign early in 1868, though he lingered on until 1871.

William Ballantine remembered him with affection: "I visited at his house, and met him frequently at the Garrick Club," he wrote. "He planted the seeds of a premature death by giving himself too little relaxation from intensely hard work. I have seen him come into the club of an evening looking worn and exhausted, swallow a hasty dinner, and rush off to further labour. He earned a high reputation, but paid a heavy price for it."

The record for Garrick longevity in that era must surely belong to another lawyer, Frank Fladgate (Garrick 1832-1892). At the time Ballantine wrote his memoir (the second edition was published in 1882), Fladgate was the "father" of the Club—indeed, he was affectionately known by the other members as "Papa"—and Ballantine described him as a man "who, for all the years it has existed, and through all its changing scenes, has never made an enemy". He was a great friend of Trollope and a lover of literature and the theatre. "No one of the present day is so conversant with the records of the stage and the lives of the greatest actors," Ballantine recorded, "and it is a real treat to listen to his pleasant talk, and note his adoration of his beloved Shakespeare."

The firm of solicitors of which he was a partner acted for the Garrick for many years, well into the twentieth century. It still bears Papa Fladgate's name, and in 2010 celebrated its two hundred and fiftieth anniversary, as Fladgate LLP, marking the occasion by moving its premises to Great Queen Street, Covent Garden, a short walk from Garrick Street.

There was also one thorough-going rogue: Edwin John James QC (1812-82, elected to the Garrick 1843), who might have been a model for George Macdonald Fraser's fictional creation Harry Flashman, a self-confessed coward who nonetheless contrives to win the VC and be caught up in any number of disasters from which he always manages to emerge not only more or less unscathed but with his reputation undeservedly enhanced. At the time James was elected to the Garrick, he was making a name for himself as a flamboyant and colourful courtroom performer who was adept at persuading juries of the strength of his case despite what his fellow lawyers felt was an extremely limited grasp of the law.

James came from a good family: his father was a solicitor and a well-known figure in the City of London. As a boy Edwin had a passion for the theatre and acted at a private theatre in Gough Street, near Gray's Inn. He went on to appear at the Theatre Royal, Bath, although his appearance was said to count against him as "he looked like a prize-fighter". His parents evidently disapproved and persuaded him to give up the stage and study for the law. In the light of subsequent events, perhaps they should have left well alone.

James was called to the bar at the Inner Temple in 1836 and practised on the Home Circuit, helped by his father's connections. "Such aids gave him the start of competitors otherwise his superiors; and in confidence and assurance he was not wanting," noted an anonymous commentator in *The Law Magazine and Law Review* after James's career had foundered in spectacular fashion. "His bold and jocund manners and his confident mien soon became noticed in the robing rooms of the Four Courts of Westminster and Guildhall." His career flourished, aided undoubtedly by his acting skills. By the mid-1850s he was a QC and involved in a series of high-profile cases but there were plenty who were sceptical about his abilities. The *Dictionary of National Biography* records: "In dealing with common juries he freely appealed with conspicuous success to their ignorance and prejudices, but his knowledge of law was very limited." *The Law Magazine* went further: "He never had any reputation as a 'Lawyer'. His Law was almost always... 'got up' for him." The writer went on to explore just what qualities James did possess. "We must however in justice admit that of late years his speeches in Court, to common Juries especially, were marked by talent. In cross-examination he was tolerably prudent, but displaying no sagacity; yet in 'flash cases' his addresses were pre-eminent. He understood an ordinary Jury, and by appeals to their ignorance, passions and prejudices how best to obtain *his* verdicts. But in the half-dozen cases only of remarkable Actions at Law and Criminal Trials in which he led, he displayed no real eloquence or safe judgment – his powers consisting only of unscrupulous assertion, confident demeanour, and sonorous voice. Discretion was no part of his valour as an Advocate."

Still, his self-confidence was unlimited. During the famous Garrick feud between Thackeray and Dickens over the expulsion from the club of the young writer Edmund Yates after he had the temerity to express mild criticism of Thackeray in a magazine article, James tried to persuade Thackeray to take the matter to court. Doubtless James viewed the case as a golden opportunity to further his own career for it would have been headline news for months had Thackeray been foolish enough to take his advice; he wisely decided not to.

From 1855 to 1861 he was recorder of Brighton and, like any lawyer with higher judicial aspirations at that time, he had political ambitions too. In 1859 he was elected MP for Marylebone and the following year visited Garibaldi's camp and witnessed the Italian rebel leader's troops take part in a skirmish outside the town of Capua as they approached the triumphant climax of their drive to unite Italy. The *Illustrated London News* wryly noted: "Mr James was a spectator of, and to a certain extent a participator in, the affair of the 19th ult. before Capua; and our Special Artist [Frank Vizetelly] took a Sketch. . .of the honorable and learned member for Marylebone as he then appeared in his half-military, half-navvy equipment, engaged, without a retaining fee, in the cause of Italian freedom." The accompanying full-length portrait of James reveals a stocky figure with indeed something of a prize-fighter's face framed by mutton-chop whiskers and topped by a navvy's cap, wearing a fairly shabby jacket and trousers, standing staring into the middle distance, supported by a stout stick, with a pair of pistols tucked into his belt; the effect is faintly comic. Something of James's bellicose temperament can be gleaned from his own description of the Italian army's retreat before Garibaldi's troops, published in the *Illustrated London News*.

> The cry arose that the "Cavalry were coming!" and the panic seized the troops. In the mêlée I lost my carriage; my servant had very indiscreetly taken shelter with some priests in the top of a convent, and during his absence the carriage disappeared. I had to walk along the high road to Caserta; a little Swiss soldier who had been wounded by a rifle-ball in the wrist, and was going to the hospital there, accompanied me. On our way I saw seven or eight soldiers among whom were two officers—the Swiss soldier told me they belonged to a Sicilian regiment—seated on one of the long agricultural carts, which they had taken from a field adjoining the road, and were proceeding at a rapid pace to Caserta. As they met troops coming from that town to relieve Santa Maria they spread the panic among them; they cried out, "The cavalry are coming!" "The artillery are close on us!" "We shall all perish!" "Back to Caserta, back!" More than one regiment wavered and turned. The officers behaved firmly and well, drew their swords, and urged their men on. I followed these mischievous and cowardly fellows to Caserta, asked for the Colonel of a regiment who spoke French, gave him my name and address, pointed out the fellows as they entered the square in front of the Palace, and although I did not request it as

> a personal favour, I certainly suggested that they should
> be marched out and shot; they were at once taken to the
> guardhouse and were seen no more by me.

Within two years of becoming an MP, James was appointed Solicitor-General despite the belief of the *Law Magazine's* writer that "as a Law Officer of the Crown he would have been woefully deficient; and thoroughly unlearned in Civil Law and the Laws of Nations he would have been utterly incompetent for any official station." Despite such misgivings, it looked as if his political career was about to take off. But at the very moment of his triumph, and even before he received the knighthood that traditionally accompanied the job, disaster struck. Although James had derived a considerable income from his legal work, he was by now heavily in debt. It emerged that, starting in 1857 he had borrowed some £35,000, an enormous sum in today's money, from Lord Worsley, the gullible young heir to Lord Yarborough, pledging life insurance policies as collateral. When Lord Yarborough got to hear of this, he put his solicitor on the case but James managed to put them off until 1861, promising first to repay the money as soon as possible and after failing to do so, while running up further loans elsewhere, by pledging most of his future professional income to pay back the debt in stages. It then emerged that he had borrowed a further £20,000 from a West Country solicitor, whom he had got to know in about 1858, and, clearly spotting a lucrative source of income, had lured into friendship by inviting him to go shooting with him. He immediately started borrowing from the poor man, who was completely taken in by James and his glamorous social connections. He even advised James on the purchase of his house in Berkeley Square, for which he presumably put up a considerable proportion of the money. This wasn't all: with breathtaking cynicism, James borrowed £1,250 from the defendant in a case in which he was acting for the prosecution, assuring him he would go easy on him during his cross-examination.

James had no scruples at all about borrowing from a fellow QC and Garrick member without the slightest means or intention of repaying him. This was Henry Hawkins, later a distinguished if controversial judge, who described the incident in his memoirs. He did not name James but he did not need to. Hawkins was from a modest background and prided himself on not trying "to lounge about amongst the socially great", as he put it, unlike James.

> The entrance-fee into the portals of the smart society temple is heavy, especially for a working man, and so found the bright particular star who had long held his place amidst the the splendid social galaxy, and then disappeared into a deeper obscurity than that from which he had emerged, to be seen no more for ever.

> He was a Queen's Counsel, a brilliant advocate in a certain line of business, and a popular, agreeable, intellectual, and amusing companion. He obtained a seat in Parliament and a footing in Society, which made him one of its selected and principal lions. In every Society paper, amongst its most fashionable intelligence, there was he; and Society hardly seemed to be able to get along without him.

Hawkins related how James had unexpectedly called on him one Sunday afternoon, and even more surprisingly asked him to lend him £1,250 so that he could meet bills for that amount which fell due the following morning. Hawkins was astonished, for he had no idea that James was in such difficulties, but he said he would see what he could do. James expressed his gratitude in fulsome terms while making clear, wrote Hawkins, that he had "not a farthing of security to offer for the loan. A man who ought to have been worth from fifty to a hundred thousand pounds!"

Hawkins went to his bankers the next morning, arranged to take out the money and met James in court to tell him the news. James looked downcast: £1,250 would not be nearly enough, he needed twice that sum. "I was a little staggered," wrote Hawkins, but nonetheless went back to his bankers and agreed on the new sum, which he himself would have to borrow at five per cent interest. Hawkins stipulated that James would repay him £500 a quarter until the loan was paid off, but he need not have bothered, as he recounted:

> The next day he pledged the whole of his prospective income to a Jew, incurred fresh liabilities, and left me without a shadow of a chance of ever seeing a penny of my money again, and I need not say every farthing was lost, principal and interest.

James's total debts were said to be more than £100,000, and in April 1861 he resigned from the House of Commons and from his clubs, and his house in Berkeley Square was seized. The appalled benchers of the Inner Temple began an inquiry into his conduct; James offered to resign from the bar but his offer was declined, and the whole grisly story came out. James offered no objection to Lord Yarborough being questioned by the inquiry but as the peer began his evidence James suddenly left the room. Shortly afterwards his clerk sent in a note that James felt "too unwell" to continue attending. It was his last public appearance in Britain for eleven years. The hearing went on without him and the Inner Temple came up with the only verdict open to it: James was disbarred. Nothing daunted, at around the same time James married the widow of an army officer, perhaps in the hope that she might rescue him from his debts. If so, he was sadly mistaken. Within two years they had separated.

However, the word "chutzpah" might have been invented for Edwin James. He immediately set off for the United States, and in November 1861, shortly before his name was formally struck off the books of the Inner Temple, he was admitted to the Bar of New York. News travelled pretty quickly by then and his disbarment in London was soon known in America. Moves were made to disbar him in New York too but displaying his customary brass neck James simply denied the allegations on oath. Many Americans harboured a strong dislike of all things English and the New York Bar took a lenient view. He was allowed to continue practising law in his adopted country, which even granted him citizenship. He soon built up an extensive and remunerative law practice. Back in London, his appointment as QC was cancelled in 1862, and it may have been that the Americans, while admiring his pluck, eventually saw through his abilities as a lawyer, for by 1865 he was back on the stage trying to ply his old trade as an actor.

In 1872, things had quietened down sufficiently for James to judge it safe to return to London. Soon afterwards he gave a lecture on America at the St George's Hall in Langham Place and petitioned to be reinstated as a barrister. His request was turned down, so he articled himself to a City solicitor. He had lost none of his bumptiousness for he then tried to stand for Parliament as candidate for his old Marylebone seat. But little went right for him in the second act of his London life; he was reduced to giving the odd lecture on Garibaldi and writing the occasional magazine article. By 1882 he had fallen on such hard times that his remaining friends in the legal profession were about to raise a fund for him when he died on 4 March at the age of sixty-nine.

5
THE LAW OFFICERS

For much of the period between the mid-1870s and the first decade of the twentieth century, members of the Garrick occupied the principal legal offices of the crown—Lord Chancellor, Attorney-General, Solicitor-General—sometimes simultaneously and sometimes succeeding one another, at least once in controversial circumstances.

Sir John Holker (1828-1882, Garrick 1873-1882) was appointed Solicitor-General in 1874 by Disraeli and promoted to Attorney-General the following year. He served in that post until the general election of 1880 when Gladstone's Liberals returned to power. Holker was an unlikely success as a law officer for his early legal career was unpromising, to say the least. He was born in Bury, Lancashire, educated at the town's grammar school, articled to a solicitor in Kirkby Lonsdale, Westmoreland, and called to the bar at Gray's Inn in 1854. He returned north to base himself in Manchester and went on the northern circuit. But work was slow to arrive and he earned himself the nickname of "Sleepy Jack" Holker among the legal fraternity. He was once described as a "tall, plain, lumbering Lancashire man, who never seemed to labour a case nor to distinguish himself by ingenuity or eloquence, but through whom the justice of his case appeared to shine as through a dull but altogether honest medium."

Holker was clearly no ball of fire: after ten years building up his practice, he finally came to wider notice by his work on a parliamentary committee on the Stalybridge and Ashton Waterworks Bill, which does not sound like a springboard to legal distinction. However it seems to have done the trick: Holker moved to London in 1864 and became a QC two years later, specialising in patent law. In 1872, he was elected to Parliament at a by-election as Conservative member for the Lancashire seat of Preston. It was no ordinary by-election: it was the first to be contested under the Ballot Act, which had come into law earlier that year and under which the ballot was for the first time secret. The Preston by-election naturally attracted widespread publicity and brought Holker almost unwittingly to public attention. Luck continued to be on his side: many of the leading barristers of the day, such as William Ballantine, were tied up in the long-running Tichborne Claimant case, which provided Holker with a great deal of work that might not otherwise have come his way.

The days of "Sleepy Jack" were long gone. Sir Edward Clarke wrote of him: "Sir John Holker was a powerful advocate, and one of the kindest and most generous of men. Tall and massive in person, slow and deliberate in movement and in speech, there was a stately simplicity in his manner and his diction which was far more effective than the dramatic gesture and ornate rhetoric of some of his contemporaries. His phrases, spoken in a full richly-toned voice, were made more musical by the slight northern accent which broadened all the vowel sounds.

But his great strength as an advocate lay in his instinctive and conspicuous fairness to his opponents. That inspired such confidence in judges and juries that in his day he was almost irresistible on the Northern Circuit."

"He was the kindliest, the cheeriest, and the most lovable of men," wrote Montagu Williams. "He was always the same, never taking any pleasure save in the happiness and comfort of his old associates, in which respect he was very unlike many others who have arrived at the greatest height of distinction in their professions, and who never seem to be happy except when they are endeavouring to consort with persons supposed to be in a higher social grade than themselves."

Having briefly served as Solicitor-General, Holker became Attorney-General on the appointment of Sir Richard Baggallay to the Appeal Court and was a great success in the post. In those days the law officers could maintain their private practice alongside their public duties and it was hugely profitable to do so; Holker's income soared. As Attorney-General, he introduced the Bankruptcy and Criminal Code Bills as well as Bills relating to summary procedure and public prosecution. When Disraeli's administration was replaced by Gladstone's in 1880, Holker returned to private practice but was elevated to the Court of Appeal at the beginning of 1882. William Ballantine recalled visiting Holker and his second wife at his country seat at Coulthurst, on the Lancashire-Yorkshire border. He wrote approvingly of Holker's appointment as a judge: "The position that he attained at the Common Law bar speaks for itself; his selection to conduct important Equity cases shows that he must possess sufficient knowledge upon that branch for appellant business... I am uttering a very safe prophecy when I predict that he will be received with a hearty welcome on every circuit in the kingdom."

Alas, by the time the second edition of Ballantine's memoirs came out, he had to add a postscript recording Holker's premature death. His tenure in the Court of Appeal was sadly brief: his health deteriorated soon after his appointment, he resigned in May 1882 and died five days later, aged only 54. Edward Clarke wrote sadly: "I last saw him early in that year on the sea-front at Brighton. He was in a bath-chair, and his beautiful and devoted wife was walking by his side ... It was a lovely spring day, and I expressed a hope that he was enjoying the sunshine. 'Ah, my dear Clarke,' said he, 'a dying man does not enjoy anything.'"

Holker was both preceded and succeeded as Attorney-General by Sir Henry James, later Lord James of Hereford (1828-1911, Garrick 1862-1902), who had the distinction of being the first boy on the roll at Cheltenham College, with which he maintained a connection for the rest of his life. He began his legal studies at the Middle Temple and soon attracted notice as a student debater, like so many other future advocates of distinction. He built a successful commercial practice but his career really took off when he entered politics as Liberal MP for Taunton in 1869 and became known in the Commons for his powerful, if protracted, oratory. Within four years he was Solicitor-General under Gladstone and only two months later was promoted to Attorney-General in a reshuffle, but the administration fell shortly afterwards. When Gladstone returned in 1880, James resumed office as Attorney-General and held the the post for the full five-year term of the government. His principal achievement was to draft and nurse through the Commons the Corrupt and Illegal Practices Prevention Act of 1883, to eradicate intimidation and bribery. Re-elected for Bury in 1885, he was pressed hard by Gladstone to become Lord Chancellor in 1886 but declined the post because of his opposition to Irish Home Rule. Gladstone had a high regard for him: Roy Jenkins described him as the "epitome of an amenable but respected lawyer politician." Through his membership of the Garrick, he was a friend of the artist Sir John Millais, the author Charles Reade and other figures in the world of arts and books; a keen cricketer in his youth, he was President of the MCC in 1889.

James returned to his successful and lucrative private practice; as one of the legal team representing *The Times* during the commission of inquiry into the allegations the newspaper had made against Charles Stewart Parnell, he summed up in a speech lasting twelve days. He was an adviser, friend and confidant of the Prince of Wales, later Edward VII, was created Lord James of Hereford in 1895 and, by now a Liberal Unionist, joined the Cabinet as Chancellor of the Duchy of Lancaster, quitting politics (and the Garrick) in 1902. He sat as a Law Lord and was much in demand as an arbitrator in industrial disputes. He died in 1911. His private life was somewhat complex: by his mistress Alice Hardwicke he had a daughter, but he never married.

Going back to 1875, the man who succeeded Holker as Solicitor-General was his fellow Garrick member Hardinge Stanley Giffard (1823-1921, Garrick 1868-1886), who went on to become Lord Chancellor and the first Earl of Halsbury. The breadth of his accomplishments was extraordinary. He lived on well into the twentieth century, dying in 1921 at the age of 98, and his name lives on into the twenty-first century: *Halsbury's Laws of England*, which he was first invited to edit in 1907, remains the indispensable encyclopaedia of English law, now available online.

He was the son of Stanley Lees Giffard, an Irish barrister turned one of the most notable journalists of his time. An arch-conservative, he was editor of *The St James's Chronicle*, then founder-editor of the newspaper *The Standard* from 1827, a post he held for 25 years. Hardinge was his third son; he was educated at home and Merton College, Oxford, but graduated with only a fourth-class degree. A short, stocky young man with a squashed face and notable lack of eyebrows, he went to work for his father at *The Standard* but while the elder Giffard had moved from the law into journalism, his son moved in the opposite direction, being called to the bar at the Inner Temple in 1850. He joined first the Western, then the South Wales circuit, and chambers at 7 King's Bench Walk where his friend Harry Bodkin Poland was already a member; they were elected to the Garrick within a year of each other the following decade. Early in his career he appeared mainly in criminal cases at the Old Bailey and the Middlesex Sessions; on circuit, he did less well, largely he believed because Lord Campbell, the Lord Chief Justice, "evinced a chronic disinclination to accept the young advocate's arguments", as Lord Birkenhead later put it in an admiring essay on Halsbury.

When Poland's uncle William Henry Bodkin was created a judge in 1859, Giffard succeeded him as junior prosecuting counsel at the Central Criminal Court, which entailed appearing for the Crown in many important cases, in the police courts and in subsequent trials. He took silk in 1865; by this time he had risen to the top of the tree. "Solicitors who felt that their clients' interests demanded a silk who could conduct a telling cross-examination and make a convincing speech, went first to Giffard, and in due course he was seen on one side or the other in all the *causes célèbres*," wrote Birkenhead.

Giffard came to public attention two years later with his skilful defence of Edward John Eyre, the noted explorer of Australia and subsequently Governor of Jamaica who was accused of exceeding his powers in putting down a violent native rebellion on the Caribbean island. The issue aroused huge public attention and sharply divided political and intellectual opinion: John Stuart Mill chaired a committee containing other notable liberal figures who were determined to prosecute Eyre for murder; Thomas Carlyle, Alfred Lord Tennyson, John Ruskin and Charles Kingsley were among his equally vehement defenders. After returning to England, Eyre was charged with murder but, represented by Giffard, he was cleared by his local magistrates in Shropshire. The campaign to arraign him continued, however, and he was tried for a misdemeanour at Bow Street court. Again defended by Giffard, he was once more acquitted; Eyre retired to Shropshire to continue to enjoy his retirement, and Giffard's career at the bar prospered. In 1871-2, he was second counsel to his fellow Garrick member William Ballantine, in the long-running Tichborne Claimant trial. His friend, political colleague, frequent opponent in court and fellow Garrick member Sir Edward Clarke wrote of him: "Short of stature, not distinguished in appearance or manner, with a voice which though loud and clear was somewhat harsh and had no persuasive tones in it, Giffard was by his industry ... by his great knowledge of law, his strong masculine sense, his indomitable courage, and his excellence in the art of arranging and narrating facts, one of the most formidable of advocates. His scrupulous and absolute fairness gave him great influence with juries, and his reply in a criminal case was always worthy of study and imitation. It has been pleasant to see my old friend and companion develop into the greatest judge before whom I ever practised."

Montagu Williams had less solemn memories of Giffard. He recalled travelling with him to Shrewsbury to fight an election challenge arising from the 1870 general election against a young friend of Williams, Douglas Straight, who had won a narrow victory which he was then accused of buying. He fielded an all-Garrick defence team—Giffard, Williams and Harry Poland—while Serjeant Ballantine led for the prosecution. "Giffard was always one of the greatest possible sticklers for the performance of the duties that are expected from a junior," Williams noted, one of which was attending to "the eating and drinking department... for the whole party." So Williams knew what was expected of him from his leader. Giffard hated smoking and the smell of tobacco (and would certainly have been delighted by the smoking ban imposed by legislation on the Garrick today) and after dinner insisted that Williams go outside for his usual cigar, even though it was snowing heavily. Williams plotted his revenge. Giffard was a stickler for other rituals too, one being that on circuit he would not start on his own breakfast before his junior had joined him. Williams didn't eat breakfast so next morning he waited until 9.55 a.m. before going down to the breakfast room, leaving Giffard no time to eat his before they had to go off to court.

Furious, Giffard accused Williams of being "the most selfish fellow I ever came across" until Williams reminded him of the smoking incident the previous evening. Giffard then laughed and they left for court together. That evening Williams made up for the lack of breakfast by laying on a dinner of Lucullan proportions, with course after course arriving until Giffard asked what on earth was going on. Williams explained that he, not Giffard, was in charge of eating and drinking, and afterwards was allowed to stay by the fire and smoke his cigar in peace. The Garrick team won their case, to the great enthusiasm of the crowd in the square outside the court, and celebrated with a prolonged dinner which ended with Williams and his delighted client (but certainly not Giffard) having "a remarkably fine snow-ball fight around the gravestones in Shrewsbury churchyard" at two o'clock in the morning.

Giffard had always been, like his father, a staunch Conservative and he stood twice for Parliament in the general elections of 1868 and 1874, each time unsuccessfully. He was nonetheless appointed Solicitor-General by Disraeli in 1875. After a further setback at the hands of the voters in 1876 he was eventually elected MP for Launceston in 1877, retaining the seat in the general election of 1880 in which, however, the Conservatives lost office. Giffard combined an active role in politics with a renewed and successful career at the bar. In the Commons he led the traditionalist case against the freethinker Charles Bradlaugh, who, when elected MP for Northampton in 1880 wished to affirm rather than swear the oath of loyalty on the Bible, a battle it took Bradlaugh nearly six years to win.

When Lord Salisbury became Prime Minister for the first time in 1885 Giffard was appointed Lord Chancellor, more as a reward for his political endeavours for the Conservative party than for his legal career, distinguished though that had been. According to Birkenhead, Salisbury favoured Sir William Baliol Brett, later Lord Esher, while Giffard was backed by Lord Randolph Churchill. Giffard was said to have demanded an interview with the Prime Minister and stated his case so passionately that he got the job. He took the title of Baron Halsbury, of Halsbury in Devon. In the event, he was a highly successful Lord Chancellor, holding the office for three periods and a total of seventeen years, and retiring in 1905 at the age of 82, still in full possession of all his faculties.

Halsbury was not a complicated man. "He was the embodiment of the Tory spirit—plain, blunt and masterful, averse to change," wrote Birkenhead. "What he seemed to be, he was. There were no secret mysteries in his life; no unsuspected depths of learning or of guile." Although a conservative in every respect, he did not stand in the way of reform when it was generally agreed to be necessary. He was Lord Chancellor, for instance, when the Criminal Evidence Act of 1898 passed into law, at last enabling those accused of a crime to give evidence on their own behalf, a cause for which equally conservative lawyers like Edward Clarke had campaigned for decades. As Lord Chancellor, he attracted most criticism for the quality of his judicial appointments, particularly when it came to members of his own family.

The characteristic that governed his judgments as Lord Chancellor was common sense, and he expressed himself with admirable clarity, as in a case in which a jury's verdict was challenged: "If reasonable men might find ... the verdict which has been found, I think no Court has jurisdiction to disturb a decision of fact which the law has confided to juries, not to judges ... The principle must be that the judgment upon the facts is to be the judgment of the jury, and not the judgment of any other tribunal."

Some of his phrases will evoke sympathy more than a century after he pronounced them, for putting in simple language what many people still instinctively feel, although the law has developed hugely since then. In a personal injury claim which went to the Lords in 1900, Halsbury declared: "How is anybody to measure pain and suffering in moneys counted? ... In truth I think it would be very arguable to say that a person would be entitled to no damages for such things. What manly mind cares about pain and suffering in the past?" But after making his feelings plain, he went on to admit: "But nevertheless the law recognises that as a topic upon which damages may be given." (And have been given in increasing amounts ever since.)

His views on trades unions were robust and straightforward but even in his era the courts were developing a sympathetic view towards protecting them from legal action. Not so Halsbury: "If the Legislature has created a thing which can own property, which can employ servants, and which can inflict injury, it must be taken, I think, to have impliedly given the power to make it suable in a Court of Law for injuries purposely done by its authority and procurement." It would be more than eighty years before a government came round to endorsing that opinion and bringing in new laws to enforce it.

It is beyond the scope of this book to provide a detailed account of the countless judgments Halsbury delivered during his long tenure as Lord Chancellor and a Law Lord, but a consistent thread runs through them all, that of plain, unadorned good sense and a fierce wish to protect the core meaning of legislation and common law. Nor did he care much about the concept of public opinion. "I am not much impressed by the question: what the man in the street would say," he opined.

Even at the age of 89, he was still capable of standing up for longstanding legal precedent in forceful language, when rebutting the suggestion that a wife could be obliged to give evidence against her husband: "If you want to alter the law which has lasted for centuries and which is almost ingrained on the English constitution in the sense that everybody would say, 'To call a wife against her husband is a thing that cannot be heard of'—to suggest that that is to be dealt with by inference, and that you should introduce a new system of law without any specific enactment of it seems to me to be perfectly monstrous."

The use of the word "constitution" is an interesting one, for it surely means not the (unwritten) English constitution but the sensibilities and common sense of the average English citizen, of whom Halsbury himself was such a shining example. He went on sitting until he was at least ninety-three, and a service was held at the Temple Church in 1920, the year before he died, to celebrate the seventieth anniversary of his being called to the bar.

At the same time as Giffard was appointed Lord Chancellor for the second time, in July 1886, his old post of Solicitor-General was filled by Edward George Clarke

(1841-1931, Garrick 1884-1931). Clarke was a remarkable figure by any standards, a man from a humble background who rose to the very top of the legal profession but whose political career suffered because he would never budge from his principles (see Chapter Six).

In 1905, Halsbury was succeeded as Lord Chancellor by another Garrick Club member, Robert Threshie Reid (1846-1923, Garrick 1869-1896). He was created Earl Loreburn and sat on the woolsack for seven years of turbulence and controversy which culminated in the drastic curtailment of the powers of the House of Lords in 1911.

Reid came from a distinguished Scottish family but he was born in 1846 on the Greek island of Corfu, then a British protectorate, where his father, Sir James Reid, was the chief justice. He, like Henry James, was educated at Cheltenham College; he went on to Balliol College, Oxford. He was a brilliant sportsman at both school and university. He represented Oxford at both cricket (he was a fine wicketkeeper) and rackets, and maintained a lifelong interest in cricket, being elected president of the MCC in 1907 (again, following in the footsteps of Henry James). The Mike Brearley of his day, he was also an outstanding scholar, taking first-class honours in classical moderations and *literae humaniores* before following his father into the law: he was called to the bar by the Inner Temple in 1871 and went on the Oxford circuit.

Henry James was to be a guiding hand in both law and politics: Reid "devilled" for him before tasting early success in commercial law. James was instrumental in getting him selected as Liberal candidate for the older man's home city of Hereford and Reid entered Parliament in 1880. He took silk in 1882 but made no great early mark in the Commons and stood down at Hereford in 1885 when it became a single-member constituency. He won the Scottish seat of Dumfries the following year and, unlike his mentor James, stayed loyal to Gladstone over Home Rule.

In 1894 he became in swift succession Solicitor-General and Attorney-General but left office in 1895 with the change in government. Ten years later, he was a perhaps surprising choice by Campbell-Bannerman to be Lord Chancellor but as Baron Loreburn he was a success in the office, his greatest achievement being the establishment of the Court of Criminal Appeal in 1907, long advocated by many criminal lawyers who had witnessed terrible miscarriages of justice which they could do precious little about. As with every such reform before and since, it also attracted huge opposition but Loreburn's performance at the head of the new institution proved the doubters wrong. A supporter of Lords reform, he presided over the Upper House's historic ceding of most of its powers in 1911. His health suffered during his period on the woolsack and was the major contributor to his retirement in 1912 though in the event he lived on for a further sixteen years.

Reid had been succeeded as Solicitor-General in 1894 by one of his closest friends and yet another Garrick member, Sir Frank Lockwood (1846-1897, Garrick 1882-1897). Lockwood was a colourful, larger than life and much-loved character, and an accomplished artist, a skill inherited from his father. He sketched compulsively in idle moments in and out of court and left a large collection of drawings of judges, barristers and other courtroom personalities. Indeed, his drawings largely took the place of a diary or even letters. "It is no exaggeration to say that he communicated with his family and friends pictorially," wrote his friend, biographer and fellow Liberal MP Augustine Birrell. Lockwood would dash them off and give them away to anyone who wanted them; they became collectors' items, and Lockwood was delighted when visiting the Prince of Wales to find that he had acquired his own personal Lockwood collection which he proudly showed to the artist. For his younger daughter Madge he invented a cartoon character called Moses, with vaguely Semitic features, who was the epitome of the naughty boy, and he would make up stories about him and adorn his letters to her with drawings of Moses up to all sorts of mischief.

Standing six feet two inches tall, Lockwood was an imposing figure, a good-looking man with prematurely white hair and a ready smile, fond of telling amusing stories against himself and a great practical joker. When for a magazine article Birrell, no mean wit himself, invented a character called the Rev Tobias Boffin, B.A. (Lond) during a dreary debate in the House of Commons, Lockwood seized upon it and gave Boffin a whole new existence, inserting his name into smart dinner parties and on one occasion placing a marriage notice in a newspaper, the ceremony having been performed by Boffin. Birrell even received a newspaper cutting reporting that the Rev T. Boffin had harangued a speaker at a political meeting and delivered a strongly-worded attack on Birrell. How Lockwood engineered that particular joke remained a mystery.

Lockwood was a proud Yorkshireman, born in Doncaster, and educated locally and at Manchester Grammar School, after his father moved to that city, and at Gonville and Caius College, Cambridge, where he was a far from diligent student. He spent more time rowing and playing cricket than at his books, being better known for his dislike of authority, good nature and propensity for high jinks. A friend recounted how, passing St John's, they noticed a crowd of Old Johnians gathering for a college event. Lockwood darted into a nearby shop, came out with an M.A.'s gown, joined the throng posing as an old boy of the college and sat down next to "a reverend gentleman old enough to be his father with whom, in awestruck whispers, he conversed about 'old times'." Lockwood eventually managed a pass degree and the distinction of being sent down after obtaining it as a consequence of a fracas with a policeman while he and a friend were trying to climb into their college after hours. Undaunted, Lockwood put on a false beard, styled himself Major Macpherson and returned to Caius to spend a couple of days with his friends before departing from Cambridge for good.

He was clearly not cut out for the life of a clergyman, as his father had hoped, and after a few months touring as an amateur actor with a group of friends (again under the name of Macpherson), he decided to study law on the spur of the moment while visiting a friend in Lincoln's Inn. He was called to the bar at the same Inn in 1872 and prospered from the start, "almost the inevitable result of his natural endowments and character," as Birrell put it. He went on:

> His manner was at once striking and engaging, nor was there in his mode of conducting a case any apparent indifference to the result, an offence seldom overlooked by the brief-giving fraternity. His jokes and quips had business in them, and never either diverted or delayed the course of what is called justice. His views of life were manly and familiar... A jury had only to look at him to see that they had pleading before them a man who, though he

did not expect too much of human nature, hated cruelty, fraud and oppression, and would not willingly be a party to any mean or paltry chicanery. Though not a great speaker... he was on occasions most impressive. In fine, he had a personality which attracted attention, and won both liking and confidence.

In 1874 he married Julia Salis Schwabe, daughter of a wealthy German-born Manchester industrialist whose wife, also Julia, was a distinguished educationalist and helped to introduce the kindergarten to Britain; they numbered the anti-Corn Law campaigner Richard Cobden, the composer Chopin, Charles Hallé (founder of the Hallé Orchestra) and Mrs Gaskell among their friends.

Lockwood was a popular figure on circuit in the North and Midlands. A jury in York, for which he was also an MP, was once reported to have declared in favour of "him as Mr Lockwood's for" without bothering to consider the evidence. He first featured in a high-profile trial when he agreed to defend the notorious criminal Charles Peace on a murder charge at Leeds Assizes in 1879. There was huge public interest in the case, fanned by the popular newspapers, for Peace had been on the run for several years. Lockwood did his best, attacking the press for its reckless coverage which, he claimed, had found Peace guilty long before his trial. But the evidence was overwhelming and Peace was hanged. Shortly afterwards, at a function at his old Cambridge college, Lockwood was congratulated for his defence of "Peace with honour", to which he retorted that it had not been "Peace at any price", as he had received no fee for his work.

After eleven years at the Bar, he became a QC in 1882, and in 1884 was made Recorder of Sheffield, in which post he distinguished himself for his leniency. That year he was elected Liberal MP for York after two earlier unsuccessful attempts, at King's Lynn and York. He was a popular candidate, with his cheerful demeanour and quick wit, and equally popular in Parliament. At the bar he was handling more fashionable divorces and libel actions, representing among others the Liberal MP and wealthy editor and writer Henry Labouchere, who regularly attracted libel writs as a result of his outspoken articles in his magazine *Truth*. During one trial, Labouchère told the court he estimated he had spent £40,000 defending himself at law. "Long may you prosper!" exclaimed Lockwood, to gales of laughter.

Along with Sir Henry James and Robert Reid, Lockwood played an important role before the Parnell Commission, which sat for more than a year from 1888 to 1889 inquiring into the truth of allegations made by *The Times* into the conduct of the Irish nationalist leader and other Irish MPs. It was not a popular tribunal with the lawyers, dragging on apparently aimlessly for month after month. In 1894 his great friend Reid was appointed Attorney-General and Lockwood took his place as Solicitor-General, a Garrick double. In 1896, the Liberals lost power and Lockwood should have swiftly given up the reins. But the man whom the new Prime Minister Lord Salisbury wished to appoint in his place, the great advocate and former holder of the office (and yet another Garrick member) Sir Edward Clarke, believed he should be allowed to retain a certain amount of private practice, which the Government had forbidden the law officers to do in 1894. Clarke was a stubborn man and would not budge, so Lockwood found himself carrying on while the situation was sorted out. A couple of months later he handed over to Sir Robert Finlay (another Garrick member, inevitably) who went on to hold all three government legal offices.

In 1896, Lockwood travelled to the United States with the Lord Chief Justice, Lord Russell of Killowen, plus his wife and elder daughter, for the annual meeting of the American Bar Association at Saratoga Springs. He kept a diary, illustrated with his sketches, and recorded how they had met President Cleveland, a very fat man whom he drew standing upright in a small boat and looking rather uneasy; Cleveland's opponent for the presidency William Jennings Bryan, whom they heard give a campaign speech and with whom they were invited to share the platform; and the great inventor Thomas Edison, whom Lockwood clearly found easily the most interesting of the three. To the shock and grief of his friends and colleagues, Lockwood died the following year after an undisclosed illness at the age of only fifty-one. "His was an intensely emotional temperament, and an imaginative nature," lamented Augustine Birrell. "He had an actor's sensitiveness and an artist's fancy."

Lord Rosebery, who had appointed Lockwood Solicitor-General, wrote: "So powerful was [his] personality that his entrance into a room seemed to change the whole complexion of the company, and I often fancied that he could dispel a London fog by his presence."

Sir Robert Finlay (1842-1929, Garrick 1871-1919) succeeded Lockwood as Solicitor-General, became Attorney-General in 1900, serving in the post for five years, and in 1916 became Lord Chancellor. He was a Scotsman who graduated in medicine from Edinburgh University but after only a few months in practice switched to the law. He became a very successful silk: more of a scholar than a courtroom performer, he was frequently in the appeal court and House of Lords. He was Liberal MP for first Inverness Burghs and then Edinburgh and St Andrew's Universities. As Attorney-General he erred in not prosecuting the financier Whitaker Wright for fraud; in the end a private prosecution went ahead and Wright was demolished in court by Rufus Isaacs. Finlay was best known as an international lawyer. As Attorney-General he handled several big international arbitration cases and after his brief (and unhappy) spell as Lord Chancellor he became the first British judge to sit at the newly created Permanent Court of International Justice at The Hague, where he commanded huge respect for his experience and learning. A keen golfer, he was Captain of the Royal & Ancient Golf Club in 1903.

Among his successors as Solicitor-General and his immediate predecessor as Lord Chancellor was Sir Stanley (later Viscount) Buckmaster (1861-1934, Garrick 1909-1934). His Garrick membership is commemorated in his *Dictionary of National Biography* entry by Geoffrey Russell, who records that he was "much beloved" at the club, but adds rather tartly: "He seldom said a witty thing and seldom told a good story, but his speeches at the famous Sunday dinners at the club were delightful in their always kindly humour." He was a long-time Trustee of the club. Buckmaster was indeed a superb orator, rated by many as the finest platform speaker in the country, although he rarely spoke from a script but merely from a few scribbled notes.

Buckmaster studied mathematics at Christ Church, Oxford. He built up a successful practice as a Chancery junior and took Silk in 1902, after which he went into politics, being elected Liberal MP for Cambridge from 1906-10 and for Keighley from 1911-15. During this period he was also an immensely successful and well remunerated Chancery silk. He was appointed Solicitor-General in 1913 and became thoroughly unpopular with the Press when at the outbreak of war in 1914 he was appointed director of the Press Bureau and took a hard line with newspapers which did not, as he saw it, show sufficient subservience to the government in its handling of the conflict. In 1915, he became Lord Chancellor but had little chance to demonstrate his ability in the role as he was replaced only eighteen months later (by Finlay) when Lloyd George became Prime Minister. After the war he acquired the reputation of being an outstanding judge in the Lords, though he was not the creative type: in the modern American parlance, he was a "strict constructionist". He was more adventurous in the political sphere, a vigorous campaigner for social reform, most notably in the field of divorce. Like one or two politicians of the contemporary era, he became more radical as he grew older.

6
SIR EDWARD CLARKE,
EMINENT VICTORIAN

❝ To succeed at the Bar a man requires three things: he must be ambitious, very poor and very much in love." So wrote Sir Edward Clarke (1841-1931, Garrick 1884-1931), who had certainly succeeded at the bar and who equally certainly qualified in all those categories. His magisterial axiom was often quoted although it may be that only the first requirement stands up to a moment's scrutiny: the latter two were disproved by the backgrounds of Clarke's rivals for the title of England's leading barrister in the last quarter of the nineteenth century. Be that as it may, one can imagine Clarke delivering his words to a rapt jury and its members swallowing every word.

Clarke was generalising from the particular, for he was describing his own early life. He came from a humble background, worked ferociously hard to forge a hugely successful career at the Bar and as a Conservative MP, and was twice happily married: when his first wife, whom he had adored at first sight since youth and who was the mother of his first three children, died young, he remarried a woman half his age within months and their marriage was successful and long-lasting. He became something of a celebrity; his severe features, adorned by long side-whiskers which cascaded well below his chin, were a familiar sight to readers of the popular newspapers who followed his courtroom exploits in the most celebrated cases of the day with the sort of rapt attention that television talent shows receive in our own era. The experts agreed about his greatest strength as an advocate. Sir Norman Birkett, as highly regarded as Clarke in a later era, wrote: "Edward Clarke had the supreme gift—the advocate's pearl of great price—the gift of persuasion." Edgar Lustgarten, the legal writer, added: "Clarke's endowment was persuasiveness, and his weapon was the speech—not the smooth persuasiveness of wheedling or blandishment, but that powerful persuasiveness that springs from deep sincerity."

Edward Clarke was the son of a silversmith who had a shop in King William Street in the City of London and who had come up to the capital from Bath, where he had served his apprenticeship; the family originally hailed from Axbridge in Somerset. The Clarkes lived above the shop with their six children, of whom Edward was the third child and oldest boy. His mother was active in the Society for the Promotion of Christian Knowledge and the atmosphere in the cramped but highly respectable household was typical of the early Victorian era, in which reading and music were encouraged. The young Edward was bookish and delicate and at the age of eight was sent away to board at Merchant Taylor's School in Edmonton, then in the heart of the countryside, for the sake of his health. He grew stronger but not happier and after two years was brought back home and sent to the City Commercial day school in Lombard Street where he thrived, excelling in elocution, though not apparently reaching the heights of a recent pupil named John Henry Brodribb, later rather better known by his stage name of Henry Irving, who was to become a firm friend and fellow member of the Garrick Club. "Whenever I had done anything particularly well, I used to hear 'Very good, Clarke, very good, but I wish you could have heard Brodribb say that,'" Clarke recalled. He had conceived the ambition to be a Member of Parliament as early as the age of nine and vividly remembered being taken by his father to join the crowd in Parliament Street where Sir Robert Peel lay dying, having fallen off his horse on Constitution Hill, and at the age of eleven standing on a box in the Strand to watch the Duke of Wellington's funeral procession. But for all his progress at school Edward had to leave at the age of thirteen to help his father in the shop.

He was still an avid reader, being particularly influenced by the novels of Benjamin Disraeli, little realising they would one day be political colleagues. "*Coningsby* and *Sybil* together made me a politician," he later wrote. At the age of fourteen, he saw Charles Dickens make his first political speech at a packed meeting of the Administrative Reform Association, formed to protest at the conduct of the Crimean War. The organisers were amused to see the boy, who was small for his age, but let him in none the less, and he was hugely impressed by Dickens's "attractive presence" and his "melodious and penetrating voice".

Fortunately Clarke was able to continue his education at evening classes which had recently been instituted at Crosby Hall in Bishopsgate. There he again excelled: he won a ten-guinea prize for English Literature and entered with gusto in the social life associated with the Hall. He starred in debate and met a girl, Annie Mitchell, whom he almost instantly—and accurately—decided he would marry. He continued to be successful in the annual Society of Arts examinations and in 1858 he went to Oxford to sit for the University's first outside examination for the degree of Associate of Arts. He came out top of all the entrants, becoming the University's first Associate of Arts. This was a remarkable coup for the silversmith's son who was taking advantage of Victorian society's slow but accelerating moves to broaden the opportunities available to talented young people. His next step was to sit a new public examination for eight clerkships in the India Office, with salary and allowances amounting to £150 a year, a decent sum for a young man. He came seventh and at the age of eighteen entered the India Office.

But Clarke's eyes were already fixed on a further horizon. His extensive reading in history had planted the seed of interest in a political career but how would a young man of his background ever get a foothold in that world? One day he attended a debate in the House of Lords and was particularly impressed by a speech by Lord Lyndhurst, a former Lord Chancellor, by then in his eighties, who was of similarly humble birth. Perhaps the law could offer the young man a path to politics? When Clarke set himself on a path there was no diverting him. Such was the case with Annie Mitchell, to whom he became engaged while he was still only eighteen, to his mother's strong disapproval. He was also determined to pursue a career in the law and the opportunity to do so arose when the India Office, on moving premises, decided to cut its staff numbers and offered generous severance terms to volunteers. Clarke forsook the safety of the clerk's life and took the £253 on offer to leave. It was a huge gamble but he never doubted the wisdom of his decision.

In June 1861 he was elected to a Tancred Studentship at Lincoln's Inn and embarked on his new life. He ate his dinners and was taken into chambers, first by a young barrister called Vernon Lushington, then by Thomas Randall Bennett. He also worked as a court reporter for a Conservative newspaper *The Morning Herald* (he had learned shorthand at evening class), which gave him valuable experience of court work. The newspaper was impressed enough by his diligence and literary ability to offer him a regular slot as a book reviewer, which gave him a welcome additional salary. He had not forgotten his political ambitions: he also fitted in some parliamentary reporting for *The Examiner*, a weekly paper, which provided him with a close-up view of the arena he hoped to enter in due course, and he polished his public speaking at the Hardwicke Society, a debating society which then met in rooms off Fleet Street (it later moved to the Middle Temple).

Clarke was called to the bar in November 1864, and moved to chambers at 3, Garden Court. Like most young barristers without patronage, his was the usual bag of mundane cases at the lowest levels of court life, the county and police courts. Now his debating skills, and contacts, came to the rescue: Clarke had led the Conservative side in the Crosby Hall debates and the leader of the Liberal faction there was a young solicitor's clerk called W.R. Stephens. While he differed from Clarke in politics, he recognised his ability and he got his firm, Freelands, to send him a prosecution brief on behalf of the South Eastern Railway. Clarke lost the case but performed well enough to get more work from the firm. His debating skills brought him his first break, from a different source: attending another debating society, he stood in for a speaker who failed to turn up, and performed brilliantly. His off-the-cuff speech impressed another member of the audience, a solicitor and former MP, J.P. Morrough. He sent him a couple of cases, the second of which brought Clarke to the notice of the most senior judges by a convoluted set of circumstances within only a few months of being at the bar. The American authorities had applied to extradite Charles Windsor, a New York bank clerk accused of making off with a large sum of money by making false entries in the bank's books. He could only be extradited if forgery could be proved: but was making a false entry the same as forgery? Clarke was briefed as junior defence counsel and did not expect to speak before the panel hearing the case, headed by no less than the Lord Chief Justice, Lord Cockburn. But another lawyer involved in the case, Hardinge Giffard, urged him to add to his leader's words, and so he did, making a decent impression. (Giffard was to go on to become Lord Chancellor as Lord Halsbury and be a great Garrick friend of Clarke's.) But this was not the end of the Windsor case. The errant clerk was released on a habeas corpus petition but his former employer brought a civil action to recover its money and the case was heard in July 1865, again by the Lord Chief Justice. But a general election had just been called and the Circuits had just started. This double set of circumstances meant that no fewer than four leading counsel (including the soon to be discredited Edwin James QC) were called away in turn either to go on circuit or fight the election. This left Clarke, at 24 a virtual novice, representing Windsor against three senior barristers. He was denied an adjournment and so had to fight the case. He lost but made a good impression on all present, including *The Times* reporter.

Clarke never wasted an opportunity to demonstrate his deft legal mind. At Surrey Sessions he represented a couple accused of keeping a brothel. He obtained the woman's discharge on the grounds that she was being coerced by her husband. But he then announced he would call her as a witness on behalf of her "husband". The chairman naturally objected, only to be told by Clarke that she was not after all the man's wife. The woman gave evidence that she was not indeed married to the accused, who was an actor and could prove that he was on stage while the activities in the brothel were allegedly proceeding. He was duly acquitted.

Clarke had suffered a setback in his personal life when Annie broke off their engagement in 1863. Although he pronounced himself resigned to being merely friendly with her, he made no attempt to find a replacement in his affections. Three years later he proposed again, and the couple were married in December 1866. Three children followed.

His legal practice slowly grew as did his political reputation. His great ability as a public speaker meant that he was much in demand in support of Conservative candidates up and down the country. Such activity on behalf of the inexperienced young Lord Randolph Churchill at Woodstock formed the basis of a lifelong friendship between the two men, despite their very different backgrounds and occasional deep political differences.

In the long vacation of 1865 Clarke wrote a textbook on extradition. It went into several editions and brought him plenty of work on the subject, including the celebrated case of Henri de Tourville, a Frenchman who had become a British citizen and led a rather rackety life. Styling himself the Count de Tourville, he married a wealthy widow whose body was found shortly afterwards at the bottom of a steep river bank in the Tyrol. De Tourville's story was that while they were out walking she had slipped and hurt herself slightly so he returned to their hotel for help. The men sent to aid her found her body. A local judge cleared De Tourville of any wrongdoing and he departed for London with a large legacy, but a higher court applied for his extradition. Representing the requesting state and exhibiting Poirot-like skills of detection, Clarke demonstrated to the Bow Street magistrate's satisfaction how the poor lady's demise was unlikely to have been an accident and De Tourville, against all expectations and despite being represented by two other Garrick men, Harry Poland and Montagu Williams, was packed off back to Austria to face the music.

Clarke's star was clearly on the rise but it was two high-profile criminal cases in 1877 that brought him to the attention of the wider public, even though in one he was on the losing side. Such trials were reported in great (and accurate) detail by the newspapers and avidly followed by their readers. Long before the advent of radio and television, the Old Bailey and the various assize courts provided daily soap operas with a cast of real people, often on trial for their lives; the existence of the death penalty added a grim backdrop to every murder trial until the 1960s. The barristers leading for prosecution and defence could also become stars almost overnight if the case had the right dramatic ingredients. That was certainly so in the trial at the Old Bailey of four young men and women accused of the murder of Harriet Staunton, who had died in a house in the Kent suburb of Penge only a few days after the death of her baby son. It emerged that Mrs Staunton had been in an appallingly emaciated and filthy state when she died, and the prosecution case was that she had been confined and starved to death by her husband Louis, a rakish auctioneer's clerk twelve years her junior, his 18-year-old mistress, his brother Patrick, and his wife. Harriet Staunton had brought to the marriage a £2,000 legacy which naturally provided her relatives with motive enough to suspect Louis Staunton's motives in marrying her. Indeed, her mother had been so concerned that she had unsuccessfully tried to have Harriet declared unfit to marry. The young woman's pitiful condition and the circumstances of her death provoked an outcry and it was Edward Clarke's unenviable task to defend Patrick Staunton. At that time, the accused could not give evidence, which Clarke always considered a legal outrage and which he eventually helped to rectify nearly twenty years later. Still a junior, he was up against the combined might of the Attorney-General Sir John Holker and the Solicitor-General Sir Hardinge Giffard. But Clarke was to be the leading voice for the defence because it was agreed that he should cross-examine on behalf of all four defendants on the medical evidence, which was not nearly as straightforward as the prosecution made out. The postmortem had shown evidence of tuberculosis in Harriet's lungs and brain. Clarke gave up his summer holiday to study the disease and he cross-examined the prosecution's medical witnesses with great skill and thoroughness. In addition, he delivered a closing speech whose peroration he considered, looking back many years later, to be the finest he ever delivered. But it was in vain, or almost. The eloquence and forensic skills of the finest barristers can mean nothing if the judge is hopelessly biased against you, as Clarke considered Mr Justice Hawkins to be in the Staunton trial. Hawkins took eleven hours to sum up and left no doubt in the jury's mind of his belief in the defendants' guilt. Clarke described it damningly: "Speaking in a gentle, clear, beautifully modulated voice, the Judge set himself to recapitulate all the facts, however trivial and unimportant, which had been related in the evidence of the last four days. As an exhibition of tenacious and exact memory it was wonderful. The narrative was complete and perfectly arranged. But of the judicial fairness which should characterise a summing-up, especially in so grave a case as this, there was not the slightest trace." Hawkins hardly dealt with the medical evidence at all and insisted on continuing his summing-up until 9.30 pm with only a quarter of an hour's break, so that the jury in the stuffy courtroom was numb with exhaustion by the time he concluded. Clarke was scandalised by Hawkins's conduct. The jury was then sent out to consider its verdict (no overnight hotels in those days) and came back ninety minutes later. All four defendants were found guilty and sentenced to death. But out of defeat, Clarke plucked a victory of sorts. So powerful had been the medical evidence which he had produced that a public campaign was mounted against the verdicts, led by another distinguished Garrick man, the writer Charles Reade, and supported by a petition signed by 400 doctors, headed by Sir William Jenner. The sentences were commuted to life imprisonment. Clarke's biographers summed it up very aptly: "So Clarke, although he had failed to win the verdict in the Court, had carried the day with this unusual Court of Appeal." There was a footnote, which spoke volumes about Clarke's humanity and generosity: many years later, after Louis Staunton had been released from prison, Clarke gave him £100 to help him join a relative's business, after which Staunton remarried and flourished. Clarke had no such merciful feelings towards the judge. "Sir Henry Hawkins continued his career of public disservice," he wrote. Clarke waited until 1898, when Hawkins retired, to take his revenge. He wrote to the Attorney-General to say that if he made a speech complimenting Hawkins, as had become the custom, "I should make a public protest." No such farewell was forthcoming.

The other trial of 1877 that helped make Clarke's name became famous as the Detectives' Case. Four Scotland Yard detectives were accused of taking bribes by a gang of fraudsters: the evidence against three was substantial but less so against the fourth, Inspector George Clarke, an officer of nearly forty years' standing against whom there had previously been not a breath of suspicion. Edward Clarke, whose junior was Charles Willie Mathews, had to convince the jury that his namesake had been framed by the gang leader, Harry Benson, alias Yonge. He did this by treating the slippery Benson with elaborate courtesy in the witness box; Benson was so flattered that he gave Clarke the answers he needed. Next, Clarke established that George Clarke's superior officer trusted him and knew of his dealings with Benson. Lastly, his final speech to the jury came to a magnificent and moving climax in defence of the Inspector's honesty. Within an hour of retiring, the jury convicted the other three but cleared Inspector Clarke. The case had exposed the rottenness at the heart of Scotland Yard and the upshot of it was the creation of the Criminal Investigation Department, the CID, which was to become world-famous. As in the previous case, Clarke's humanity was evident long after it had concluded. When one of the guilty detectives, having served his time in prison, applied to open a pub in Surrey, Clarke helped to persuade the local magistrates to grant him a licence.

After two such prominent cases, Clarke's career prospered but life was not all plain sailing. He applied to be Recorder of Brighton but was unsuccessful, and his private life was in turmoil. His little daughter Mabel died of tubercular meningitis and his wife fell ill with the TB from which she never recovered. He also declined an offer from the Attorney-General Sir John Holker to be appointed to the coveted post of Junior Counsel to the Treasury, the "Treasury Devil", because his long-term ambition was to become first a Conservative MP and then Solicitor-General.

He achieved the first goal at a by-election early in 1880 in the Southwark constituency, where he had been a prominent figure for some time. Clarke overturned the Liberal majority and was briefly the toast of the Conservative Party. He was invited to lunch by his hero, Disraeli, the Prime Minister, who congratulated him on "a brilliant campaign". But his triumph was short-lived. As frequently happened to him, Clarke fell ill through stress and overwork and was prescribed absolute rest by his doctor, Sir William Jenner, at precisely the moment he achieved the goal of being appointed QC. Encouraged by Clarke's Southwark victory, Disraeli called a general election in which the Conservatives were soundly beaten. The convalescing Clarke was unable to campaign and within six weeks of being elected was thrown out by a fickle electorate.

But all was not lost. In those days many challenges were made to results by means of an election petition and Clarke was frequently in demand to mount them in the Conservative interest. He was very busy in this line of business after the 1880 election, a thoroughly corrupt affair, and succeeded in overturning several results in favour of his party. He was also to benefit personally from a successful petition against the Conservative winner at Plymouth, a case in which he was not involved. A by-election had to be held and Clarke was invited to represent the Conservatives. He accepted and was elected by a wafer-thin majority. But his wife did not share his triumph for long. Her illness worsened and she died in March 1881. Before she died she had expressed the hope that her husband would remarry and that his bride should be a young cousin of hers, Kathleen Bryant, then only twenty-two, who had cared for her in her final illness. Clarke, eighteen years her senior, did not take long in coming round to the idea himself. After taking her to a performance of *Romeo and Juliet* starring his Garrick friend Henry Irving, Clarke proposed to her. They were married only a few days later and enjoyed a happy and successful union that lasted for fifty years.

Happy once more in his private life, Clarke was now where he had always wanted to be in his public one. He was a successful QC and developing a good reputation as a loyal and capable opposition backbench MP. In 1886 he took on a case that gripped the country for months and came to be regarded as his greatest achievement as a defence counsel: the trial of Adelaide Bartlett for the murder of her husband. She was an attractive and slightly mysterious young woman, the illegitimate daughter of a Frenchwoman and an Englishman, who was married at nineteen to Edwin Bartlett, a successful provisions dealer more than ten years her senior. On the surface they had a happy marriage though it later transpired that it was essentially a sexless union: on the one occasion they had intercourse she became pregnant but their child was stillborn. Nor was this the only unusual feature of their marriage: it became a threesome (though probably still an asexual one) with the involvement of their clergyman in Merton, south London, George Dyson, rather a wet-sounding young man who developed a strong affection for Adelaide, with the active encouragement of her husband. After they had been married for a decade, Edwin Bartlett's health declined: the cause was found to be mercury poisoning. Mrs Bartlett looked after him devotedly but confided in his doctor, Alfred Leach, that she was worried she would be suspected of poisoning him. Edwin Bartlett made a partial recovery, but in late December 1885 Adelaide asked Dyson to get her some chloroform to help her husband sleep at night. He did so but some time on New Year's night Edwin Bartlett died at their Pimlico home. Adelaide said she woke to find him lying on the floor but could not revive him. A post-mortem was held next day and the doctors present noticed a strong smell of chloroform when the body was opened. After more tests, an inquest returned a verdict of wilful murder against Adelaide Bartlett, and against Dyson, who had come clean about his role during the hearing. Edward Clarke was entrusted with the defence of Mrs Bartlett, and swiftly realised that the case would turn on the medical evidence, and on the use of chloroform as a murder weapon. As with the Staunton case, he steeped himself in all the medical literature available until he was confident he had mastered the subject.

The trial at the Old Bailey generated huge public interest, with the public devouring the lengthy daily newspaper reports of the proceedings. The defence was entirely a Garrick affair: Dyson was represented by Frank Lockwood QC. The prosecution was led by the Attorney-General Charles Russell QC, acknowledged to be the finest advocate of the day (though Clarke ran him close). But he was not perhaps ideally suited to this particular case, depending as it did on minute scrutiny of complicated medical matters, at which Clarke, with his meticulous attention to detail and capacity for sheer hard work, excelled. As an Irish nationalist, Russell may have been distracted by the fact that at the same time Gladstone's first Home Rule Bill was being introduced in the Commons, requiring long hours of attendance in the House after each day's adjournment at the Bailey. His first move was a surprise: he offered no evidence against Dyson, who was formally acquitted. Russell went on to outline the prosecution case: that Adelaide Bartlett had first sedated her husband with chloroform, then when he was unconscious poured more chloroform, in liquid form, down his throat.

Clarke marshalled the defence skilfully before the climax of the case, the examination of the medical evidence. (It must be remembered that defendants could not, at that time, appear as witnesses so Adelaide Bartlett could not go into the witness box and tell her side of the story.) First, he adroitly got the dead man's father, who had always opposed the marriage, disliked his daughter-in-law and wanted the jury to share his belief in her guilt, to discredit himself in comprehensive fashion. Then he went easy on Dyson when cross-examining him, realising that to destroy him (as he could easily have done, for his behaviour had left him wide open to criticism) would reflect badly on Adelaide Bartlett too. That left the medical evidence. First to be cross-examined was Dr Leach. Before getting on to chloroform poisoning, Clarke elicited from him the revelation that in his last days Edwin Bartlett believed he was receiving a "vital force" from his sleeping wife as he stood over her; in other words, that he might have been becoming deranged, and raising the possibility that he might have committed suicide (which Russell had raised, then dismissed). Under Clarke's patient cross-examination, Leach agreed that administration of chloroform was a very difficult operation which required skilful handling, and that it was usually accompanied by vomiting, depending on what the patient had eaten. Pressed by Clarke as to whether Bartlett would have been likely to have done so, Leach agreed that it was "a very likely suggestion". Leach was merely a humble general practitioner; Clarke now had to question Dr Thomas Stevenson, Professor of Medical Jurisprudence at Guy's Hospital, and a leading authority on toxicology. His cross-examination of such an expert was a masterpiece. In his brief questioning by Russell, Stevenson stated that it was quite possible to administer liquid chloroform to a man who had been sedated by a previous dose. Clarke's purpose was to show that this operation was very difficult and well-nigh impossible for someone without medical training (such as Adelaide Bartlett). Every time Stevenson made an assertion, Clarke was able to come up with a textbook which qualified it in some way, culminating in Stevenson tacitly admitting that the administration of liquid chloroform could only be done successfully by a skilled operator. Finally, Clarke got Stevenson to agree that it would also be likely to burn the unconscious man's windpipe: no such trace had been found in the post-mortem. Furthermore, had the post-mortem been held on the day Bartlett died, as his wife had wished, Stevenson agreed with Clarke that there would have been more chance of determining the cause of death. It was a most effective parting shot.

Clarke's final speech to the jury lasted five hours and held the jury rapt throughout. He started with an attack on Russell's right to the last word before the judge summed up and followed with a gratuitous and perhaps uncharacteristic dig at Russell's Irish roots: "My learned friend, coming from a country distinguished far more for its advocates than for its judges, may import the combative instinct into the conduct of this case." While Russell might try to sway the jury's emotions, Clarke would rely on the science—and also construct a plausible scenario showing how Edwin Bartlett could well have administered the chloroform to himself and that his wife had done her desperate best to revive him. His peroration to the jury was intensely moving: "I believe that, as a case like this goes on from day to day, there comes into your hearts a deep desire which is in itself a prayer that the spirit of justice may be among us and may guide and strengthen each to play his part. That invocation is never in vain. The spirit of justice is in this court today to comfort and protect her [Adelaide Bartlett] in the hour of her utmost need. That spirit will speak in firm and unfaltering voice when your verdict tells to the whole world that in your judgment Adelaide Bartlett is not guilty." As he sat down exhausted and almost overcome by emotion, the onlookers packed into the public gallery burst into a spontaneous and prolonged round of applause. The jury took two hours to come to a rather long-winded verdict, finding Mrs Bartlett not guilty although it thought she merited "grave suspicion" and there was insufficient evidence to show how the chloroform was administered. Another ovation ensued, to the judge's fury, and as the news spread to the people outside they too erupted. As Clarke left the court, the jurymen shook his hand, and the enthusiastic crowd cheered him as he emerged, many of them running alongside his carriage as it travelled away from the Old Bailey. Another ovation greeted Clarke at the theatre that evening to crown his greatest court triumph. That great twentieth-century advocate Norman Birkett regretted that he had never heard Clarke speak but, he wrote, that whenever members of the bar fell to discussing the great cases and the great advocates, "it was Clarke who lived in the memory and imagination. Men spoke of him with a kind of admiring wonder—'Ah! But you should have heard Edward Clarke when he defended Adelaide Bartlett'—just as though one of the great experiences of the world had been missed."

In 1885 Gladstone resigned and the Conservatives prepared for another spell in office. Hardinge Giffard became Lord Chancellor, with the title Lord Halsbury, and Clarke was strongly tipped to be Attorney-General. But the post went instead to Richard Webster, a less well-known barrister who was not even an MP. Before the appointment was announced Clarke fired off an angry letter to the new Prime Minister, Lord Salisbury, pointing out his own superior qualifications for the job. Salisbury stuck to his guns, though he did add the emollient qualifier, "You have a long future before you and under any political circumstances you cannot have long to wait." Webster was duly appointed and Clarke was even passed over for the junior post of Solicitor-General. As before with his attempts to enter the House of Commons, he did not have to wait long to enter the government ranks. At the general election of 1886, the Conservatives were returned with a comfortable majority and Salisbury invited Clarke to become Solicitor-General. He accepted, received the customary knighthood accompanying the office and served loyally under Webster, reappointed Attorney-General, for the next six years. The jobs did not carry the political weight which they do nowadays and the holders of the two offices were allowed to maintain their private practices. In Clarke's case, his income from his private practice nearly doubled in his first year in office despite the restrictions he imposed on himself to ensure there was no conflict of interest between his bar work and his political duties. The ending of this custom in the following decade angered Clarke and led him to decline further political office.

One of Clarke's self-imposed restrictions while in office was on criminal work. But there was no barrier to divorce work, and he appeared in a succession of high-profile cases. Lord Colin Campbell, a son of the Duke of Argyll, and his wife sued each other, she charging him with adultery with a former maid, he accusing her of adultery with no fewer than four well-known men, including the Duke of Marlborough and a surgeon named Bird. Clarke represented Bird, dismissing the charge with style and wit:

"A great point has been made about Dr Bird falling asleep in Lady Colin's bedroom. It is said Lord Colin found him asleep. Well, I do not think there is much in that to prove improper conduct. Had Lord Colin found him awake the case might perhaps have been stronger." Bird was cleared of impropriety but so was everybody else so the case, which featured a veritable galaxy of Garrick lawyers, ended in an expensive stalemate.

The most dramatic and far-reaching divorce case of the era was that involving the Irish politician Charles Parnell and his mistress Kitty O'Shea which destroyed Parnell's career when it was at its peak. Clarke represented Kitty's husband, Captain William O'Shea, and had little difficulty in proving his client's case as Parnell's affair was common knowledge.

Clarke was also entrusted with the onerous task of defending the Prime Minister, Lord Salisbury, against a charge of slander brought against him by the fiery Irish Nationalist MP for Cork, William O'Brien, over a speech in which Salisbury had accused O'Brien in the bluntest terms of inciting his countrymen to murder (Ireland being the dominant political issue of the day). Clarke took a brave gamble: he decided to plead justification rather than fair comment and persuaded Salisbury to agree to this approach despite the risk of greatly increased damages if the jury declared for O'Brien. His cross-examination of O'Brien, who was a clever man and a fine public speaker, lasted the best part of a day and was a classic of its kind. Clarke had also lined up thirty witnesses who would testify to murderous violence in Ireland. After fourteen had given evidence, O'Brien's QC stopped cross-examining and Clarke said he would call no more: he had made his point.

After an eloquent closing speech by Clarke, the jury took only six minutes to clear Salisbury, and the Appeal Court confirmed the verdict, with Clarke again representing the Prime Minister.

He was intimately involved too in the slander action that climaxed what has been described as the greatest scandal of the late Victorian era, the Baccarat Case, in which the Prince of Wales himself was obliged to give evidence. The Prince was the leading figure in the rakish, fast-living, amoral circle that dominated high society and which was laid bare to a fascinated public by the newspaper reporting of the case. Clarke had the fiendishly difficult task of representing Sir William Gordon-Cumming, a baronet, gallant soldier, distinguished member of the Scottish gentry, respected London clubman and friend of the Prince, who was accused of cheating at baccarat by five young fellow members of a house party at the imposing Yorkshire country pile Tranby Croft during the Doncaster autumn race meeting in September 1890. The Prince of Wales was the principal guest and an enthusiastic participant in the games of baccarat that followed dinner. Gordon-Cumming was confronted with the accusation and denied it, but eventually agreed to sign a confession and a declaration that he would never play cards again. The agreement was that the document would remain confidential but of course the story soon leaked out, and Gordon-Cumming sued his accusers for slander. Clarke was engaged to represent him. Things looked bleak for Gordon-Cumming because of the signed confession; he argued that he had only signed to keep the matter quiet in order to save the reputation of the Prince of Wales. He also claimed his accusers were novices at baccarat (he on the other hand was a vastly experienced player) and had misunderstood his actions in pushing forward counters representing his bets. When the case opened, the packed courtroom was treated to the extraordinary sight of Queen Victoria's heir sitting on a special chair between the judge and the witness box. On the other side of the judge, Lord Chief Justice Coleridge, sat his wife, Lady Coleridge, there to nudge him in case he fell asleep as he was increasingly wont to do. Clarke's initial tactic was to make a conciliatory opening speech in the hope that the accusers would withdraw their allegations and settle out of court, thus saving the Prince from giving evidence. But Sir Charles Russell, Clarke's opponent, did not take up the offer and so the trial went ahead. After questioning his client, who admitted his stupidity in signing the confession but repeated his innocence, Clarke called the Prince of Wales. He said he had noticed no skulduggery at the card table but felt he had to believe the accusers when they came to him with their charges. Clarke's final speech to the jury was one of his finest, drawing on all his powers of oratory to try to save Gordon-Cumming's reputation, and he sat down to an ovation from the gallery, which pleased Lord Coleridge not at all. He adjourned proceedings overnight to let the atmosphere cool, then delivered his summing-up, which, though fair, leaned subtly towards the defendants. Clarke later wrote ruefully: "It has often been a subject of discussion among lawyers whether Charles Russell or John Duke Coleridge was the greater advocate. I am not sure that Russell was quite at his best in the Baccarat Case, but so far as that case was concerned I think no careful student of the trial would deny the supremacy to Coleridge." The jury thought so too and swiftly found against Gordon-Cumming. The crushing effect of the verdict was that he was effectively banished from society; he retired to his Scottish estates where he lived for the next forty years until his death. Clarke was deeply saddened by the outcome, writing in his memoirs many years later, "I believe the verdict was wrong, and that Sir William Gordon-Cumming was innocent of the offence charged against him."

Clarke's six-year tenure as Solicitor-General ended in 1892 when the Conservatives lost office at the general election but having retained his Plymouth seat he remained an active member of the Opposition front bench. He had the honour (and onerous task) of replying to Gladstone's three-hour speech setting out the Home Rule Bill, the Old Man's last great Commons performance (he was by then eighty-four), and his much briefer effort drew wide praise. Clarke still had hopes of returning to political office and he thought the chance had come in 1895 when Gladstone's government fell and Salisbury returned. He wished to reappoint the law officers in his previous administration— Lord Halsbury as Lord Chief Justice, Sir Richard Webster as Attorney-General and Clarke as Solicitor-General, with an assurance to Clarke of the reversion to Attorney if the job fell vacant, as it did. But there was a snag as far as Clarke was concerned: Gladstone's government had stopped the Attorney-General and Solicitor-General from accepting private briefs while in office, putting them on a higher salary instead to compensate for loss of private earnings. But Clarke, who was always opposed to such a ban, refused to accept office on those terms. Webster eventually caved in but Clarke typically stuck to his principles and declined the job. He believed he should have been appointed Attorney-General when the post became vacant in 1897 and would have gone on to be Lord Chief Justice in 1900. He also turned down the post of Master of the Rolls in 1897, believing it to be less important than that of LCJ. So he ended up with nothing, apart of course from his private practice which, after his long period in political office, naturally thrived even more.

He appeared in yet more high-profile cases, none more dramatic, of course, than the two trials involving Oscar Wilde in 1895. In the first, Wilde sued the Marquess of Queensberry for criminal libel after he left a card at the Albemarle Club addressed "To Oscar Wilde, posing as a somdomite (sic)". Clarke showed himself to be rather an innocent at large by initially being confident that his client had nothing to fear. But during Edward Carson's lacerating cross-examination of Wilde the playwright approached him at the luncheon adjournment on the second day to admit that his private conduct did in fact lay him open to the charge he had thus far stoutly denied. Carson's cross-examination grew progressively more devastating and by the end of the day's proceedings Clarke realised the game was up. Next morning he advised Wilde to withdraw, thus admitting that Queensberry was right. Clarke assumed that Wilde would then flee the country but unaccountably he stayed on in London. The Director of Public Prosecutions issued a warrant for his arrest, homosexuality then being illegal, and Wilde was detained. Clarke immediately wrote to Wilde's solicitors offering to defend him without charge, an offer gratefully accepted by Wilde, who was bankrupted by the costs of his disastrous libel action. But Clarke's eloquent defence of Wilde at his trial was in vain. Interestingly, Clarke made no reference to either trial in his otherwise exhaustive memoirs, probably because such an upright Christian gentleman did not wish to be reminded of their sordid nature, and of the fact that he had initially been grievously misled by his client.

It was Clarke's integrity that led to the end of his political career. He was utterly opposed to the Boer War, believing that a deal could have been struck with the Boers without resort to military force. In this stance he was a lone voice in the Conservative Party. He had unsuccessfully defended Dr Jameson, whose famous Raid into the Transvaal in 1895-6 was part of the run-up to war. Jameson was brought to London to face charges under the Foreign Enlistment Act; he was sentenced to fifteen months' imprisonment but returned to South Africa a hero. Clarke was not so fortunate; many in his Plymouth constituency were angered by his anti-war stance and rather than lose the next election Clarke resigned from Parliament early in 1900. It was not quite the end for him politically. In 1906 he was adopted as Conservative candidate for the City of London seat and was voted back to the Commons. But once again he would not deviate from his principles: he had always been a staunch free trader and his party had now backed special treatment for Empire trade. His relationship with his leader, Balfour, chilled to such an extent that within four months of re-entering Parliament Clarke again resigned. This time there was no comeback.

With no further prospect of or aspiration to high political or legal office, Clarke was able to combine his lucrative bar practice with his passion for literature and the theatre, which included friendships with the great names of the theatre like Henry Irving and Herbert Beerbohm Tree, with whom he would often dine at the Garrick. In court he also came up against a future Garrick member, the rising silk Edward Marshall Hall, in two Appeal Court cases which resulted in strong criticism of Marshall Hall by the court and did his reputation no good at all. In May 1914, at the age of seventy, Clarke announced his retirement from the bar. To mark his departure, an unprecedented farewell dinner was held, presided over by the Lord Chancellor, Clarke's old friend Lord Halsbury, with the Attorney-General Sir John Simon speaking on behalf of the bar. "I finish as I began, as a private member of the English bar. To some that will look like failure," said Clarke in his own speech but he comforted himself with the words of Archbishop Trench, "Not all who seem to have failed have failed indeed." Many barristers since then would gladly have swapped their success for Edward Clarke's failure. He had a long and busy retirement: he sat on a government commission of inquiry into German atrocities in Belgium at the start of the First World War, and wrote a popular biography of his hero Disraeli after his application to write the official one was turned down. He even paid for a new Anglican church to be built next to his Thames-side house at Staines. He died in 1931, soon after reaching his ninetieth birthday. His elder son, Sir Percy Clarke (1872-1936, Garrick 1894-1936), was also a distinguished lawyer, senior Treasury counsel at the Old Bailey and chairman of the County of London Sessions.

What made Clarke such a significant figure on the legal and political stage? In many respects he was the perfect Victorian, born at the start of the Queen's long reign, his career spanning her reign (and some way beyond). He was the ultimate self-made man: everything he achieved was through his own merit and legendary hard work, while never deviating from his high principles. His biographers summed up: "He satisfied, to an extent never perhaps equalled by any other lawyer, the ideal of contemporary opinion. The Victorian age looked with respect and admiration on his unquestioning acceptance of those high standards of conduct which it prescribed."

7

SIR JAMES FITZJAMES STEPHEN, JOHNSONIAN JUDGE

Many contemporaries compared Sir James Fitzjames Stephen (1829-1894, Garrick 1872-94) to Dr Johnson, so broad were his interests and his friendships, and so eloquent and forceful was he in expressing his views, allied to a rather brusque manner. He ended his distinguished career as a judge, before which he had been best known within the law as a writer on legal affairs and a codifier, most notably in India. He was, however, much more than a distinguished lawyer: he was a prolific journalist and a friend of some of the most important literary figures of the day, such as Carlyle and Froude. He was a great bear of a man, a tremendous walker, with a deep and sonorous voice, and above all a man of enormous integrity and principle.

He came from distinguished legal, political and academic stock: the Stephen family tree links in with some of the greatest names in eighteenth, nineteenth and twentieth century English history. His grandfather, James Stephen, was a Master in Chancery, brother-in-law and close ally of William Wilberforce, and like him a lifelong campaigner against slavery. His father, also Sir James Stephen, was a lawyer turned civil servant, who became Under-Secretary for the Colonies and was said by a colleague to have "ruled the colonial empire"; he went on to become Regius Professor of modern history at Cambridge. James Fitzjames Stephen (always known by his second name to distinguish him from his illustrious namesakes) was his second son; his third was Leslie Stephen, who was to become a Cambridge don, pioneering mountaineer, noted journalist, mentor of writers like Robert Louis Stevenson and Thomas Hardy, and first editor of the *Dictionary of National Biography*. He also married Thackeray's daughter and wrote a bulky biography of his older brother shortly after Fitzjames's death. The next generation were just as distinguished: Virginia Woolf was Leslie's daughter, and Fitzjames's daughter Katharine became Principal of Newnham College, Cambridge. Two of his sons were judges.

Fitzjames and Leslie Stephen were sent to Eton as dayboys but neither retained fond memories of the school. Fitzjames was mercilessly bullied there and as a result retained a lifelong sympathy with the underdog which came to the fore when he eventually became a judge. Via King's College, London, he went up to Trinity College, Cambridge, where he was not a particularly good student. "I utterly loathed examinations, which seem to me to make learning all but impossible," he once said. He did, however, distinguish himself at the Union where his powerful oratory and invective led him to be nicknamed "the British Lion" and goaded one enraged opponent into attempting to attack him physically during a debate, to the delight of the undergraduate audience. He was also invited to join the elite and secretive discussion group known as The Apostles, which was a sign that an undergraduate was among the cleverest and most promising members of the university, whatever his academic record might be. It was perhaps typical of Fitzjames Stephen that he decided to go down without taking his degree. Having decided that he should either become a clergyman or a lawyer, he eventually settled for the latter and was called to the bar at the Inner Temple in 1854; he also studied for an LL.B at London University. However, he thought little of the standard of legal education he received in chambers. He went on the Midland Circuit, slogging round the Lincolnshire, Nottinghamshire and Derbyshire sessions, where his plain speaking and commonsensical approach stood him in good stead. The life of the barrister on circuit led him to reflect on his fellow practitioners in a magazine article a few years later: the English bar was "exactly like a great public school, the boys of which have grown older and have exchanged boyish for manly objects. There is just the same rough familiarity, the same general ardour of character, the same kind of unwritten code of morals and manners, the same kind of public opinion expressed in exactly the same blunt, unmistakable manner." It is a description which many will think as true of the English bar today as it was then.

At the same time, Stephen was building up a reputation as a journalist. He had taken the first steps with articles for a worthy evangelical publication called the *Christian Observer*. The most satisfactory outcome of his relationship with the magazine was that he married the editor's daughter, Mary Richenda Cunningham, with whom he enjoyed lifelong happiness (they had eight children, two of whom died in infancy). In the winter of 1851-2 he wrote a few articles for the *Morning Chronicle* but little more until 1855 when a new magazine, the *Saturday Review*, was launched by disaffected staffers and supporters of the *Morning Chronicle*. The editor, John Douglas Cook, gathered round him a group of brilliant young men of whom Stephen was one. He wrote extensively on law and literature but it was in the *Edinburgh Review* that he wrote a critical piece about Charles Dickens and what he saw as his inaccurate and unfair sending-up of the legal system in such novels as *Little Dorrit*, in which Stephen discerned a satire on the elite caste represented by his own father. The journalistic connection was helpful in Stephen securing an important post in 1858, that of secretary to the Royal Commission on the state of popular education. The chairman was the Duke of Newcastle, a patron of Cook, who probably recommended Stephen. The commission took three years to gather a mass of information and statistics, sending Matthew Arnold and the Oxford academic and writer Mark Pattison to Germany, France and Switzerland to report on how schools were run there. One of the commission's members said of Stephen: "Though under thirty, he brought to the task a combination of talents rarely found in any one individual. To his keen insight, wide grasp, accurately balanced judgment, and marvellous aptitude for details, was due much of the success with which we were able to lay down the future lines of popular education."

In 1859, Stephen was made Recorder of Newark, again probably via the patronage of the Duke of Newcastle, and in the early 1860s he combined working as a barrister in the North Midlands with his career as a prolific journalist, extending his range of outlets to another new journal, the *London Review,* and to the *Cornhill Magazine*, which had been launched in 1860 with Thackeray as editor; the two men became firm friends. Stephen's articles on the law in the *Saturday Review* were collected in a short book, *Essays by a Barrister*, published in 1862. His reputation was enhanced by his defence of an Anglican clergyman, Dr Rowland Williams, who was tried by an ecclesiastical court because he had written that there were mistakes in the Bible. Although Williams was found guilty, he was cleared on appeal by the Privy Council. Stephen was extremely interested in religion and met John Henry Newman at the Birmingham Oratory to engage in a robust argument with him about Newman's and the Roman Catholic Church's claim to speak for Almighty God. Stephen remained unconvinced by the great man's defence.

In 1863 Stephen published his first substantial book, *General View of the Criminal Law of England*, which he had been mulling over for five years. Its basis was the connection between law and morality, an issue which fascinated Stephen and occurred again and again in his writing. In the book he compared the English and French criminal justice systems, concluding that the English was superior while admiring some aspects of the French inquisitorial approach, and proposed a Ministry of Justice a century and a half before that institution finally came into being. As a journalist he continued to be recruited by new magazines, the next being the *Pall Mall Gazette*, which was launched in 1865. Under the editorship of Frederick Greenwood, another Garrick member, Stephen contributed many lengthy leading articles in which he extended his reach beyond the law and literature to politics and current affairs. He was extraordinarily prolific, writing before breakfast, then walking to the *Gazette*'s offices off the Strand on his way to chambers to discuss things with

Greenwood and sometimes write another article on the spot. He kept up the pace even when out of London on circuit.

In 1866 Stephen was deeply involved in the legal action in England that followed on from the native uprising in Jamaica the previous year, which was put down with the utmost severity by the island's administration under its Governor, Edward Eyre; the rebel leader George Gordon was swiftly hanged after a court-martial. Stephen and his fellow Garrick member Edwin James gave evidence to a committee under the chairmanship of John Stuart Mill: Stephen believed Eyre had exceeded his authority in court-martialling Gordon, and that his hanging should therefore be considered as murder. At Bow Street Magistrates' Court he applied for the committal of the officers responsible for the court-martial, Nelson and Brand, on a charge of murder. He succeeded there but failed to persuade the magistrates in Eyre's home county of Shropshire to commit the former Governor: they preferred the defence arguments put forward by Hardinge Giffard, later Lord Halsbury. At the trial of Nelson and Brand at the Old Bailey, the Lord Chief Justice, Lord Cockburn, largely agreed with Stephen's exposition of the law but not so the grand jury, which cleared the two officers. Stephen declined to pursue the matter further, which led to a lasting breach with Mill.

Stephen took silk in 1868. He enjoyed his occasional spells on the bench but found the day-to-day work of a barrister humdrum and unfulfilling. Since childhood, he had been fascinated by India, the jewel in the British Empire. One of his dearest friends since Cambridge and a fellow Apostle, Henry Maine, had gone to India in 1862 to work on codifying the law there. In 1868 Maine suggested to him that he should be his successor in this complex task, and in 1869 Stephen accepted the post. He arrived in Calcutta in December of that year and immediately got to work. As a disciple of Bentham, Stephen was ideally suited to the job of codifying the mixture of Indian and English legal codes and regulations which had developed higgledy-piggledy since the arrival of the East India Company and the gradual spread of British rule. A penal code and a code of criminal procedure, defining the British administration of justice in India, had been enacted in the previous decade, and Stephen at first thought he could revise them lightly. But on closer examination of the code of criminal procedure he declared he had never read "a more confused or worse-drawn law". With a small working group of British officials he laboured to draw up a better one. Over a period of two and a half years Stephen worked on this and other codifying Acts, and in the last few months of his stay in India his drafts became law: as well as laws on land and native marriages, an Evidence Act, a Contract Act and a Criminal Procedure Act came into effect in 1872, a herculean accomplishment on Stephen's part. He attracted some criticism for not remaining in India for the full five years he had been expected to but many thought he had crammed five years' work into half the time. Although his wife had made several visits, he missed his family and he knew that the longer he was away from England, the more difficult it would be to regain his place on the legal ladder.

He arrived back in London in May 1872 and immediately got back into the old routine, calling on Greenwood at the *Pall Mall Gazette*'s office to hand over an article he had written en route in Paris. At a dinner of the legendary Cambridge club to which he and Maine had belonged, he proposed Maine's health and suggested that the legislation they had drafted in India should from now on be called "the Acts of the Apostles". He resumed his career at the bar, reappearing at the Old Bailey in June for the first time in eighteen years, though to his amusement his achievements in India did not impress the court. His brother and biographer Leslie recorded: "The judge, he says, 'snubbed' him for some supposed irregularity in his examination of a witness, and did not portray the slightest consciousness that the offender had just composed a code of evidence for an empire." Elsewhere, though, his abilities were being fully recognised. He was appointed counsel to Cambridge University, and was elected to the Athenaeum, while he resumed his friendship with Carlyle and Froude. His codifying skills were also in demand: he was asked to draw up a bill on homicide, in light of a recent Royal Commission on capital punishment. This led to some confusion when he was staying with Froude in a remote part of Wales and needed a copy of his draft. He telegraphed to the Recorder of London, "SEND HOMICIDE BILL," which request was rejected as the official who received it thought it meant he was required to dispatch a murderer to the Froude residence. The Attorney-General, Sir John Coleridge, also asked him to draft an Evidence Bill, drawing on his work in India. He also published as a book a series of essays he had written for the *Pall Mall Gazette* on the journey home from India, under the title *Liberty, Equality, Fraternity*, in which he attempted to define his own politico-socio-legal philosophy, which was essentially a variation of the Benthamite utilitarianism he had espoused since youth. Perhaps unwisely, in 1873 he allowed himself to be talked by Coleridge and others into standing for Parliament as a Liberal candidate at a by-election in Dundee, on the understanding that he would be appointed Solicitor-General if elected. All three candidates supported the government one way or another; Stephen came bottom of the poll. Perhaps he was too much of a plain speaker to succeed in politics, perhaps he was not at heart a Liberal. One well-qualified to opine on the matter thought he could have been a successful politician on the other side. Lord Beaconsfield, formerly Benjamin Disraeli, wrote in a private letter some years later, by which time Stephen had been elevated to the bench: "It is a thousand pities that J.F. Stephen is a judge; he might have done anything and everything as leader of the future Conservative party."

Stephen himself never displayed any regret that his one foray into politics had been so brief and unsuccessful. His real ambition was to be appointed a judge, having acted as a part-time judge for several years and enjoyed it. In 1874 he thought he had a strong chance but a vacancy hinted at did not materialise and he did not realise his ambition until 1879. Meanwhile, it was back to codifying. Disraeli's new administration of 1874 asked him to consolidate the Acts relating to the government of India and he set to work with a will, drafting a single Act of 168 sections to replace the jumble of Acts which had accreted since the previous century. But objections from the Legislative Council in India killed it.

In 1875 he was appointed Professor of Common Law at the Inns of Court. At the same time he was working on a much expanded version of his book on criminal law, published a dozen years earlier; the new book eventually appeared in 1877 (the same year he was knighted for his work in India) as *A Digest of the Criminal Law*, and it led to Sir John Holker, the Attorney-General, asking him to draw up a penal code and a code of criminal procedure, for which his new book provided the foundations. A commission of three senior judges plus Stephen was set up to go through it line by line and it produced a report by the summer of 1879. But any hope of it being turned into legislation vanished with the change of government of 1880, and so ended Stephen's last opportunity to codify English law. He did not repine, for in January 1879 he was at last appointed a High Court judge; at the end of the first case over which he presided, at the Old Bailey, he had to pass the death sentence.

The general opinion in the legal world was that Stephen was a better judge than an advocate, for which role his uncompromising honesty and dislike of sophistry were at heart unsuited. As a judge he was something of a paradox: he developed a reputation for tough sentencing but was also noted for his fairness and keenness to help the underdog, a trait he had possessed ever since he was bullied as a schoolboy. In one case, for example, he had just passed a seven-year prison sentence on a man who had pleaded guilty, against Stephen's advice, to a charge of stabbing a policeman to avoid arrest. As he was about to be taken down, the prisoner clutched the rail and shouted, "You can't do it! You don't know what you're doing!" Most judges would doubtless have ignored such an outburst but Stephen's instincts were otherwise. He called the man back and questioned him at length about why he was complaining, even calling back witnesses to confirm his story. Stephen eventually reduced the sentence to nine months, admonishing the man for pleading guilty in the first place, and asking him if he was satisfied with the reduced sentence. "Thank you, my Lord," he replied, "that's quite right." Stephen was just as fair to the advocates in his court: he once stepped down from the bench to sit beside Montagu Williams QC so that he did not have to raise his voice, which had been affected by illness. The fact that they were both members of the Garrick probably did Williams's cause no harm, but Stephens would have applied the same courtesy to anybody.

Stephen excelled in trials in which he could exercise both his powerful intellect and his deep knowledge of legal history, although his acquaintance with popular culture was somewhat sketchier: he once innocently asked, "What is the Grand National?" at Liverpool Assizes of all places. One trial that enabled him to display his talents to the full and had profound and long-lasting implications was that of a colourful Welsh nationalist, radical and self-styled Archdruid, William Price, who was accused of trying to cremate the body of his five-month-old son in 1884 (Price, incidentally, was 83 years old when the boy was born). Stephen concluded in his summing-up that although cremation had not been legalised, it was not illegal if it did not cause a public nuisance. Price was cleared and returned to Wales a hero. He was allowed to proceed with his son's cremation (the boy's body had earlier been rescued by an angry crowd), and the first official cremation took place in Woking in 1885.

The most high-profile trials Stephen presided over came towards the end of his time on the bench. The first, in 1887, was that of Israel Lipski, a 22-year-old Polish-Jewish man living in the East End who was charged with murdering a young woman by forcing her to take nitric acid. He was found guilty and Stephen sentenced him to death. His lawyer disputed the verdict and wrote a pamphlet laying out his reasons for doing so. Lipski's cause was taken up by the newspapers, and the execution postponed, while the Home Secretary, Henry Matthews, and Stephen himself considered new evidence. A hundred MPs signed a motion requesting commutation of the sentence, and three members of the jury also intervened on Lipski's behalf. But both Matthews and Stephen concluded that the original verdict should stand, and on the same day Lipski confessed his guilt. He was hanged next day, justice being administered with dispatch in those days.

The second case was that of Florence Maybrick, an American-born woman who was accused of murdering her much older English husband, James Maybrick, a wealthy Liverpool cotton broker, by administering arsenic to him. The trial had many echoes of that of Adelaide Bartlett, whom Edward Clarke so memorably and successfully defended just three years earlier, but the great Charles Russell, who had led for the prosecution in that case, failed again with the Maybrick trial, this time for the defence. Mrs Maybrick was found guilty by the jury and sentenced to death by Stephen. The public had taken Mrs Maybrick's side; Stephen was booed and jeered at by a crowd as he left the court, and was again bitterly criticised by the press and in many anonymous letters for his handling of the case. Such was the outcry that the matter was again referred to the Home Secretary, Henry Matthews: this time, he and the Lord Chancellor, Lord Halsbury, concluded that Mrs Maybrick had indeed administered arsenic to her husband, but that the dose which killed him was not necessarily the same one. Her sentence was commuted to life imprisonment, of which she served fourteen years, being freed in 1904. During her incarceration, Russell, by then elevated to Lord Chief Justice, tried to have her sentence overturned, for he remained convinced of her innocence, but he was again unsuccessful.

The widespread criticism levelled at Stephen after the Lipski and Maybrick verdicts, that he had been prejudiced against the defendants, was probably unfair. But was he entirely compos mentis by then? He had suffered a stroke in 1885: in a letter he wrote of a "dreadful tale of my getting up in the morning and finding that my right hand had either forgot its cunning or had turned so lazy that I could not write with it..." He made what appeared to be a full recovery, but his powers were not what they were. His summing-up in the Maybrick trial took two days to deliver and was rambling, prejudicial to Mrs Maybrick, and in places completely meaningless. "From first to last, the judge seemed all at sea," wrote Edgar Lustgarten. By early 1891, comment was being made in the press and in legal circles that his mind was failing him. It would appear that Lord Coleridge, the former Attorney-General and now Lord Chief Justice, who was on circuit with Stephen in March 1891, put these concerns to him; Stephen immediately consulted his doctor and resigned from the bench soon afterwards. He was created a baronet, retired to a nursing home in Ipswich and died in 1894.

8

THE JUDGES: FROM HENRY HAWKINS
TO TRAVERS HUMPHREYS

The most controversial judge of the nineteenth century was probably Sir Henry Hawkins (1817-1907, Garrick 1855-1886), eventually ennobled as Baron Brampton. Before his elevation to the bench in 1876, he was a leading member of the bar, a rival and frequent opponent of Ballantine and Parry, but it was as a judge that he left a lasting mark.

Hawkins was the son of a country solicitor in Hitchin, Hertfordshire, and educated at Bedford School. In his lengthy memoirs, he described a scene from his school days that left a lifelong impression on him: from a first-floor window in the school, he saw a horse and cart proceeding slowly down the street, watched by a silent crowd, with a grief-stricken couple walking behind it. It bore the body of their seventeen-year-old son, hanged that morning in Bedford Gaol for setting fire to a stack of corn. Such was the state of English justice in the 1830s. "Years afterwards, when I became a Judge," wrote Hawkins, "this picture, photographed on my mind as it was, gave me many a lesson which I believe was turned to good account on the judicial bench. It was mainly useful in impressing on my mind the great consideration of the surrounding circumstances of every crime, the *degree* of guilt in the criminal, and the difference in the degrees of the same kind of offences."

For all that, he became known as "Hanging Hawkins", renowned for the severity of his sentencing, although his biographer in the *DNB* took a more balanced view. "Hawkins was an admirable criminal judge," he recorded. "Extremely patient and thorough, he took care that both the case for the Crown and that for the accused person should be exhaustively stated and tested to the utmost." That view was contradicted by one of the leading silks to appear before him, Sir Edward Clarke, who made no attempt to hide his outrage at the manner in which Hawkins conducted one of the most famous trials of the mid-Victorian era, the so-called Penge murder trial, and subsequent cases. "Sir Henry Hawkins was the worst judge I ever knew or heard of," Clarke wrote in his own memoirs. "He had no notion whatever of what justice meant, or of the obligations of truth and fairness." These were strong words indeed from a man who was known for his unbending principles. One wonders if they ever met at the Garrick centre table and if so what they talked about.

Hawkins was clearly a prickly character, who could nurse a grievance for a lifetime. He was always bitter at being deprived of the plum role of defending the Tichborne estate against the Tichborne Claimant at the last minute: he was replaced by the newly-appointed Solicitor-General Sir John Coleridge, whose right it was to take over the case. Hawkins had to act as Coleridge's junior and for ever afterwards believed that had he been allowed to cross-examine the claimant, Arthur Orton, he would have brought the trial, which lasted a ludicrous and unnecessary 188 days, to a much speedier end. Hawkins could be a devastating cross-examiner and he may well have been right.

Soon after he first became a judge, in 1876, he was transferred from the Queen's Bench division to the newly-created but short-lived Exchequer division, which replaced the Court of Exchequer. Judges of the latter court had been styled "Baron" and Hawkins thought the title should have remained. If he couldn't be Baron Hawkins, he declined to be called Mr Justice Hawkins, preferring Sir Henry Hawkins.

He had a long career on the bench, though Edward Clarke preferred to put it that "Sir Henry Hawkins continued his career of public disservice." However, Travers Humphreys (himself to become a leading judge) thought that on balance Clarke was probably being unfair. "The evidence was all before the Jury," he wrote of the Penge murder trial, stressing that he had not been present, "and no allegation is made of any impropriety on the part of the Judge during the hearing of the evidence and speeches." Although Hawkins had been a judge for only three years, the case encapsulated his way of doing things. He was keen on the outdoors (he was a great racing enthusiast), but he had a horror of fresh air in his court, demanding that any apertures be sealed tight and the temperature kept as high as possible. On circuit, he would often sit for unreasonably long hours, sometimes just to spite counsel who had evening engagements elsewhere. He frequently sat until 11pm or later: on one such occasion, when delivering sentence on a man and a woman found guilty of murder, he droned on and the woman fainted several times in the dock. Hawkins merely waited until she recovered before he continued, finally passing sentence of death at 11.30pm.

Eventually the judicial authorities took him to task, after which he rose promptly at 4pm although the court could never be certain when he would arrive in the morning.

As a young barrister, Travers Humphreys often appeared before Hawkins in the last nine years on the bench. He left this portrait:

> What I saw was an elderly but vigorous man, very sure of himself, very certain of the law, willing to hear argument, but once his view had been stated, allowing no further discussion upon the matter: what I heard was a beautiful voice with a slight purr in it which seemed to resemble the sound made by a pleased cat; when there was an interruption or a sound of any kind displeasing to the speaker, which is the same thing as saying any sound but that of his own voice, the resemblance to a domestic cat vanished. There was no raising of the voice, still less anything resembling a feline spitting of rage, but the voice would be heard murmuring that the *slightest* interruption from *any* quarter would be followed by a clearing of the Court, and if necessary a further step which would have the effect of making the interrupter *very* sorry for himself.

Hawkins was not without a certain dry wit. One defendant who had just been found guilty started weeping in court, saying that he had never been to prison before. "Don't cry about that, my good fellow," replied Hawkins, briefly raising the man's hopes, "you are going there now," and sent him down for five years.

He was also devoted to his fox-terrier Jack, to such an extent that several chapters in the second volume of his rather tedious and unrevealing autobiography purport to be written by the dog. Sir Frank Lockwood is described by the animal as "a very amusing counsel, whom I always liked, because he often sketched me and my lord in pen and ink".

Even odder was the disparity between his performance in criminal and civil cases. Although Sir Edward Clarke doubtless had good grounds for his animosity, many thought Hawkins a superb criminal judge, fair, patient and thorough. His summings-up, generally delivered without recourse to notes, were thought to be models of lucidity and impartiality, and he made no secret of believing in leniency for first offenders. Many of his comments on the subject could be those of a liberal reformer of a century later. But his lucidity seemed to desert him in his civil judgments. "In delivering a considered judgment he was verbose and tautological," recorded the *DNB*. "He failed to grasp the principles of the law and to deduce from them the true effect of the facts before him, and he involved himself in contradictions." His judgment in *R. v Lillyman* (1896) "was so unsatisfactory that for nine years, while it remained a leading authority, it was invariably construed as meaning the contrary of what it said."

He converted to Roman Catholicism late in life, was a great friend of Cardinal Manning, the Archbishop of Westminster, and donated large sums of money for the decoration of the gloomy brick interior of the neo-Byzantine Westminster Cathedral.

A similarly dominant judicial figure, though without the personal eccentricities, was Sir Horace Avory (1851-1935, Garrick 1897-1935). He sat on the Bench for twenty-five years and became the best-known criminal judge of his era. He had been a leading criminal silk and he went on to hear a huge number of criminal cases and to deliver many sentences of death. It is hard to believe he was much fun to sit next to on the Garrick centre table for he was a dry man of few words; he deplored judges who used their courts to display what they imagined to be their wit. "The stage is the place for witticisms," he once said, "not a court of justice." F.W. Ashley, who was his clerk for fifty-four years, wrote perceptively of him in his memoirs. Ashley admired Avory enormously and was utterly devoted to him but he harboured no illusions about his personality:

> He had no small talk and little interest in events which did not find their ultimate expression in briefs. The alert manner, the almost ascetic figure, and the boyish plumpness of his features, may have concealed from strangers the prematurity of his development and the strain of hardness in his disposition, but if they ever came to know him they quickly realised that to Horace Avory nothing mattered except his work, and that outside a very limited circle of friends and acquaintances he preferred to be left alone. All through his life only three men ventured to address him by his Christian name, and of the notable trio Sir Charles Mathews was the one he liked most. I had almost written loved, but perhaps the word would be out of place in writing of a man who detested sentiment.

Avory's other intimates, by the way, were Sir Charles Gill and Sir Edward Marshall Hall.

Avory came from a distinguished legal line. His father, Henry Avory, was a solicitor and clerk to the Central Criminal Court at the Old Bailey and famous for his knowledge of the law: Montagu Williams remembered him leaping up, after taking "a huge pinch of snuff", clutching the appropriate statute, in order to correct an errant judge. Horace, his second son, studied at a day school in Clapham and King's College, London, before going up to Corpus

Christi College, Cambridge, to study law. He went straight on to read for the bar and was called by the Inner Temple in 1875. He was a ferociously hard worker who was soon in demand as an advocate in the police and county courts and who would do everything in his power on behalf of his clients, however lowly. He had, said Ashley, a hatred of injustice: "not one of his contemporaries gave greater service and loyalty than he did." Ashley provided an account of a typical day, with Avory scheduled to appear at five different London courts—including Bow Street, Clerkenwell, Thames Police Court and Shoreditch, Ashley preceding him by hansom cab to assure the court the young barrister was on his way.

A pillar of rectitude, Avory was shocked to learn from his clerk that a bailiff had called to his chambers in Paper Buildings and removed all its contents in lieu of two years' unpaid rent. The explanation was that Avory had taken over the rooms from the wily old Serjeant Ballantine, to whom Avory had naively paid the rent. Ballantine, who was constantly in financial trouble, had neglected, however, to pass on the money to the treasurer of the inn.

In 1889 Avory was appointed Junior Counsel to the Treasury. "He was recognised already as one of the men at the Bar who could handle difficult and complicated cases," noted Ashley. "A quick reader, he had such a good memory and could assimilate facts so rapidly that it was seldom necessary for him to read a brief twice." Throughout his life, Avory prized conciseness and precision in his own speech and that of other lawyers. "He disliked anything savouring of the theatrical either in language or in action," wrote Ashley. "A very ready speaker with a clear and attractive voice he never ventured on the heroic, rarely raised it, and

I cannot recall, even in very pathetic cases, any attempt at a peroration." Avory believed that "the jury when they retire are more affected by facts than by eloquence."

He spent twelve years as Treasury counsel prosecuting the whole gamut of crime, including major fraudsters like Jabez Balfour, an MP who raised money from small investors via the Nonconformist chapel network, left thousands destitute when his financial empire crashed in 1892 and had to be extradited from Argentina to face trial (he got fourteen years).

Avory had a deserved reputation for diligence and fairness, both as barrister and judge, but there was always one large black mark against his name: the strange case of Adolf Beck, a terrible miscarriage of justice which was a big factor in the creation of the Court of Criminal Appeal in 1907. Before that the unfortunate Beck had to serve most of a seven-year sentence, although the Home Office had known for the last three years of it that he was undoubtedly innocent. Avory prosecuted Beck, a Norwegian by birth, in 1896 for posing as an aristocrat and robbing by deception a string of women of money and valuables. Beck was assumed to be a fraudster named John Smith, who had been found guilty of similar frauds in 1877 and served five years in prison. Beck could prove that he had been in South America in 1877 but Avory objected to the defence attempting to introduce this alibi on the grounds that it would be unfair to the defendant to have previous convictions revealed to the jury. The judge, the Common Serjeant, Sir Forrest Fulton, upheld this bizarre argument, and Beck was convicted. While he was in prison, his solicitor attempted many times to have the case re-examined but without success. The vital piece of evidence that should have cleared Beck was that he was not circumcised whereas Smith, a Jew, was, as his medical records showed. Extraordinarily, three years after his release in 1901, Beck was rearrested for similar offences and again found guilty at the Old Bailey. However, this time the judge, Mr Justice Grantham, was concerned about the case and postponed sentence while he reviewed the papers. Meanwhile, in another twist the original John Smith (his real name turned out to be Wilhelm Meyer and he was Austrian) was arrested at the same time in London for defrauding two women and eventually identified as the real guilty party back in 1896. Beck eventually received £5,000 in compensation which he rapidly squandered, while a committee of inquiry strongly criticised Sir Forrest Fulton's conduct but exonerated Avory. Many thought him fortunate. Indeed, in the London Library's copy of Ashley's book, an anonymous commentator has written in blue ink: "Avory knew perfectly well what he was doing and should have gone down for a long stretch himself."

Avory survived this to take silk in 1901, becoming KC rather than QC as Queen Victoria died between the Lord Chancellor's decision being made known and the award itself. His first case as a KC was the defence of Earl Russell in the famous bigamy case heard by his peers in the Lords. He played a key role in the great Whitaker Wright fraud case, in which his fellow Garrick members Sir Edward Carson and Sir Robert Finlay, then the Law Officers, did not distinguish themselves by deciding there was no case for a prosecution. Some of the shareholders of Wright's insolvent companies did not share this view and they retained Avory in 1901 to see if a private prosecution could be brought. Avory concluded that they had a case and presented it to a judge, who agreed. Wright fled the country and it was not until 1904 that he stood trial, was found guilty and promptly committed suicide by taking poison in a courtroom lavatory.

Avory's decade as a KC was highly successful but it is as a judge, which he became in 1910, that he achieved lasting fame. "He took his position with ease in the King's Bench Division and dealt with emergencies in a manner which was to become one of his noted characteristics," wrote Ashley. "Novel points of law neither puzzled nor alarmed him. He was calm, judicious and painstaking and knew when to be silent. His patience, learning and alertness helped by an analytical turn of mind enabled him to find the answer to any question if an answer existed."

He was fifty-nine when he took up his new position and he was to stay in harness until he was eighty-four, a term of nearly a quarter of a century. Like Hawkins, he soon developed a reputation as a "hanging judge", and certainly the statistics bore that out: he heard one-hundred-and-sixty-three murder trials and sentenced sixty-nine people to death. He was keen on flogging too, if the offence merited such a harsh punishment (it was not abolished in Britain until 1948).

Henry Leon, later a judge himself but better known as the author Henry Cecil, observed him as a young barrister:

> Avory was a very small man with a parchment-like face and a rather rasping Cockney accent. He was quite a good criminal lawyer but nothing like as good as his reputation supposed him to be. This reputation sprang from the fact that the standard of lawyer at the Criminal Bar was not high and that Avory was far above it. He was a stern judge, but would decide a point of law quite dispassionately and

would not attempt to twist the law to the disadvantage of the prisoner.

Avory became the most famous judge in England, at a time when judges were probably much better known to the public than they are today, partly because he presided over so many high-profile trials, partly because he was an assiduous circuit judge, who visited every Assizes in the country except, for some reason, Oakham. "On circuit he expected counsel and the officials to do their work as it ought to be done," recorded Ashley. "Everyone knew that nothing slipshod was permitted."

His fellow Garrick member George Pleydell Bancroft was Avory's marshal—the official who organised the judge's life on circuit—for his first three years on the bench and left an intimate portrait of him in his memoir *Stage and Bar*.

> On the small side in stature, with acutely sloping champagne-bottle shoulders, a long upper lip, legal corners to a strong set mouth, small alive blue eyes, closely cropped short whiskers, he was distinctly impressive in appearance and manifestly a lawyer.
>
> Upon the Bench he had great natural dignity without a trace of pomposity; the gift of silence; repose amounting almost to stillness; extraordinary patience; a big dislike of bad court jokes, and good ones had not to be too many; an innate dislike of the limelight; an infinite capacity for taking pains; a defiant fearlessness; and a determination to see that justice was done.
>
> He possessed too a further quality when trying a case—a total unawareness of the existence of a Court of Criminal Appeal.

Bancroft thought he lacked only one quality: "a musical voice".

Avory's only distraction was golf. He loved to play on the local links when on circuit and it was perhaps fitting that he should die suddenly in the Dormy House Club at Rye in the summer of 1935, still working at the age of eight-four, having hinted to Ashley that he would retire in the autumn after completing twenty-five years on the bench.

Avory's successor as the leading criminal judge was Sir Travers Humphreys (1867-1956, Garrick 1909-1956, and a Trustee of the club). Even more than Avory, he was born to the purple: his father and two uncles were partners in one of London's leading firms of solicitors, which had been in the Humphreys family for generations. Indeed, Travers would have joined them if his older brother Carl had not drowned in a boating accident in the Thames. He had been destined for the bar; with his death, the mantle was passed on to his younger brother. Hardinge Giffard was a sort of honorary uncle: he came to live with the Humphreys family after his first wife died (in another accident) and stayed on until he remarried.

After Shrewsbury and Cambridge, where he was a keen rower, Humphreys went into the chambers of E.T. Besley, along with Archibald Bodkin, and learnt his trade at the Middlesex and North London Sessions and the South-Eastern Circuit, graduating to the Central Criminal Court where he played an increasingly significant role for nearly thirty years, first as a junior, then senior Treasury counsel, prosecuting on behalf of the Attorney-General. He developed a reputation for fairness (which he carried on to the bench) and he appeared in some of the most famous trials of the late nineteenth and early twentieth centuries, some of which have been referred to already in these pages: the Oscar Wilde trials, as junior to Edward Clarke and Charles Willie Mathews, the trial of Dr Crippen, the "Brides in the Bath" case, the prosecutions of Sir Roger Casement and of Horatio Bottomley, the arch-swindler who had so often previously cheated justice.

At the highest level of the judiciary there was, in those days, still a notable lack of criminal experts, so with Avory visibly ageing, Humphreys was appointed to the King's Bench in 1928. "Commonsense as we all know is the foundation of the common law," he once wrote and that was the essence of his great strength as a judge. He went circuit three or four times a year; in those days judges were allowed to take a friend to keep them company, an echo of the era when they were accompanied by a marshal, or armed bodyguard. Travers Humphreys (now Sir Travers) once took along his son Christmas (later a judge himself) but a more frequent companion was Christmas's Cambridge friend Harold Abrahams, the Olympic gold medallist sprinter whose story was immortalised in the film *Chariots of Fire*. A keen statistician, Abrahams would pull out his stopwatch and time the undefended divorce cases, urging Sir Travers to speed up and break the record.

Humphreys presided over some of the great criminal trials of the 1930s and '40s: the murder prosecution of Elvira Barney in 1932, Patrick Hastings's greatest criminal defence triumph; another exotic figure accused of murder, Alma Rattenbury, and her teenage lover George Stoner, in 1935; the complex trials in 1939 of eighteen IRA members accused of a murderous bombing campaign; and perhaps most famously the sensational trial at Lewes of the serial killer John George Haigh (when Humphreys was eighty-two). In all of them, Humphreys distinguished himself by his objectivity, thoroughness and courtesy. As his obituarist in the *DNB* wrote: "By the end of his life Humphreys had become in the public mind the embodiment of English criminal justice."

He was also a valued member of the Court of Criminal Appeal, particularly welcomed as a counterweight to Lord Chief Justice Hewart, who was more prone to racing to conclusions and fairly overt bias. One such panel heard the appeal in 1931 of Alfred Rouse against his conviction for murder of a drifter whose body was found in Rouse's burnt-out car. The appeal judges were Hewart, Avory and Humphreys, all Garrick members at some time, and Rouse was represented by another, Hastings: the case might almost have been heard over lunch in the Coffee Room.

Humphreys retired at eighty-four in 1951. He was a great believer in the jury system and a thoughtful commentator on legal issues, as he showed in his book of reminiscences *Criminal Days*, published in 1946. He was a conservative and a traditionalist—he wore a top hat every day on his way to court until 1939, long after it had gone out of fashion—but he was not a hidebound reactionary. He believed in leniency for first offenders and was generally not a savage sentencer. He had a delightful sense of humour, as is evident from his writings, but he took great care not to show it in court; like Avory, he left no doubt of his dislike of judges who insisted on inflicting their laboured witticisms from the bench. His biographer Douglas Browne called him "a born mixer and maker of friends, with strong affections and loyalties". He lost his elder son in the First World War but the family legal tradition was continued by his son

Christmas Humphreys, who in his turn became one of the country's best-known and best-loved judges.

"Justice should not only be done, but should ... be seen to be done" is probably the legal maxim best known to and most quoted by the general public. It was first enunciated by Lord Hewart (1870-1943, Garrick 1921-1933, 1935-1937), Lord Chief Justice from 1922 to 1940. He was a great clubman but he preferred the Reform and the Savage to the Garrick. His immortal pronouncement was made in a routine appeal by a Hastings man found guilty of dangerous driving. His lawyer then discovered that a partner in a solicitors' firm seeking damages for injuries caused by the driver was also clerk to the Hastings magistrates. Hewart quashed the conviction in the Divisional Court. "A long line of cases shows that it is not merely of some importance, but it is of fundamental importance, that justice should not only be done, but should manifestly and undoubtedly be seen to be done," he said.

Gordon Hewart was yet another lawyer to make it to the very top after starting out in life in a very different direction. In his case, it was journalism that first attracted him. He was a Lancashire lad, born in Bury in 1870, the son (like Norman Birkett) of a successful draper who ran the biggest such business in the town. Another Garrick lawyer son of Bury was Sir John Holker, who too went on to become Attorney-General some time before Hewart. Indeed, at the age of twelve Hewart was much moved by a speech in memory of Holker, who had just died, delivered to the pupils of Bury Grammar School by the headmaster. He was said to have gone home and told his father he would be Attorney-General too one day. A precocious but delicate boy who loved the Classics (a passion that was to remain with him for the rest of his life), Hewart went on to Manchester Grammar School and University College, Oxford. His father wanted him to read for the bar and he was attracted by the idea but wanted to be financially independent. He had always been fascinated by journalism and had written articles for the local paper while still at school. Now he borrowed £5 from his father and headed for London to try his luck as a freelance. It was tough going but he found work writing articles about London life for provincial newspapers and landed a staff job writing parliamentary reports and leaders for the *Star*, a brash, lively new daily paper, as well as a weekly column for the *Bury Times*. He moved on to another new paper, the *Morning Leader*, and spent eight years in total on Fleet Street. But his thoughts started turning towards the law and he started reading for the bar in what little spare time his journalistic duties afforded. Finally, he reckoned he had saved enough money to abandon journalism and was called to the bar at the Inner Temple in 1902. He went back to Manchester to embark on his new life, and soon acquired a reputation for diligence and thorough preparation, however small and badly-paid the case: it was not just the content but its presentation that he would study for hours. George Pleydell Bancroft, Garrick member and Clerk of Assize on the Midland Circuit, said after watching him in action: "That man would have made a really first-class actor. When he stands up in court, it is as though he is in the middle of a stage. He moves nothing but his eyes."

Hewart's first case to attract widespread coverage came in 1908 in a libel case that was still being cited in law lessons for young journalists well over half a century later, and indeed concerned a former journalist, Thomas Jones.

He was a friend of Hewart and had enjoyed a similar career, being a parliamentary sketch writer before becoming a barrister, when he had used his middle name Artemus rather than Thomas to give himself a more striking byline. To his astonishment and embarrassment, the *Sunday Chronicle* ran an article on the colourful atmosphere at the Dieppe Grand Prix in France, and singled out a man called Artemus Jones who "turns night into day, besides betraying a most unholy delight in the society of female butterflies." The newspaper, as sometimes happens, made matters worse by publishing a flip apology. Jones sued for libel. The newspaper claimed that the use of the name was a pure coincidence but Hewart, representing his friend, produced a string of witnesses who said they believed the article to refer to Thomas Artemus Jones. The judge and jury agreed and awarded Jones £1,750, a handsome sum. The case went all the way to the House of Lords, which backed the original verdict, and the case of Artemus Jones went into the lawbooks as a warning to journalists to do everything in their power to check that a fictitious name was just that – or risk the consequences.

Hewart was soon established as one of the busiest and most in-demand advocates at the Manchester bar. He took silk in 1912 and in 1913 was also elected Liberal MP for East Leicester at a by-election. His political ascent was rapid. He was a great admirer of Lloyd George and the feeling was mutual: when Lloyd George became Prime Minister in 1916 he appointed Hewart Solicitor-General. He rapidly became an irreplaceable ally for Lloyd George and performed so well in the post and in Parliament that after the end of the First World War (in which he lost his eldest son Gordon at Gallipoli) he was promoted to Attorney-

General in the reshuffle involving F.E. Smith's elevation to Lord Chancellor. His own elevation to Lord Chief Justice in 1922 was a tortuous affair that displayed Lloyd George at his most devious. The vacancy arose because in 1921 the Prime Minister wished to appoint another Garrick man, Lord Reading (formerly Sir Rufus Isaacs), Viceroy of India, but he did not wish to lose Hewart as Attorney. So he proposed to appoint an elderly judge as Lord Chief Justice who would give way when the moment came for Hewart to take over. Hewart was naturally anxious that if he agreed to wait circumstances might change and he would be deprived of a job he craved. F.E. Smith (now Lord Birkenhead) chipped in the unwelcome opinion that the Prime Minister had no right to sack a judge when he was felt to have outlived his usefulness. Hewart eventually, and reluctantly, agreed to the deal, and Mr Justice A.T. Lawrence found himself Lord Chief Justice at the age of seventy-four. In due course he read of his own resignation in the newspaper one morning in 1922 and Hewart duly succeeded him.

Hewart had a brisk and efficient manner. A typical judgment was one he delivered in the Divisional Court. "Counsel for the appellant has raised six points in support of this appeal," he pronounced. "In the first point there is nothing, and the same applies to the others. Five times nothing are nothing. The appeal is dismissed." But he also acquired the reputation of taking sides in certain cases, and as he aged he became, his biographer Robert Jackson noted, "autocratic and irascible" in court. Jackson wrote:

> His obstinacy sometimes drove to despair counsel in whose favour he was about to find; he could scarcely bear to have his authority on a legal point questioned. "Why on

earth did you differ from me yesterday?" he would greet members of the Court of Appeal, who had reversed one of his judgments. The less strong-willed judges avoided him, so as not to be involved in a scene…

Like many brilliant and successful men, Hewart was undoubtedly difficult to work with. He could command a scourging turn of phrase, and he had a gift for irony which he did not hesitate to use, often with small provocation, in private. His brilliance and his swift rise to the head of the profession had made him many enemies. He had come up the hard way and had earned his success, but in the eyes of some who, aided by influence, had had an easier passage, he was an "outsider"… To the world Hewart was tough, imperturbable, untouchable almost. But, in fact, his brilliance and aggressiveness cloaked a sensitive nature. He might pretend in public that the calculated insults of his enemies in the Temple meant nothing, but his friends knew that they hurt him deeply.

Henry Leon, better known as the novelist Henry Cecil, had mixed feelings about Hewart. "I think he had the greatest command of simple English of any judge whom I've heard," he noted, "and it was a delight to listen to the way in which he chose his language." He rated him a successful Attorney-General but not a good Lord Chief Justice. In fact, thought Leon, "he was a shockingly bad judge."

Hewart's tendency to over-hastiness in coming to judgment was clearly shown in a notorious libel case in 1928 when William Hobbs, a former solicitor's clerk jailed for conspiracy to blackmail, sued a string of newspapers on his release from prison for having published lurid stories about him which, he claimed, went well beyond what he had been convicted for. The *Liverpool Daily News* was the first paper to reach court, in what was regarded as a test case. Hobbs was represented by the distinguished Irish advocate Serjeant A.M. Sullivan, who had defended Sir Roger Casement, but he never had a chance. Hewart took against Hobbs completely and Sullivan later described how a "continuous snarl" from the bench had accompanied his opening speech. Hewart invited the jury to come to a verdict before Sullivan had finished his case and although Sullivan protested and was allowed to finish, Hewart's utterly biased summing-up left the jury little alternative but to find for the newspaper. Sullivan's list of objections to the Appeal Court was a lengthy one and the verdict was set aside. (The accumulated Hobbs cases were eventually settled out of court.) It was a stinging rebuke for the Lord Chief Justice, who had by then realised he had gone too far.

Hewart was much preoccupied by the belief that Britain's growing bureaucracy, empowered by Parliament with an ever-increasing amount of legislation, was undermining the judiciary, and in 1929 he published a book, *The New Despotism*, setting out his fears. One of his particular bugbears was that the Lord Chancellor's department was, so he believed, bent on creating a Ministry of Justice. The book created a public stir and was perhaps ahead of its time in its warnings of the gathering power of the unelected; it was said to have influenced Margaret Thatcher. Oddly enough, in his last years Hewart disowned the book, believing that the nascent welfare state needed all the bureaucratic strength that could be mustered to get it off the ground. Suffering from increasing ill-health, he retired in 1940, aged seventy, and lived for only another three years. He was irascible to the end. Spring had arrived, and his last words were: "Damn, it's that cuckoo again."

Sir Thomas Noon Talfourd, by John Lucas, c.1840

Sir John Adolphus, published in *The Monthly Mirror*, February 1803

JOHN ADOLPHUS ESQ.ᴿ F.A.S.

William (Mr Serjeant) Ballantine
Hand-coloured Talbot-type, c.1854

John Humffreys (Mr Serjeant) Parry
Carte-de-visite, c.1875

Sir John Holker, by Sir Leslie Ward,
published in *Vanity Fair*, 9 February 1878

Sir James Fitzjames Stephen, carte-
de-visite by London Stereoscopic &
Photographic Company, 1870s

Edwin John James, as an observer with
Garibaldi's forces in Italy, published in *The
Illustrated London News*, 13 October 1860

Sir Henry Hawkins (Baron Brampton),
Carte-de-visite, c.1880

Sir Harry Poland, by Harry Furniss,
published in *The Garrick Gallery of
Caricatures*, c.1910

Sir Henry James, by John St Helier Lander

By kind permission of the Masters of the Bench of Honorable Society of the Middle Temple

Sir Charles Willie Mathews

by Harry Furniss, published in *The Garrick Gallery of Caricatures*, c.1910

Garrick Club / Art Archive

Sir Edward Clarke

by Harry Furniss, published in *The Garrick Gallery of Caricatures*, c.1910

Garrick Club / Art Archive

Robert Threshie Reid (Lord Loreburn)
by Henry Harris Brown, 1911,

Courtesy of the Masters of the
Bench of the Inner Temple

Hardinge Stanley Giffard, 1st Earl of
Halsbury, by Harry Furniss, c.1890

© National Portrait Gallery, London

Sir Frank Lockwood, by Arthur Stockdale Cope

By kind permission of the Masters of the Bench of the
Honorable Society of Lincoln's Inn

"Sir Henry Irving meets his first
pheasant", by Sir Frank Lockwood

Garrick Club / Art Archive

Sir Horace Avory
by Harry Furniss, published in *The
Garrick Gallery of Caricatures*, c.1910

Garrick Club / Art Archive

Sir Robert (later Lord) Finlay
by George Fiddes Watt, 1917

Courtesy of the Masters of the Bench of the
Honourable Society of the Middle Temple

Sir Rufus Isaacs (Lord Reading)
by George Fiddes Watt

Courtesy of the Masters of the Bench of the
Honourable Society of the Middle Temple

Sir Edward Carson

by Harry Furniss, published in *The
Garrick Gallery of Caricatures*, c.1910

Garrick Club / Art Archive

Sir Edward Marshall Hall

by Harry Furniss, published in *The
Garrick Gallery of Caricatures*, c.1910

Garrick Club / Art Archive

Sir Archibald Bodkin

by Harry Furniss, published in *The
Garrick Gallery of Caricatures*, c.1910

Garrick Club / Art Archive

F.E. Smith
(Lord Birkenhead), by Glyn Warren
Philpot c.1919

Reproduced by kind permission of the Masters
of the Bench of the Honourable Society of
Gray's Inn

Sir Patrick Hastings
by "Quiz" (Powys Evans)

Mary Evans Picture Library

Sir Gordon (Lord) Hewart, by Sir Oswald Birley, 1935

Sir Norman (Lord) Birkett
by Claude Rogers, 1958

Sir Hartley (Lord) Shawcross putting the prosecution case at Nuremberg, 1946

Christmas Humphreys
by Ockinden, 1950

James Crespie, from the menu card
for a dinner in his memory at the
Garrick Club, 12 October 1992

Sir Peter (Lord) Taylor, by Andrew Festing

Courtesy of the Masters
of the Bench of the Inner Temple

Sir Michael Davies, from *The Garrick* No 20, November 2006

Garrick Club LIbrary

Peter Carter-Ruck, by Bryan Organ, 1995

Courtesy of Carter-Ruck

Sir David Napley, by Michael Noakes

Kind permission of The Law Society

George Carman upon his appointment as a QC, December 1971

Central Press / Hulton Archive / Getty Images

Richard Ferguson

Courtesy of Carmelite Chambers

John Mortimer, by Tai-Shan Schierenberg, 1992

9
TOP OF THE TREE:
EDWARD CARSON AND RUFUS ISAACS

The trials of Oscar Wilde in 1895 crop up repeatedly in these pages because so many Garrick lawyers were involved on one side or the other. The first trial destroyed Wilde's reputation and made that of Edward Carson (1854-1935, Garrick 1896-1921) in England. It was a task Carson approached with no eagerness for he and Wilde were fellow Irishmen and indeed had been contemporaries at Trinity College, Dublin. But once committed to an undertaking, whether legal or political, Carson gave everything of himself and was single-minded in the pursuit of his goal. When Wilde heard that Carson would be cross-examining him, he remarked: "No doubt he will perform his task with all the added bitterness of an old friend." Wilde was, as usual, exaggerating for effect, for he and Carson had never been friends, merely acquaintances, and bitterness played no part in Carson's cross-examination of Wilde. But it was devastating and led, as we have seen in Chapter Six, to Sir Edward Clarke withdrawing Wilde's criminal libel action against the Marquess of Queensbury and to his inevitable criminal indictment for gross indecency. Wilde's distinguished defence team's efforts on his behalf foundered on the rock of Carson's relentless questioning. It lasted for two days and finally drew from the playwright the fatal, offhand remark, when Carson asked him whether he had kissed a young man called Grainger in Lord Alfred Douglas's rooms at Oxford, "Oh dear no, he was a peculiarly plain boy. He was, unfortunately, extremely ugly. I pitied him for it." Carson closed in for the kill after that, and once he had revealed that he proposed to call various young men as witnesses, Wilde knew the game was up. The trial judge, Mr Justice Collins, was bowled over by Carson's performance. He sent him a personal note: "I never heard a more powerful speech, or a more searching cross-exam. I congratulate you on having escaped most of the filth." For all his unbending integrity, Carson was a merciful man. He declined to take part for the prosecution in Wilde's first trial for indecency, and when it ended in a hung jury, Carson approached the Solicitor-General, Sir Frank Lockwood, who intended to submit Wilde to a retrial, and pleaded for mercy with the words, "Cannot you let up on the fellow now? He has suffered a great deal." Lockwood ignored his request and pressed on with a prosecution that led to Wilde's imprisonment, ruin and early death.

Little could young Ned Carson have imagined that he and Wilde would end up confronting each other at the Old Bailey in the trial of the decade, if not the century, when they were students at Trinity. Wilde was the flamboyant star of the university, gaining first-class honours before departing for Oxford, while Carson was a run-of-the-mill classics student and oarsman who scraped a pass degree and gave no indication that he would not only become one of the most glittering and highest-paid figures of the English bar but the leader of the fight against Irish Home

Rule and the father of modern Ulster, idolised to this day by the Protestants of Northern Ireland for saving the Six Counties from incorporation into what became the Irish Republic. He might even have become Prime Minister during the First World War, had he wanted. But one activity in which he did excel was debating, as a member of Trinity's famous College Historical Society; the Auditor (President) in the year Carson joined was Bram Stoker, future author of *Dracula*. It is interesting to note how many great advocates were mediocre students but keen university debaters.

Probably few people today realise that this champion of Ulster Unionism was a Dubliner, the son of an architect. Having gone on to study law, Ned Carson was called to the Irish bar in 1877 and like most lawyers who went on to make a great name for themselves endured several years of low-paid drudgery on circuit, in Carson's case the county courts of Ireland. It was on circuit that Carson developed the highly personal cross-examining technique that would become so well-known in the English courts: asking only a few but highly relevant and searching questions and then sitting down. It was risky, in that the advocate had to be certain he had isolated the key points of the case that he needed to highlight, but in Carson's hands it was to prove extraordinarily effective. It was helped in good measure by his imposing personal presence: he was tall, dark-haired, slightly stooping, with a jutting jaw, piercing blue eyes and a serious, almost grim expression, and he had a beautiful Irish brogue combined with a quick mind and wit that was capable of turning the tables on his opponent or even the most eminent judge in an instant.

Carson was learning his trade during a period of the most intense political ferment in Ireland, much of it centring on the land issue and the struggle between landlords and tenants. Carson started to acquire a reputation as an able advocate in the newly-established Land Commission, representing first tenants, then landlords when they realised how good he was. His first big break as a criminal barrister came in 1882 when he defended two young men accused of murdering a third in the snug bar of a Dublin public house. The atmosphere in Dublin was volatile because of a spate of violent killings and attacks but Carson's eloquence resulted in a hung jury, and the men eventually pleaded guilty to manslaughter. The following year, Carson made his name in a notorious murder trial when he was junior defence counsel for four men accused of murdering Mrs Henry Smythe, sister-in-law of a well-known landowner in County Westmeath who was the intended victim; their carriage was attacked by gunmen as they returned home from church on Palm Sunday. The family was very well-connected: Queen Victoria and the Prime Minister, Gladstone, had sent messages of condolence, so naturally the trial, based on evidence from informers, attracted massive coverage in the press around the world. The lead defence counsel had a bad-tempered exchange with the prosecution, so deemed it prudent to let Carson make the final speech to the jury. His eloquence won widespread praise, although it cannot be said to have saved his clients; a juryman suffered a breakdown and a retrial had to be ordered in which Carson played no part. It did not matter; his name was made, and he was not yet thirty. More important, his performance impressed the prosecution counsel, Peter O'Brien (1842-1914, Garrick

1888-1902), a colourful character and hate figure for Irish nationalists who was known as "Peter the Packer" for his skill at excluding nationalists from juries in agrarian trials. He was to serve as Lord Chief Justice of Ireland for twenty-four years. When he became Solicitor-General for Ireland, he recommended Carson for the post of Counsel for the Attorney-General of Ireland, i.e. his chief prosecutor, with the vital task of enforcing the draconian Crimes Act of 1887, which was meant to suppress the violence that was then rampant in every corner of the country. Carson set to with a will, showing himself to be utterly fearless and earning the nickname "Coercion" Carson. (He seemed to attract sobriquets: later on, he was known in Ulster as "King" Carson.) His performance attracted the attention of the new Chief Secretary to Ireland (and future Prime Minister), A.J. Balfour: a strong friendship ensued and Balfour became Carson's political mentor. The relationship, both personal and political, lasted for the rest of Balfour's life.

Remarkably, given the course of his later career, Carson had no greater ambition than to be an Irish judge, but others, in particular Balfour, had other ideas, recognising the young barrister's qualities. Balfour pressed Carson, a Liberal-Unionist, to stand for the UK Parliament as one of the candidates for the Trinity College seat, which in those days returned two members to Westminster. Within the space of a few days in 1892 Carson was appointed Solicitor-General for Ireland and elected to Parliament. This was the turning point in his life: as the Conservatives, now led in the Commons by Balfour, had lost the election, he soon lost his new official post, and decided that as he would be an MP at Westminster he would try to forge a new career at the English bar. Carson thought he was unknown in London but a chance meeting in the Commons with Charles Darling QC MP, later a distinguished judge, led to an invitation to join Darling's chambers. Darling allayed Carson's misgivings by telling him he would have five times his (Darling's) practice within a year. Carson demurred but bet him a shilling if he did so: he paid Darling a year later. It is not within the scope of this brief chapter to give an account of Carson's political career but suffice it to say that he made an equally extraordinary impact in both Parliament and at the bar. His maiden speech, on Home Rule, was judged to be a triumph. Joseph Chamberlain, leader of the Liberal-Unionists, sent him a personal note: "It was the best debating speech I have heard for a long while in the House of Commons, and for a maiden speech I think it was unprecedented." The newspaper coverage next day echoed Chamberlain's praise.

Leaving his wife Annette and their four children in Dublin, Carson embarked on his legal career in London after going through the formality of being called to the bar at the Middle Temple. Within three months, in July 1893, he had made his mark in a big libel trial. He represented the *Evening News*, which had been sued by Joseph Havelock Wilson MP, founder and general secretary of the National Amalgamated Sailors' and Firemen's Union, which later become the National Union of Seamen. The newspaper had accused Wilson of pocketing union money and of chaotic financial organisation verging on the corrupt. Among Wilson's team was a junior barrister called Rufus Isaacs who was to rise swiftly to the top of his profession and oppose Carson in many important (and lucrative) cases in the years ahead; like Carson, he had a parallel political career in which he also rose to the heights. Isaacs was also a member of the Garrick, albeit only for seven years. This was the first occasion they had met, and so Isaacs was able to witness Carson from close-up. It was quite a spectacle, for Carson submitted Wilson to such a ferocious and forensic cross-examination that at the end of the day the union boss burst into tears and had to be led sobbing from the witness-box. Next day, the jury threw out all but one of his claims, for which he was awarded one farthing. The press was unanimous in its praise for Carson and his performance did not go unnoticed by the English bar either. Travers Humphreys, who was often his junior, noted: "His reputation as a great-hearted fighter for his client, a master of the epigram and the verbal quip, a deadly cross-examiner and the possessor of a voice which charmed all hearers, is safe for all time. He took risks, but they generally came off."

In 1894, Sir Henry Hawkins told him he ought to be a QC (which he was already, but only in Ireland). Carson duly applied for silk but was turned down by the Lord Chancellor Lord Herschell, who thought it premature. Carson was outraged and Hawkins not much less. The press weighed in on Carson's behalf and Hawkins wrote to Herschell asking him to reconsider. Herschell relented and Carson received his patent from the Lord Chancellor alone. This led to a fine example of Carson's sharp wit. By tradition as a newly-created QC, he had to go from court to court in the law courts in full fig bowing to the judges and counsel. But in the last court, the judge, Mr Justice Kekewich, had already gone home. By coincidence, Carson was in his court next morning. He embarked on his case but the judge, a stickler for formality, kept interrupting and saying, "I can't hear you, Mr Carson." Carson raised his voice until he was shouting, to no avail. The judge pointed out that Carson had not been called as a QC within the bar of his court and so he could not "hear" him. However, he added, "I don't propose to send you home to put on your knee-breeches, as perhaps I should."

"I should hope not," retorted Carson.

"What's that you say?" cried the affronted judge. "I shall tolerate no impertinence."

"I thought your Lordship could not hear me," replied Carson, which provoked laughter in court and even forced a smile from the judge.

After the Wilde case the following year, Carson was in huge demand, and able to command the highest fees, along with Rufus Isaacs. Not every case was as desperately serious as that of Oscar Wilde: in 1898 Carson represented a theatrical magazine called *The Era* which was sued for libel by the great W.S. Gilbert (a Garrick member for the last five years of his life, from 1906 to 1911). Edward Marshall Hall was Gilbert's junior defence counsel. The case might as well have been put on by the D'Oyly Carte Opera Company at the Savoy Theatre as in the High Court. It arose from an article in *The Era* criticising Gilbert in rather harsh language after he had given an interview to a Scottish newspaper criticising some of the greatest contemporary names in British theatre, including Irving and Tree. (Irving was called to give evidence, which was then ruled inadmissible by the judge.) *The Era* accused Gilbert of ingratitude and an "abnormal protuberance of self-esteem", among other things. Gilbert was extremely thin-skinned, as he freely admitted in cross-examination by Carson, and proved the point fairly conclusively by walking out during Carson's closing speech and snubbing him whenever they ran into each other thereafter. The jury could not agree on a verdict, so nobody won. The only thing the case lacked was a final chorus composed by Sir Arthur Sullivan.

In 1900 Carson had to forego most of his income when, the Conservatives having been returned to office, his friend Balfour invited him to become Solicitor-General; with some misgivings Carson accepted. He served until the end of 1905, prosecuting in a wide variety of cases for the Crown, such as Earl Russell's trial for bigamy before the House of Lords in 1901, for which the peer got three months in Holloway Prison, though he eventually received a free pardon. There were a couple of trials arising from the Boer War, including that of a fellow Irishman, Colonel Arthur Lynch, for high treason, for which Lynch received the death penalty, rapidly commuted to life. Lynch served only a few months in prison, and eventually ended up in the House of Commons, where one of his anti-German speeches during the First World War was praised by none other than Carson.

The principal criminal case which Carson prosecuted was the trial for murder in 1903 of George Chapman, when he led an all-Garrick team, his juniors being Charles Willie Mathews and Archibald Bodkin, both of whom went on to become Director of Public Prosecutions. Chapman was a Pole by birth who had done away with by poison a series of women with whom he lived. He was found guilty and hanged; there were many at the time who believed Chapman was also Jack the Ripper, and they included the Scotland Yard detective in charge of the hunt for the Whitechapel murderer.

In 1905 Carson was offered the Presidency of the Probate, Divorce and Admiralty Division by Lord Halsbury, the Lord Chancellor, but after long consideration he turned it down, saying he preferred life at the bar. This was undoubtedly true but had he become a judge the future of Irish politics might have been very different. At the end of that year, he was granted his wish: Balfour's government fell and he returned to his lucrative private practice. Over the next few years he was invariably pitted against Rufus Isaacs (1860-1935, Garrick 1905-1912) in the most celebrated cases of the day.

Like a surprising number of great advocates of the period, Isaacs's path to the top had been by no means a straight one. The son of an affluent Jewish fruit merchant, he was brought up in comfortable circumstances in Hampstead but was taken out of school at fourteen to learn the family business, although the headmaster of University College School, where he spent his last year in formal education, thought he had the makings of a good lawyer, being lively and clever if undisciplined. Inevitably, office work bored him, so his father decided a spell at sea might straighten him out. He signed on as ship's boy, the lowest form of maritime life, on a sailing ship bound for Brazil, where, bored again, he jumped ship. He was tracked down and brought back to the ship, spending a month ashore at Calcutta, the next port of call, little imagining that one day he would return as Governor-General of India. Back in England, he returned to the family business with the same outcome: this time, he stayed on dry land and went to work for his brother-in-law's stockbroking business. He then struck out on his own as a foreign stock jobber, but ran into trouble and was "hammered"— thrown out of the Stock Market—and effectively made bankrupt. But though the future looked bleak, his time in the Stock Market was not wasted. He had learned a great deal about finance and business which was to prove invaluable. He decided on a fresh start abroad but his mother, remembering his old headmaster's advice, thought he should study law and he was, literally, hauled back from the Liverpool train at Euston, and enrolled at the Middle Temple.

His progress thereafter was little short of meteoric: he rapidly built up a busy and lucrative High Court practice, hugely aided by the establishment of the Commercial Court in 1892, where his knowledge of the intricacies of the Stock Market and the financial world proved invaluable. Within a few years he was addressing—and greatly impressing— the House of Lords in a landmark industrial relations case which had started with Isaacs giving a legal opinion for a fee of one guinea. Within ten years of being called to the Bar, he was a QC at the age of thirty-seven. The fraud trial of the millionaire businessman Whitaker Wright in 1904 showed Isaacs's talents at their finest. Wright was the most colourful financier in Britain: thousands of ordinary people had invested in his companies for it appeared he could do no wrong. The sense of public shock and outrage when they suddenly collapsed was therefore deep; many small investors had lost everything. It was a case of extraordinary complexity, involving Wright switching funds between his many enterprises to enable them to appear solvent until the inevitable crash. Isaacs's opening speech lasted five hours and his closing one a day and a half but it was his cross-examination of Wright that proved the financier's undoing. "This was advocacy of a very rare and special kind," wrote Lord Birkett, "seen at its best in the grasp of detail combined with the superlative gift of explaining complicated figures with complete lucidity to lay minds." Wright was found guilty and sentenced to seven years' imprisonment. He asked to be allowed to go to the lavatory, and there swallowed a potassium cyanide capsule. He was dead within minutes.

Isaacs achieved results without bluster or emotion. He was always courteous to those he was cross-examining, calm, restrained, patient and superbly well-prepared. He was known as one of the hardest workers in the profession but he always had time for those in trouble. When Edward Marshall Hall, another frequent opponent in the top trials of the day, fell on hard times Isaacs offered support and financial assistance, which was eventually but gratefully declined.

Isaacs and Carson faced each other at Liverpool in 1907 when the soap magnate William Lever (later Lord Leverhulme) sued Lord Northcliffe and Associated Newspapers for alleging, particularly in the *Daily Mail*, that Lever Brothers had cornered the market and thereby exploited consumers. The court action lasted only a day, in which Carson questioned his client Lever, who put up a good performance. Isaacs, representing Northcliffe, realised he was going to lose and offered to settle for £10,000. An entertaining bout of bargaining then ensued, with Carson bidding Isaacs and Northcliffe up to £50,000, which Lever accepted, as well he might: it was the largest sum offered until that date by an English court. The press baron bore no grudge against Carson, and later supported him in his fight against Home Rule. In 1909,

Carson defended three newspapers, including the *Evening Standard*, against Cadbury's, the chocolate manufacturer and pillar of do-gooding paternalism, who sued for libel after the newspapers accused them of employing slave labour on the Portuguese islands of São Tomé and Príncipe, off West Africa. The trial was held on Cadbury's home turf, Birmingham, and William Cadbury was felt to have performed well under examination by his own lead counsel, Rufus Isaacs. Carson followed him and ruthlessly exposed Cadbury's hypocrisy: he admitted he had known the appalling truth about conditions on the islands, with men, women and children marched up to a thousand miles from the interior of the Portuguese mainland territory of Angola to the coast to be shipped in shackles to the islands. The jury awarded Cadbury's a derisory farthing, which was seen as a victory for Carson: he certainly viewed it as one.

The following year came the case which Carson regarded as his greatest triumph, and is commemorated for posterity by a much-loved play (and film). In contrast to Carson's innumerable cases involving the reputations or divorces of millionaires or socialites, it revolved round a thirteen-year-old boy and a five-shilling postal order. The boy was George Archer-Shee, a cadet at the Royal Naval College at Osborne on the Isle of Wight, whose epic battle to clear his name of theft was the inspiration for Terence Rattigan's play *The Winslow Boy*. Archer-Shee was expelled from the college, accused of stealing a postal order from a fellow cadet and cashing it at the local post office by forging the recipient's signature. George maintained his innocence throughout, and on the advice of his elder son, who was, like Carson, an MP, the boy's father consulted Carson. He was intrigued by the case, partly because his own son Walter had just left the college and partly because he was impressed by the boy's steadfastness after he had subjected him to a searching examination. But how to clear his name? It took Carson eighteen months of patient work, a successful visit to the Appeal Court and an application before the Lord Chief Justice to get the case heard by a judge and jury. The long battle to get the case heard at all was not Carson's only preoccupation: his wife was very ill, his own health was not good (he suffered from ill-health and a certain hypochondria all his life), he had recently been elected leader of the Irish Unionists, which brought a huge amount of extra responsibilities, for the issue of Home Rule was coming to a head again, and yet he pressed on with this apparently trivial case. Once committed to a cause, whether Unionism or the reputation of a teenager, Carson could not be deflected from his path. Again he was up against Isaacs, who was by now Sir Rufus Isaacs, Solicitor-General (he was advanced to Attorney-General later that year). Once young George had stood up well to cross-examination, the case came down to the evidence of the postmistress who had cashed the five-shilling postal order. It was Carson's delicate task to show there was room for doubt about her identifying the person who had cashed the order without impugning her integrity. He managed this feat triumphantly with one of his brief cross-examinations. On the fourth day of the trial, Isaacs announced that the Admiralty accepted George's complete innocence: Carson had won. He also helped to secure substantial, if grudging, compensation for the boy's father from the Admiralty. The sad postscript was that George Archer-Shee, who was never accepted back by the college, lived only another four years before perishing at Ypres in 1914.

Sir Rufus Isaacs had reason to be grateful to Carson in 1913 when he represented his brother Godfrey Isaacs, managing director of the Marconi Company, in two libel actions arising from the Marconi scandal, in which Sir Rufus and Lloyd George were accused of profiting from the wireless company's rocketing share price. The French newspaper *Le Matin* admitted libel and paid damages but a British journalist, Cecil Chesterton, editor of a magazine called *The Eye Witness* denied criminal libel after accusing Godfrey Isaacs of corruption in the plainest terms. Carson persuaded the jury to find Chesterton guilty, and he also abstained in the Commons on a vote of censure on Sir Rufus and Lloyd George, even though it was proposed by Carson's Conservative allies, many of whom criticised him and F.E. Smith for missing a chance to attack the Government by representing Isaacs. Carson ignored the criticism: he saw himself as "a lawyer first and a politician afterwards". At any rate, the taint of the Marconi affair did not prevent Isaacs from becoming Lord Chief Justice in 1913, although there was some scarcely-veiled anti-Semitic comment, notably from Rudyard Kipling in his poem "Gehazi", which ended with the words, "Stand up, stand up, Gehazi,/Draw close thy robe and go,/ Gehazi, Judge in Israel,/ A leper white as snow." Isaacs took the title Lord Reading of Erleigh: he had represented Reading as its Liberal MP since 1904.

All this was happening during a tumultuous period in Carson's life: his wife died and the situation in Ulster was nearing boiling point, with the threat of civil war. As Ulster threatened to go it alone, Carson indeed faced the very real possibility of being arrested for rebellion, an extraordinary situation for such a distinguished lawyer to find himself in but one which he regarded with equanimity. "I should have pleaded guilty," he said, reasoning that no jury would have convicted him for pledging loyalty to the Crown.

The crisis was sidelined by an even larger one, the First World War, and in May 1915 Carson joined Asquith's Government as Attorney-General with a seat in the Cabinet. He lasted only until October when he resigned over the Government's failure to go to the aid of Serbia, recently invaded by Germany; Carson was always a man of inflexible principle. He became the Government's chief critic in the Commons and played a key role in forcing Asquith out in 1916. He might have succeeded him if that had been his ambition; instead, he backed Lloyd George and joined his Cabinet as First Lord of the Admiralty, but he was excluded from the small War Cabinet which he had been instrumental in creating. He resigned again, in January 1918, to resume the fight for Ulster remaining within the United Kingdom.

Lord Reading's role during the war had been no less notable. Lloyd George was always calling on him for advice on the government's finances, and he headed the Anglo-French Financial Mission to America which negotiated a $500 million loan to help pay for the war. He then returned to the US as High Commissioner, standing down temporarily as LCJ, with the remit of co-ordinating more loans, ensuring that America stepped up its vital military and financial aid, and doing everything he could to persuade President Woodrow Wilson to enter the war. A natural diplomat, he carried off these tasks triumphantly.

Lloyd George pressed Carson to return to the Cabinet after the war but he declined, preferring to return to the bar. In 1914, he had remarried; his new wife, Ruby Frewen, was, at thirty, exactly half his age. In 1920, she gave birth to a son, also named Edward, Carson's fifth child. Perhaps it is the reason he resigned from the Garrick that year. He was greeted the day after the birth became known by cheers from both sides of the House of Commons. His son was to follow him into Parliament as a Conservative MP in 1945.

In 1921 Carson was appointed a Lord of Appeal in Ordinary and was introduced to the House of Lords as Baron Carson of Duncairn, the Belfast constituency which he had represented since 1918. He watched with grief as the Irish Free State finally came into being, denouncing in the Lords what he saw as Britain's betrayal of the Irish Unionists in the strongest possible terms, but at least his beloved Ulster was not included. He served as a Law Lord for eight years before his health started to fail. He died in 1935 but not before he had witnessed the unveiling of a statue to him outside the Northern Ireland Parliament at Stormont.

Rufus Isaacs too had a vigorous public life after the war. Resuming life as Lord Chief Justice after his Washington mission, he now found the duties undemanding and accepted with alacrity the offer to become Viceroy of India in 1921 where he found himself dealing with Mahatma Gandhi's growing influence. Successively Baron Reading, Viscount Reading, the Earl of Reading and finally the Marquess of Reading, he had a two-month stint as stand-in Foreign Secretary in Ramsay MacDonald's first National Government and saw out his days as Lord Warden of the Cinque Ports until his death in December 1935. He outlived his old friend and rival Carson by just three months.

10

GARRICK MEN WHO BROUGHT DOWN A GOVERNMENT: PATRICK HASTINGS AND ARCHIBALD BODKIN

Sir Archibald Bodkin and Sir Patrick Hastings were distinguished barristers and Garrick members of very different temperament who unwittingly contrived to bring down Britain's first Labour government in 1924. Two less likely revolutionaries would be hard to imagine: at the time Bodkin was Director of Public Prosecutions and Hastings Attorney-General, and the issue which ended Ramsay MacDonald's first administration was an essentially minor legal case which somehow blew up into a political crisis through the maladroit handling of it by all concerned.

Archibald Bodkin (1862-1957, Garrick 1889-1957) was a dry workaholic who came from a long line of lawyers which included his uncle Sir Harry Bodkin Poland (whom he was to follow as both head of chambers and Recorder of Dover). He was educated at Highgate and was always determined on a legal career, being called to the bar at the Inner Temple. Along with Travers Humphreys, a future judge who was a lifelong friend and also a member of the Garrick, he was a pupil of another busy advocate, E.T. Besley. Thanks to his appetite for work, he progressed smoothly up the career ladder, becoming junior Treasury counsel in 1902 and senior counsel in 1908. In this capacity he led for the prosecution in many of the great criminal cases of the period, such as George Smith, the "Brides in the Bath" murderer, and helped send a succession of German spies or traitors to the firing squad or the gallows in the First World War, including Sir Roger Casement. In 1920 he succeeded Willie Mathews as Director of Public Prosecutions, a post he had not expected but at which he (largely) excelled: it was estimated that some 18,000 cases passed across his desk in the ten years in which he held the job.

His social life, though, was virtually non-existent. He had been elected to the Garrick as a young man, presumably through family connections, but rarely went to the club. His junior, Vernon Gattie, once suggested they go there for dinner. Bodkin agreed but said, "I pay my subscription but I never go." The hall porter, nicknamed "Money-brand", asked Gattie if he wouldn't mind signing in his guest, only to be told that Bodkin had been a member for many years. "I can see I shall have to come here more often," observed Bodkin.

Sir Patrick Hastings (1880-1952, Garrick 1916-1952) was a very different figure, vying with Sir Edward Marshall Hall for the title of the most charismatic silk of the first half of the twentieth century, although his route to success was anything but conventional. He was the son of a London solicitor who constantly flirted with bankruptcy, and an artist mother, who painted several portraits of Ellen Terry: the actress would occasionally bring along the aged Henry Irving, who insisted on telling the same stories and would not be interrupted until he had finished. Hastings retained a love of the theatre all his life and indeed wrote several plays, some of which were put on in the West End with varying degrees of success. He hated his time at Charterhouse, from which he was removed early when family funds ran low to live a peripatetic life with his mother and brother in Corsica, France and Belgium. Unemployed and unemployable back in England, the Hastings brothers volunteered for the army when the Boer War broke out and spent two years soldiering in South Africa. "We were perpetually chasing or being chased, shooting or being shot at, with as far as I could see, very little result on either side," Hastings remembered. Returning to London, he resolved to study law, and being penniless, he financed his studies at Middle Temple with journalism, writing drama notes for a variety of newspapers and magazines. After he qualified, he was still without any financial means, but he attended court every day to watch three leading advocates—Carson, Isaacs and Henry Duke—and learn from them. He continued to live on his wits after he qualified: he secured an introduction to a leading barrister in whose chambers he wanted to work, Charles Gill, by writing a book on moneylending and presenting the manuscript to the surprised silk. Gill gave him his first brief, possibly out of admiration at his nerve. Hastings displayed similar chutzpah to secure a permanent booth in chambers with Horace Avory, then a leading criminal silk, and he was on his way. When Avory became a judge, he generously allowed the young Hastings to take over the tenancy for nothing: Hastings paid him when he could.

He got his big break when he was retained almost accidentally to defend John Williams, known as "the hooded man", who was accused of murdering a police inspector in Eastbourne. Hastings did not get his man off but he fought for him through to the Appeal Court, and the case became something of a cause célèbre, leading to an adjournment debate in the Commons and an appeal to the Home Secretary for clemency. It was all in vain; Williams was hanged, but Hastings won many admirers for his conduct of the case. Despite this, he disliked murder cases and his practice was largely a civil one: he was involved in a string of high-profile divorce, libel and slander cases featuring such public figures as Marie Stopes, Winston Churchill, the Hon John Russell and Lord Alfred Douglas (Oscar Wilde's Bosie). In 1916 he was elected to the Garrick, and his relationship with the club was very different from Bodkin's. His biographer H. Montgomery Hyde wrote: "Hastings loved the Garrick … and he would drop in there and relax over a game of bridge or a drink on his way home from chambers, after the courts had risen for the day, a practice in which he was very sensibly encouraged by his wife, who considered it an admirable way of filling in 'that uncomfortable hour before dinner'."

Unlike Bodkin, who seldom invited colleagues to dine at home, Hastings was a social animal who, with his vivacious wife Mary, loved to entertain actors and writers, as well as his fellow lawyers at his Georgian house in Curzon Street (a site now occupied by the Curzon cinema) and was wont to organise party games if he felt the evening needed livening up. His behaviour occasionally bordered on the eccentric: if he was bored by his guests, he would sometimes disappear off to bed. Halfway through tea with Lady Hastings as the guest of King George V at Buckingham Palace, he startled the monarch with the words, "Well, I must be off now, as I have some work to do."

Much as he enjoyed society life, there was another side to Hastings. The horrors of the First World War sparked a desire to involve himself in social reform. He briefly joined the Liberal Party, but resigned in protest at Lloyd George's "coupon election" deal with the Conservatives in 1918, and joined Labour instead. He was adopted for the Tyneside seat of Wallsend, elected to Parliament in 1922 and re-elected with an increased majority in 1923. When the Baldwin government fell in January 1924, he became Attorney-General the following month in the minority Labour administration headed by Ramsay MacDonald, despite his political inexperience and relative youth (he was only forty-three). The next nine months were the most hectic and gruelling of his career: much of his time was devoted to the constitutional problems arising from the creation of the Irish Free State, and as the Solicitor-General was not an MP the task of dealing with the most minor legal questions in the House of Commons fell on his shoulders. He also had to lead the prosecution against a Frenchman, Jean Pierre Vaquier, accused of murdering his English mistress's husband at his hotel in Byfleet, Surrey, the sort of suburban murder case (this time with a faintly exotic foreign twist) which would fill many newspaper columns at the time. Vacquier went to the gallows protesting his innocence.

It was in late July that the apparently innocuous issue that led to the premature demise of the Labour government had its origins. Sir Archibald Bodkin (he was knighted in 1917) had by now been in office as DPP for four years. He received from the police a copy of a Communist newspaper, the *Workers' Weekly*, which contained an article urging British soldiers, sailors and airmen to refuse to take action in industrial disputes against their fellow-workers. Bodkin considered it an offence against the Incitement to Mutiny Act of 1798, under which the Attorney-General's permission was needed to proceed with a prosecution. Perhaps a less legalistic man would have thought twice about using such an ancient Act, and the ensuing crisis could have been avoided but Bodkin had no doubts. He sought a meeting with Hastings, who agreed with him that "it seemed to afford ground for proceedings", and gave his consent. Bodkin told the police the matter was urgent. A magistrate issued a warrant, and the police raided the magazine's office and arrested the acting editor, John Campbell. He turned out to be a First World War veteran who had lost both feet in action, and he told the police he took full responsibility for the article. Bodkin told the magazine's printers they too would be prosecuted and set off on holiday. He thought the affair so trivial he did not even mention it to his deputy, Sir Guy Stephenson.

Labour MPs took a different view. One raised the matter in the Commons, and Hastings gave an account of what had happened. The firebrand Independent Labour Party MP Jimmy Maxton leapt up and asked if the Prime Minister had read the article and was he aware that "that point of view is shared by a large number of Members sitting on these benches?" Other MPs joined in, and the fat was truly in the fire. Hastings was surprised and shaken by the fuss and had a private meeting with Maxton, who told him about Campbell's exemplary war record. Hastings started to have second thoughts, after discussing the matter further with Stephenson. The Prime Minister now got involved. He met Hastings and, in typically petulant mood, blamed Bodkin. Hastings insisted on assuming full responsibility.

MacDonald grumbled that the row could only benefit the Communists but they should press on. Hastings, however, said he had changed his mind and would apply to withdraw the prosecution. MacDonald agreed. Bodkin was recalled by telegram from his holiday and was dispatched to Bow Street to ask the magistrate to drop the charge. He agreed that he would, the barrister Travers Humphreys made the official application on behalf of the DPP and Campbell was freed. Thinking the matter settled, Hastings went off on his summer holiday and Bodkin resumed his.

Neither had foreseen that the withdrawal of the charge against Campbell would intensify, not diminish, the political outcry. The press and Conservative MPs, delighted to be handed a stick with which to beat the fledgling government, claimed that the action had been taken for political purposes, and the affair rapidly grew into a major scandal. The King, on holiday at Balmoral, asked the Prime Minister for his view. MacDonald replied that there had been "a muddle somewhere", the Communists should have been ignored and he had given the Attorney and the DPP "a piece of my mind". When Parliament reassembled, the row grew even more heated. Asked in the House why the prosecution had been dropped, Hastings provided a number of reasons, including Campbell's war record, that he was only the temporary editor, and that the Government did not wish to create martyrs. Then MacDonald was asked about his own role. He replied that he had not been consulted "regarding either the institution or the subsequent withdrawal of the proceedings" and had left the matter entirely to his Law Officers. It was a downright lie, and it naturally shocked Hastings. With the bit between their teeth, the Conservatives tabled a censure motion on the issue, which was arranged for 8 October. A few days before the debate, Hastings told MacDonald that in his forthcoming speech he could not support the Prime Minister's previous statement in the House. MacDonald was thus obliged to make a personal statement before the debate to "correct the impression" that he had not known about the proposed withdrawal of the prosecution. In his one-hour speech replying to Sir Robert Horne, who opened for the Conservatives, Hastings had a difficult start, being constantly heckled and interrupted, but he persevered and was generally thought to have done as well as he could in defending his actions, which led to some Conservative wavering. The Liberals, who held the balance of power, then proposed the matter be shunted off to a Select Committee investigation. The debate raged on until, just before the vote was due, the Conservative leader, Stanley Baldwin, rose and said his party would accept the amendment proposing an inquiry. This was generally felt to let Hastings, who was admired and respected on all sides, off the hook. Baldwin sent word to MacDonald that if the offer was accepted, the Conservatives would withdraw the censure motion and the Government could remain in office. Hastings was dismissive of the proposal: the Government would set up the inquiry "to enquire into the propriety of their own actions; in other words, to put themselves upon trial before a tribunal consisting mainly of their opponents in order to decide whether or not they were fit to remain in office." He was summoned to MacDonald's room, where the Prime Minister was huddled with his senior colleagues. He asked Hastings for his view on Baldwin's offer. Hastings was defiant and decisive: Baldwin could "go to hell," he replied, writing later that he had been longing to tell his Commons tormenters that all evening. He thought MacDonald might have disagreed but his colleagues backed Hastings. "I was heartily disgusted with the whole affair," he later wrote. The censure motion was put, the Liberals voted with the Conservatives, and the Government fell. H.H. Asquith, the former Liberal leader, who made his last Commons speech during the censure debate, said: "The Government has wantonly and unnecessarily committed suicide."

Why did Hastings not accept Baldwin's offer, given that the Government's very survival was at stake? The answer must be that he was a lawyer, not a politician. He was a proud man who was not used to being criticised and had not yet developed the politician's thick skin; as a good lawyer, he could not recommend such a dubious tribunal. The whole ridiculous controversy should never have been allowed to develop as it did. Bodkin would have done better to ignore the *Workers Weekly* article altogether, as his more easygoing predecessor Willie Mathews might well have done. Hastings's mistake was to change tack in midstream and withdraw the prosecution. If it had gone ahead, it might have created little stir. As it was, an unholy combination of the Communist Party and the Garrick Club might be said to have brought down the first socialist government the United Kingdom had ever had.

Understandably, Hastings became thoroughly dis-illusioned with politics. In the ensuing general election and Conservative landslide, he retained his seat and remained on the Opposition Front Bench, but his relationship with MacDonald was dead. He resigned from the Commons in 1926, and returned to the bar. The most successful period of his legal career was still ahead of him, but while he was re-establishing his reputation he decided to try his hand as a playwright. Many years previously he had written a play called *The River*, which he now dusted off. To his amazement, it was accepted for production in the West End, with modest success. It ran for a month before coming off but Hastings had the consolation of selling the film rights to Hollywood. He felt like giving up but was encouraged to have another go by a string of distinguished friends, including Sir Gerald du Maurier, Michael Arlen, Frederick Lonsdale and Edgar Wallace. He sat down and wrote a second play, *Scotch Mist*, which starred Tallulah Bankhead and Godfrey Tearle. The omens after the first night were not good: the critic St John Ervine called it "the worst play I have ever seen". But when Hastings visited the theatre expecting to be told it was coming off, he found people flocking to buy tickets. The explanation was simple: the Bishop of London had denounced it as immoral because it appeared that Tallulah Bankhead was about to be raped as the curtain fell on the second act. The play ran for months. His next two efforts flopped and Hastings abandoned his new career for the moment to concentrate again on the law.

In 1928, Hastings's performance at a public tribunal inquiring into the heavy-handed police treatment of his client, a young woman named Irene Savidge, won wide praise and led to important changes in the way police handled interrogations in future. In the course of the proceedings, Hastings cross-examined Bodkin, who was still DPP and had authorised the police investigation which had led to the tribunal being set up. Although Bodkin was exonerated by the tribunal's report, the press and Parliament were not so kind, and Ramsay MacDonald, still smarting from the Campbell case, weighed in to attack him too.

The 1930s were Hastings's apogee as a star silk. He represented a string of glamorous clients in high-profile cases, and usually won. He won damages for his friend Edgar Wallace when he was accused of plagiarism; he did the same for the Russian aristocrat wife of Rasputin's killer, libelled in a Hollywood film *Rasputin the Mad Monk*; he secured the acquittal of a well-known socialite Elvira Barney for the murder of her lover; and he was twice successful on behalf of Sir Oswald Mosley, then at the height of his rabble-rousing powers, first winning substantial libel damages against the *Star* newspaper, and second on a charge of riotous assembly. These are just a handful of his principal cases, in which he was frequently opposed by Sir Norman (later Lord) Birkett, the other great name of the day, whose quiet but relentlessly effective style of cross-examination was in stark contrast to Hastings's more flamboyant manner.

Birkett was a good friend of Hastings and his greatest admirer, calling him "one of the outstandingly brilliant advocates of his day and generation". Birkett addressed the difficulty of explaining the qualities of great barristers: only those who see them in action can understand how good they were; transcripts of speeches can never recapture the atmosphere of the court and the influence they exerted on it. "Patrick Hastings was a law unto himself," he wrote. "He was a master of plain unadorned English speech and he knew the immense value of brevity. Simplicity, lucidity and brevity marked all his speaking, but the reason he could rely so confidently on these things was because of the supreme gift he possessed: the power of a deadly cross-examination." Birkett recalled the first time he had seen Hastings in action, cross-examining Handel Booth MP in 1917. Booth, a Liberal, was being sued by John Gruban, a German-born man who ran a successful engineering firm, essentially for stealing the company from him during the First World War; otherwise he would be interned. Birkett described the impression Hastings left on him: "Ruthless, relentless, eager, vehement, scornful, satirical, contemptuous, he destroyed the Liberal member for Pontefract as effectively as if he had stabbed him."

Hastings had volunteered to serve in the Great War but was turned down for health reasons: he suffered from chronic asthma. When the Second World War broke out, he volunteered again, at the age of fifty-nine, and was accepted as an RAF intelligence officer, working at Fighter Command headquarters, Stanmore, with men and women thirty years or more his junior: he was invalided out in the winter of 1940 with bronchitis and asthma, and returned to the bar, where there was still plenty of demand for his services despite the war. In 1943 he won (paltry) damages for the West Indian cricketer Learie Constantine, who had been turned away by a London hotel because of the colour of his skin. Soon after the war, in which he had lost his eldest son David in the Far East, Hastings showed he had lost none of the talent for destruction noted by Birkett when he dismantled the left-wing socialist Professor Harold Laski, chairman of the National Executive of the Labour Party. Laski sued the *Newark Advertiser* and a number of other newspapers for reporting that he had urged violent revolution in a speech in Newark during the 1945 general election campaign, which returned Labour to power. The jury found against Laski, who faced costs of £13,000 which, fortunately for him, were raised by a public appeal to Labour supporters.

It was in the Garrick Club, where he was playing bridge, that Hastings suffered the minor stroke in 1948 that persuaded him that he should retire from the bar. But though his health was in decline, he at last had a decent success with his final play, *The Blind Goddess*, which centred on a libel action. It was staged at the Apollo Theatre, starred Basil Radford, and played to packed houses for four months. It was then made into a Rank film, starring Eric Portman and a number of other leading names, plus one then unknown, Claire Bloom. A disastrous and over-ambitious trip to Kenya to see his younger son Nicholas, who farmed there, ended in Nicholas's farmhouse burning down, with all Sir Patrick and Lady Hastings' belongings, and Hastings suffering a relapse. During the last two years of his life he would make the occasional trip to the Garrick, where his card-playing friends presented him with a silver salver inscribed with their names. He died in 1952, and did not leave much in his will, though he had been generous to his five children during his life. "I'm a poor man, but I've had a rich life," he said just before his death.

Archibald Bodkin's last major case as DPP was to seek to ban for obscenity the lesbian novel (now a classic of the genre) *The Well of Loneliness* by Radclyffe Hall, published by Jonathan Cape. The case displayed Bodkin's intense Puritanism at its worst: he involved himself deeply in it, expressing the wish, when he heard that a number of famous authors wanted to testify on behalf of the book, that he could prosecute the case himself. "I should like to get this fellow Arnold Bennett in the box. He would masquerade as an expert witness and I should say to him:

'Mr Bennett, you are here as an expert witness but on what? On women?' Then I should say, 'Tell me then, what happens between these women? You must surely know. Do they take their clothes off and how do they go about it? If you're an expert, you must know.'"

We can only regret that Bennett, a legendary womaniser, was not called and asked precisely those questions: his answers would have been worth going a long way to hear. In vain did Norman Birkett plead that expert witnesses be called to attempt to show the book's outstanding qualities as a literary work. No expert witnesses at all were allowed by the Chief Magistrate at Bow Street, Sir Chartres Biron, who declared the book to be an obscene libel, and ordered all copies to be destroyed. An appeal committee agreed. Bodkin took a close interest in rounding up as many copies of the book as he could and witnessed their burning himself. He left office without fanfare in 1930 and retired to Sidmouth, was reappointed Recorder of Dover and also sat as chairman of Devon Quarter Sessions. While Hastings enjoyed the Garrick, Bodkin preferred the Sidmouth Gardening Club, which he founded and presided over. And while Hastings earned a fortune and spent most of it, Bodkin watched every penny and left an estate worth £124,000 when he died in his armchair aged ninety-five.

11
A STUDY IN CONTRASTS:
EDWARD MARSHALL HALL
AND NORMAN BIRKETT

Who was the greatest British advocate of the twentieth century? The choice probably came down to three: Patrick Hastings, Edward Marshall Hall and Norman Birkett, all members of the Garrick Club. No two barristers could have had more contrasting courtroom styles than Marshall Hall and Birkett. Marshall Hall was flamboyant, erratic, rash and impulsive, a showman who could move a jury to tears. Birkett was quiet, understated, logical, a man who took witnesses and juries into his confidence and persuaded them to see things his way. They were both much loved by the public.

Almost everything Edward Marshall Hall (1858-1927, Garrick 1891-1927) did attracted publicity, good or bad. He was brilliant, impulsive, quick-tempered and often his own worst enemy in court. He was good-looking —"one of the handsomest men whom I ever saw," thought Lord Birkenhead—six feet three inches tall with a commanding physical presence, an effective if not particularly stylish speaker with a wonderfully melodious voice who could wring the maximum emotion out of a case. He was also notorious for upsetting judges to such an extent as to endanger his chances of success, and prone to let slip throwaway remarks that could have devastating effects. One such nearly ruined his career: it brought it to a shuddering halt when he was at the height of his powers, and only a meeting at the Garrick Club several years later put him back on track. He was a member of the Garrick for thirty-six years and regarded the club as his second home. His greatest virtue was courage: he feared nothing and nobody and would fight his corner to the end. Like many great courtroom performers, he was not much of a lawyer: "You must take this point, there's some law in it," he would murmur to a junior when some tricky legal question arose.

He was born in Brighton, the son of a doctor, and he retained a lifelong interest in medical matters which stood him in good stead in several big murder trials in which the medical evidence, particularly about poisons, was a key issue. He was also an enthusiastic and expert shot, which proved useful in cases involving firearms. Watching the opening stage of a notorious murder case at the local magistrates' court at the age of fourteen was his introduction to the law and the start of his long journey to stardom, but his route there was a roundabout one. After a year at Cambridge he went abroad for two years, to Paris and then Australia, before returning to Cambridge to study law. He was called to the bar at the Inner Temple in 1883, and learned his trade on the South-Eastern Circuit, earning a reputation in his native Sussex as a man who would fight tooth and nail for his client and get him off even when he was clearly guilty. He also earned the hostility of several judges, notably Mr Justice Mathew, a dry Irishman. Eventually Marshall Hall tired of this and endeavoured to put things right. Frank Lockwood agreed to help and they followed Mathew to his club. Lockwood went in to say that Marshall Hall was outside and hoped to make things up. He returned a couple of minutes later, shouting across the street, "It's no use, Marshall, the judge says he hates you."

However a future judge, adviser to and friend of the Prince of Wales and Garrick member, Sir Charles Hall, later Recorder of London, had an altogether more benign view of Marshall Hall and took him under his wing, offering him a place in his fashionable chambers at No 3 Temple Gardens. Marshall Hall stayed there for thirty-nine years. His first chance to make a name for himself came in 1894 at the Old Bailey when he was entrusted with the defence of Marie Hermann, a fading, middle-aged Austrian-born prostitute accused of battering to death an elderly client, Henry Stephens, whose body had been found in a blood-soaked trunk. Marshall Hall was up against Willie Mathews and Archibald Bodkin, a formidable team. It seemed a straightforward enough case of a prostitute killing an old man with an iron bar, the motive being robbery, but having shown that Stephens was a violent drunk with a record of attacking women, Marshall Hall got to work on the medical evidence: cross-examining two eminent doctors, he came up with a convincing alternative scenario that Hermann had been defending herself from an assault by the portly, overweight Stephens; the young advocate's analysis of the bruises on Hermann's body and the wounds on Stephens's matched it perfectly, and Marshall Hall physically (and dramatically) re-enacted Hermann's actions as she defended herself, leaving a profound impression on the court. His closing speech was in the style that would become his trademark, a passionate three-hour appeal not only to the jury's minds but to their hearts. With tears flowing down his cheeks, he concluded with the ringing phrase, "Let them remember that these women are what men make them. Even this woman was at one time a beautiful and innocent child." As if on cue, the accused woman burst into tears, and now Marshall Hall displayed what Norman Birkett defined as one of his greatest strengths, "his sometimes irresistible impulse to act on the spur of the moment" (though Birkett added that it also led to some of his failures). He turned to sit down but saw the woman weeping in the dock, straightened up, pointed to her and said in his most emotional tones: "Look at her, gentlemen of the jury, look at her. God never gave her a chance. Won't you? Won't you?" The packed public gallery broke into loud applause, and better still, the judge, who until then had appeared convinced of the prisoner's guilt, changed his mind and summed up in favour of a manslaughter conviction, which the jury duly returned after only fifteen minutes. The newspapers were delighted to unearth a new star, and Marshall Hall's name was made. He took silk in 1898, the year, incidentally, that the law was changed to allow the accused to give evidence on his or her behalf, a reform for which many lawyers had been campaigning for decades. How to use this new legal tool would be a key issue for defenders like Marshall Hall from then on.

For a few years it seemed as if nothing could go wrong for him. In addition to his glittering performances in court, he was elected Conservative MP for Southport at the general election of 1900, largely through a barnstorming performance on the stump in which his wit and ability to think on his feet made up for his lack of political experience. His time in the Commons was, however, not a success: he was not really interested in politics and he was no placeman. (He lost the seat in 1906, regained it in 1910 and eventually retired from the Commons in 1916.) But the bar was different. Sometimes his reputation was enhanced even in a losing cause, as with his defence of H.J. Bennett, charged with murdering his estranged wife in Yarmouth, also in 1900. It was a sensational case, notorious for the appalling conduct of the popular press, which decided Bennett was guilty long before his trial, a salutary reminder that at the very end of the Victorian era many newspapers behaved even worse than they do today. Marshall Hall's vigorous defence of Bennett was in vain but won widespread praise: the judge, the new Lord Chief Justice, Lord Alverstone (formerly Sir Richard Webster), wrote to him: "No man could have been more ably defended."

But Marshall Hall's weakness for a throwaway remark led to disaster, though he did not realise for several years what he had done wrong. He had already severely criticised the *Evening News*, one of Alfred Harmsworth's newspapers, for its conduct during the Bennett case. He then won substantial damages for a popular young actress, Hettie Chattell, against another Harmsworth paper, the *Daily Mail*. It really was much ado about nothing but like many libel actions, then and now, it spiralled out of control and led to bitterness and long-lasting repercussions. The *Mail* had printed a paragraph of showbusiness gossip in which it said that another actress, Rosie Boote, was Hettie Chattell's daughter, a ludicrous mistake as Miss Chattell was only twenty-eight years old. She issued a writ and the *Mail* instantly published an apology which managed to compound the error. The *Mail* then unwisely asked for three weeks to prepare a defence, which Marshall Hall, representing Miss Chattell, seized on, claiming that the newspaper's solicitors had used the time to trawl for evidence against her (a tactic not unknown to the press). He told the court: "My client may have to work for her living, but her reputation is entitled to the same consideration as that of any other lady in the land, including Mrs Alfred Harmsworth." Those last three words did the damage— not to Harmsworth but to Marshall Hall. In the short term, all was well: the jury added £1,500 to the £1,000 Miss Chattell sought in damages, along with some strong words about destroying someone's character. Harmsworth was furious at Marshall Hall's reference to his wife, and sparing no expense he hired a galaxy of the best lawyers in town, headed by Sir Edward Clarke, to launch an appeal. They argued that Marshall Hall's language had been unnecessarily violent and they denied his allegation that the *Mail* had been trying to gather material detrimental to the actress. Unfortunately for Marshall Hall, one of the appeal court judges was Lord Justice Mathew, who still harboured an intense dislike for him. Marshall Hall believed it was because he was a passionate Unionist while Mathew, an Irishman, supported Home Rule. Many leading legal figures, including Lord Birkenhead, believed Mathew should not have been allowed to hear the appeal. Mathew's hostility is plain to see from his exchanges with Marshall Hall: he called his accusations against the newspaper's solicitors "disgraceful", and although Marshall Hall and his junior, Montague Lush, stoutly defended their language, they were wasting their breath.

Delivering judgment, the Master of the Rolls, Sir Richard Henn Collins, was equally scathing, calling it "a monstrous imputation". Most of the press, fickle as ever, backed the Appeal Court's condemnation of Marshall Hall, but many of his legal confrères disagreed. "I have always been of the opinion that they [the Appeal Court] exaggerated the whole matter and that their censures were ludicrously overdone," wrote Lord Birkenhead. "I have no doubt that the Court of Appeal on this occasion was guilty of a great injustice." The judgment had a catastrophic effect on Marshall Hall's practice. His reputation and his income plummeted. It was now that he showed his true greatness, in Birkenhead's view, and it was from this period that the great affection held for him at the bar derived, for he never let his problems show. "He was always cheerful, always friendly," wrote Birkenhead. "He never complained to anyone of the bitter setback which he had experienced, or of the anxieties which at that time must have preyed upon his mind ... I can see him now ... sitting at lunch in the Inner Temple, generally surrounded by the young men in his Chambers, apparently in the highest spirits of them all, gay and full of delightful anecdotes."

Another adverse judgment in the Appeal Court followed, with more criticism being heaped on him; whenever a case went against him, the *Mail* would run the story with a mocking headline. Finally came the ultimate insult: when he did win a libel case against the *Daily Chronicle*, the *Mail* left the first part of his name blank. Marshall Hall wrote a letter of protest to the editor, Thomas Marlowe, who was also a member of the Garrick. They met at the club soon afterwards, and Marshall Hall asked Marlowe why Harmsworth was running a personal campaign against him. Marlowe said it all stemmed from his words in the Chattell case three years previously. Marshall Hall was astonished: he had no memory of having mentioned Harmsworth's wife at all. He immediately wrote an apology (presumably on club notepaper), he and Harmsworth met, the apology was accepted, and indeed they became friends; as Lord Northcliffe, Harmsworth entrusted Marshall Hall with several important libel cases in later years.

His situation began to improve but it was not until 1907 that he was given a murder case that would restore his name. It became known as the Camden Town Murder case and contained all the ingredients necessary to grip the public imagination: a pretty young former prostitute, Emily Dimmock, known as Phyllis, who had drifted back into the game despite a stable relationship with a railway dining-car steward, was found by him one morning on his return from work with her throat savagely cut. The only clues were a postcard, inviting her to meet at a local pub indicated by a little sketch, and the charred remains of a letter in the grate, apparently by the same hand. A young artist, Robert Wood, who worked for a glass manufacturing firm in Gray's Inn, was eventually arrested after a tip-off from his girlfriend Ruby Young. He admitted sending the postcard and meeting Phyllis several times but denied the murder; he agreed he had met her in the pub the evening before she was murdered but said they had gone their separate ways after a drink. Unfortunately, he asked Ruby to provide him with a false alibi, and that was his undoing. He was charged with murder, and Marshall Hall was engaged to defend him. The Old Bailey courtroom was packed, the public gallery including many leading figures from the arts and literature, some of them

Marshall Hall's Garrick friends like the playwright Sir Arthur Wing Pinero. Charles Willie Mathews led very effectively for the prosecution but the trial was a tour de force for Marshall Hall. One by one, he undermined the prosecution's witnesses so comprehensively that by the time it came to hear the defence case there had been a perceptible shift in the public mood. Wood himself nearly ruined it all by his own performance in the witness box, but Marshall Hall's closing speech—"I do not merely ask for a verdict of 'not guilty', I demand it"—redressed the balance and to everyone's surprise the judge came down on the side of acquittal, and the jury took only fifteen minutes to agree. A huge crowd had gathered outside and became rowdier by the hour on the final day. There were fears that Ruby Young would have been lynched had she not been smuggled out in an Old Bailey charwoman's dress. To cap it all, the *Daily Mail* ran an adulatory article by the popular playwright and author Sir Hall Caine: "The defence was constructed with a strenuous and impetuous power which I have rarely seen excelled ... Mr Marshall Hall made an almost overpowering appeal to the intellect as well as to the heart of his audience." Truly, he was forgiven at last.

Brilliant though his performance in the Wood affair was, Marshall Hall regarded a subsequent murder trial as a greater victory: his defence of Edward Lawrence, a wealthy, alcoholic and dissolute Wolverhampton brewer accused of shooting dead his young mistress, a barmaid called Ruth Hadley, with an old revolver of his. At first the evidence looked grim for Lawrence but under cross-examination by Marshall Hall a convincing scenario emerged of Lawrence first shooting wide of Hadley to frighten her during a typically violent argument but unintentionally grazing her, and then grappling with her when she got hold of the weapon (which he thought he had hidden). The revolver was defective and went off, killing her. But it was Marshall Hall's final speech that was the pièce de résistance. First he re-enacted the situation Lawrence had faced when he was confronted by the enraged woman pointing a gun at him, Marshall Hall dramatising it by picking up the very revolver that had killed her and pointing it at the jury. Then he used a dramatic device that was to feature in several more of his closing speeches and became known as "Hall's scales of justice act." He was by no means the first defence counsel to pray in aid the scales of justice but his method of doing so was unique and spectacular: he stood in front of the jury with arms outstretched, his body swaying from side to side as he described how during a case the balance would appear to favour first one side, then the other. "Then in the one scale, in the prisoner's scale, unseen by human eye, is placed that over-balancing weight, the weight of the presumption of innocence." It took the jury only twenty minutes to acquit Lawrence, and the judge referred to his "brilliant counsel" in urging him (unsuccessfully) to mend his ways in future.

Many wise legal observers thought Marshall Hall's finest hour came in a losing cause, in that one of the defendants was hanged. This was the trial of Frederick Seddon, accused of murdering his lodger Eliza Barrow by arsenic poisoning. Marshall Hall defended Seddon and his wife, a rather pathetic figure, and very nearly pulled off the astonishing feat of disproving the evidence of an eminent scientist, Sir William Willcox, who had examined Eliza Barrow's exhumed corpse and discovered a large enough concentration of arsenic remaining in the body to have been the cause of her death. Some was also found in her hair and Marshall Hall got Willcox to admit that this meant that Miss Barrow could have ingested the poison over a long period, perhaps even a year, and not, by inference, in a short, concentrated period as it would have to have been if it was administered deliberately by Seddon. Marshall Hall's biographer Edward Marjoribanks believed that had he then sat down, Seddon might have been acquitted. But he went on to ram home the point and Willcox came up with a brilliant alternative scenario which he tested and convinced the jury of when he was recalled some days later. "He very nearly tied me up," Willcox admitted later. "It was extraordinarily clever of him." Marshall Hall did however manage to persuade the jury (and indeed the judge) of Mrs Seddon's innocence with another bravura closing speech, doubtless aided by her breaking down in the dock, like Marie Hermann, and sobbing helplessly. But her husband was undone by a brilliant cross-examination by Sir Rufus Isaacs, the Attorney-General, in a rare foray into the criminal world. After the trial was over, Isaacs wrote to Marshall Hall that "it was a really magnificent forensic effort, and the whole defence was conducted by you in accordance with the highest traditions of our profession." So widespread was the public interest in the case that 300,000 people signed a petition for Seddon's reprieve from the death sentence. Marshall Hall argued his case in the Appeal Court (a tribunal he disliked appearing before) but to no avail.

During the First World War Marshall Hall unsuccessfully defended George Smith, the "brides in the bath" murderer, a case which showed his enormous sense of honour. He was promised a proper fee through the sale of Smith's story to a newspaper, to be published after the trial, in which there was massive public interest. When the Home Secretary vetoed the deal, Marshall Hall did not pull out as he was entitled to but fought the case (and the subsequent appeal) for a pittance.

By now, he had largely learned to control his tongue when confronted with an unsympathetic judge—but not entirely. In 1916 he walked out of Mr Justice Bray's court during a libel action after being repeatedly interrupted by the judge, and his junior counsel courageously followed suit rather than replace him. The case had to be adjourned and heard by a different judge, but it was the last time Marshall Hall behaved in such an extreme manner. The establishment had clearly forgiven him for such behaviour because the following year he was knighted. He aspired to sit on the bench too but that call never came. He had, however, another decade at the top of his profession, never so fully illustrated as by his schedule in 1920, when he acted in four highly publicised murder trials, winning acquittals in two of them against the odds, despite experiencing increasingly poor health: he suffered so badly from varicose veins that in the last few years of his career he was often allowed by sympathetic judges to conduct his case while seated, an ironic outcome for an advocate who in his stormy younger days had often been told by the bench to sit down against his will.

He regarded one of the 1920 cases as one of his finest, along with the Lawrence case. This was his defence of Ronald Light, charged with murdering a young woman called Bella Wright whose body was found beside her bicycle in a Leicestershire country lane in 1919; she had been shot in the head. A bullet was found nearby.

Witnesses recalled her being in the company of a young man riding a green bicycle; the following year, such a bicycle was retrieved from a local canal, and traced back to Ronald Light, a schoolteacher who had served in the First World War. A gun holster was also dragged up from the canal, containing cartridges of the same type found in the road near the body. Light's problem was that he at first lied to the police about owning such a bike or gun. Marshall Hall did his own extensive detective work on the gun and cartridges, once again using his own deep knowledge of the subject, and was able to cast plenty of doubt on the prosecution scenario that Bella Wright had been shot at close quarters. He also declined to cross-examine a number of prosecution witnesses; after several had come and gone unquestioned by him, Marshall Hall passed a note up to the Clerk of Assize, George Pleydell Bancroft: "Wasn't dear old Montagu Williams right when he said to me: 'My boy, remember the real art of cross-examination is *not* to cross-examine.' " But Marshall Hall's inspiration was to ensure that one man certainly did go into the witness box: Ronald Light himself, who freely admitted that he had lied out of fear of being accused of murder. He cut a convincing figure and was duly acquitted. Pinero, who along with many people had been following the trial closely, sent Marshall Hall a telegram: "Congratulations on the Light that did not fail." Marshall Hall replied warmly, concluding, "Personally, I think it is the greatest success as an advocate I ever had." The judge, Mr Justice Horridge, told Bancroft privately that Marshall Hall "did not make a single mistake".

Despite advancing age and illness, Marshall Hall was still capable of coming up with a dramatic courtroom incident that could turn a case in his favour. Such a one came in 1923 at the end of the trial for murder of a beautiful Frenchwoman accused of shooting dead her wealthy aristocratic Egyptian husband, Fahmy Bey, in the Savoy Hotel. The participants and the setting might have been dreamt up by Edgar Wallace, and Marshall Hall played his part in developing the melodrama. He researched in depth the mechanics of a Browning automatic pistol, the weapon used in the killing, with all the enthusiasm and expertise of the expert shot that he was. His examination in chief of Madame Fahmy was masterly, coaxing from her a moving and convincing account of how she had been abused and threatened with death by her overbearing husband during their brief marriage; and his summing-up surpassed even that. It culminated in another of his re-enactments of the murder, crouching and pointing the actual murder weapon at the jury as he demonstrated how his client had waved the gun at Fahmy Bey as he advanced towards her with deadly intent and how the pistol had gone off accidentally. At the climax, Marshall Hall allowed the gun to drop, hitting the floor with a loud crash that startled everyone in the crowded, silent courtroom. He claimed afterwards that this was an accident, but it was still tremendously effective. "The sudden breaking of the intense stillness of the court by the noise of the falling pistol produced the most extraordinary effect on everybody present, almost as though they had witnessed the actual tragedy itself," wrote Norman Birkett. The jury took little more than an hour to find Madame Fahmy not guilty of either murder or manslaughter.

Marshall Hall died in harness: he had just started a complicated case at Derby in 1927, defending a gang of local men accused of receiving stolen cars, when he fell ill with influenza, which developed into pneumonia. The King inquired after his condition as he lay dying at his London home. "He was the last of his kind; his mantle has fallen on no successor," wrote Edward Marjoribanks. That was in 1929 and his verdict stands. Marshall Hall's style of advocacy went out of fashion with him but his memory lives on: two courtroom stars of the modern era, George Carman and Richard Ferguson, were both inspired to become barristers by reading of Marshall Hall's exploits. So was the distinguished former High Court judge Sir Hugh Bennett, who told the author (over supper at the Garrick) how he resolved to become an advocate after reading Marshall Hall's biography in the school library. Patrick Hastings was somewhat sniffier than most. "Marshall Hall was perhaps not the great advocate that popular opinion supposed him," he wrote, but allowed that "he was a great personality, and had many qualities that brought him admiring and devoted friends." His great contemporary and friend, Lord Birkenhead, wrote of him: "He was a loyal and devoted friend ... He had a long, stormy, and eventful life. He excited many animosities, but he lived to survive them. No one at the Bar had more friends, no one among the lay public more numerous or more ardent admirers. He died, I believe, without an enemy."

Like Patrick Hastings and Marshall Hall, Norman Birkett (1883-1962, Garrick 1942-1948) came to the bar relatively late, having earlier seemed destined for a life as a minister in the Methodist faith in which he had grown up. He was born in Ulverston in the Lake District, a part of the world he loved all his life, and after leaving school at the age of fifteen went to work for his father, who ran a successful drapery and millinery business in the town. A tall, bespectacled, rather earnest lad, Norman had a sideline as a Methodist lay preacher and was also a keen reader; Dickens was a lifelong interest. He was twenty-four, and about to leave the shop to study for the ministry when a local pastor suggested he try for Cambridge instead. He was accepted by Emmanuel College and the course of his life was decisively changed, though that would not be apparent until towards the end of his studies. His preaching had given him a taste for public speaking and he became an enthusiastic member of the Cambridge Union. Birkett was not without a sense of humour: he devised a memorable practical joke by apparently fielding G.F. Haddock, the Conservative MP for North Lonsdale (in the Lakes) as a guest speaker in a college debate against Caius. Haddock was a real person but the guest speaker, heavily disguised, was another Emmanuel undergraduate, Miles Malleson, who later became a well-known actor; he carried off this particular role with great aplomb.

Birkett went on to become President of the Union but also lost his faith, and switched from history and theology to law. He financed his studies for the bar examinations by working as secretary to George Cadbury junior, son of the Birmingham chocolate tycoon and philanthropist, and helping with his political campaigning (Birkett, like Cadbury, was a keen Liberal and would remain so all his life). On the advice of the Liberal MP Stanley (later Lord) Buckmaster, he sought chambers in Birmingham and launched his legal career there, joining the Midland Circuit. Only two days before Birkett joined, a new Clerk of Assize for the Midland Circuit had been appointed: George Pleydell Bancroft (1868-1956), son of the great actor-manager Sir Squire Bancroft and his wife, the actress Marie Wilton. The younger Bancroft was a member of the Garrick for a total of fifty-one years and wrote a play with a legal theme, *The Ware Case*, which another Garrick man, Gerald du Maurier, produced and acted in; it had a successful West End run in 1915.

It was Bancroft's job to allocate the defence of poor prisoners to counsel, and he arranged for Birkett to appear in his first murder case, at Bedford Assizes. The case was hopeless as the defendant was clearly insane but Birkett's performance still won glowing praise from the trial judge. It was the first step on the long road to acquiring the reputation of being the finest defence counsel in Britain, particularly in murder trials. The case which brought him to the notice of the general public was not, however, one of murder but of abduction. An army captain was charged with luring a fifteen-year-old girl from Nottingham to his flat in London, but Birkett managed to persuade the jury at Nottingham Assizes that it was mostly the girl's idea. Although the judge summed up against him he won the day, prompting the people in the public gallery to applaud and cheer, much to the judge's fury.

Birkett's reputation in the Midlands swiftly grew; he appeared as the junior prosecution counsel in the Green Bicycle murder trial at Leicester in 1920, which provided him with a front-row seat to watch Sir Edward Marshall Hall in one of his most brilliant defences. Later, Birkett recorded the excitement and "strange magnetic quality" that Marshall Hall brought to the court, and doubtless absorbed some of the lessons of the master class in defence that the great man delivered. Realising that he had achieved all he was ever going to achieve in Birmingham, Birkett shortly afterwards took the gamble of moving down to London, joining Marshall Hall's chambers at 3 Temple Gardens in 1920. In another nice touch, his first big case at the Old Bailey after the move was a big fraud trial before the Common Serjeant, Mr (shortly afterwards Sir) Henry Dickens, son of Birkett's favourite author. He got his man off and drew a warm letter of praise from Dickens for his conduct of the case.

Birkett had Marshall Hall to thank for his big chance, which came in a high society High Court case in 1925, involving the wealthy Countess of Carnarvon, widow of the man who financed the discovery of Tutankhamen's tomb. Her second husband was a penniless soldier, Lieutenant-Colonel Ian Dennistoun, on whom she settled a fortune, whereupon his first wife sued him for the alimony she had agreed to pass up when they were divorced several years previously, plus various other amounts she had lent him. The case should have been quietly settled; instead, it ran for seventeen days and kept the readers of the popular press enthralled throughout. Marshall Hall represented Dennistoun but on the eve of his closing speech was forced to withdraw through illness. His junior was Birkett, and he had to step in and prepare his own speech overnight, fortified by sandwiches and black coffee. Without having had a wink of sleep, he spoke all day and won the admiration of the court, and more importantly, the jury, although the eventual verdict was a complete muddle. The only real winner was Birkett. "He left the Court that day at the top of his profession," wrote his clerk, A.E. Bowker.

Birkett's courtroom manner was the total opposite of that of Marshall Hall's theatrics and Hastings's icy ruthlessness. He was courteous and gentle, teasing out the answers he wanted without browbeating the witness. A very humane and decent man in his personal life, he treated witnesses the way he treated everyone. "I wonder if you could help me in this matter?" would be a typical opening remark to a nervous witness. "It was precisely the attribute of restraint that made Birkett this [the twentieth] century's greatest criminal defender," was the verdict of the veteran crime writer Edgar Lustgarten. "He had Marshall Hall's virtues without any of his failings. He was as colourful, but less quarrelsome; as tenacious, but less touchy; as eloquent and persuasive, but vastly more discreet." David Maxwell Fyfe (later Lord Kilmuir), who often appeared against him, wrote: "He was the last great example of the 'biblical' tradition which is a strong strand in English advocacy. Whoever his client, his cross-examination was possessed of a moral earnestness which hushed many a crowded court, and his speeches always had a flavour of the Authorized Version." His approach brought results. Birkett took silk in 1924 and was soon inundated with work, mainly well-paid civil briefs. But he found himself unexpectedly defending an Essex farmer's wife, Harriet Crouch, charged in 1926 with murder, once again because Marshall Hall was ill (he died a few weeks later, in February 1927). The briefing solicitor was dubious about Birkett, virtually unknown in the south-east as a criminal specialist, taking over the case, which as so many murder trials at the time seemed to, centred on a wrestling match in which a gun went off, but he was soon won over, as was the jury, which took only fifteen minutes to find Mrs Crouch not guilty.

Birkett soon built up a fashionable practice but unlike many silks in a similar position he also took on a number of unremunerated cases over the years under the Poor

Person's Act, which typified his innate decency and belief in the common good (he was also twice briefly elected to Parliament as a Liberal). He had "a passionate desire for justice and fair play", according to Lustgarten. Probably his most celebrated murder case was his defence of Tony Mancini, a Brighton pimp charged in 1934 with murdering his prostitute mistress Violet Saunders, also known as Violette Kaye. The case against Mancini looked overwhelming: Violet's decomposing body was found in a trunk in Mancini's room; he had disappeared. He had headed for London but was soon picked up by the police. His defence was that he had come home, found her dead body and panicked, thinking that the police would never believe him, as he had three minor convictions, albeit for non-violent offences. He told his friends she had gone off to France. Coincidentally, part of another woman's dismembered body was found in the left-luggage department at Brighton Station and the police, thinking it might be Violet's, interviewed Mancini. He managed to convince them of his innocence but then lost his nerve and fled. Birkett defended him for a very low fee, and against all the odds managed to persuade the jury of alternative scenarios: that Violet might have been murdered by an unknown male visitor, or that morphine, traces of which were found in her body, might have contributed to her death, or that she might have been injured by falling down the steps leading to the flat under the influence of drink and/or drugs and staggered inside to die. Mancini was acquitted. "That Birkett's record of remarkable acquittals has never been surpassed I have very little doubt. That Mancini was the most remarkable of these I have no doubt at all," wrote Lustgarten.

A rather different client was Mrs Wallis Simpson, mistress and future wife of King Edward VIII. Birkett handled her divorce from her second husband, Ernest Simpson, heard at Ipswich (a venue carefully chosen to avoid publicity) to the initial bewilderment of Mr Justice Hawke, whom Birkett succeeded as a High Court judge in 1943. Birkett was a natural choice for the bench, given his innate modesty and sense of fairness, as well as his outstanding judicial ability, although he himself was initially plagued by doubt as to his suitability; he was prone to occasional bouts of depression throughout his life. At the start of the Second World War he had given up his practice to chair the Home Office committee on appeals from internment orders, a task he undertook unpaid for two years. He also delivered a series of weekly radio broadcasts on the BBC as a counter to Lord Haw-Haw, in which he greatly endeared himself to the British public. At the end of the war, he was invited to be Britain's alternate judge on the Nuremberg War Crimes trial panel, on hand throughout the proceedings in case the senior judge, Lord Justice Lawrence, was incapacitated in any way. He was initially invited by the Lord Chancellor, Lord Jowitt, to be the senior judge but to his disgust was overruled by the Foreign Office, who wanted a more establishment figure. Typically, Birkett swallowed his pride and, in the event, was heavily involved in the tribunal's work, which took him to Germany for nearly a year. He left a fascinating diary, which revealed in particular the constant difficulty in dealing with the Russian judges and lawyers, whose concept of justice was rather more primitive and brutal than that of their Western colleagues. Birkett was bitterly disappointed to receive no honour as reward, while Lawrence was made a Baron. A few months later Birkett became a Privy Councillor but still felt he had been snubbed, a feeling that was intensified when he was passed over for the Appeal Court when two vacancies arose in 1948. Perhaps his disillusionment was a factor in his resigning from the Garrick that year. He was not promoted until 1950, retired in 1956, and was given a barony in 1958 before dying suddenly in 1962. Rarely was a lawyer and judge so widely loved and esteemed, not only by his peers but by the wider public.

12
THE GREAT ADVENTURER:
F.E. SMITH, LORD BIRKENHEAD

Lord Birkenhead (1872-1930, Garrick 1921-1930) was at the height of his formidable powers when he was elected to the Garrick: he was Lord Chancellor, an office he had assumed at the age of forty-six, making him the youngest man to sit on the Woolsack. His appointment, by Lloyd George, came as a surprise and was heavily criticised on all sides; the *Morning Star* called it "carrying a joke too far". Although perhaps the most successful lawyer of his generation and arguably the most brilliant man in Britain, he was not thought to have the necessary gravitas to be a successful Lord Chancellor. In the event, he proved the critics wrong. Although the formal side of the job soon bored him, he was a reformer who got things done, a hard-working and effective administrator, and an excellent judge to boot.

But it is not for his achievements as Lord Chancellor, however considerable, that the legend of F.E. Smith (always known as just F.E.) lives on, eighty years after his premature death at the age of fifty-eight. He is remembered for his star qualities, his meteoric rise to legal and political fame (and fortune), his razor-sharp mind, his close friendship with Winston Churchill, whose career his in many ways mirrored, and above all his wit. His instant quips, whether real or apocryphal, have gone into legal folklore. He had no fear of judges. When one of them unwisely said he was none the wiser after having read Smith's case, F.E. replied, "Possibly not, My Lord, but far better informed." After a prolonged exchange, another judge asked, "Why do you suppose I am on the bench, Mr Smith?" Came the answer, "It is not for me, Your Honour, to fathom the inscrutable workings of Providence." His wit was not reserved for the courtroom. When the newly-elected Labour MP Jimmy Thomas asked F.E., the Conservative member for Liverpool Walton, the way to the nearest Commons lavatory, Smith gave him directions, concluding: "You'll see a door marked 'Gentlemen', but don't let that deter you." Thomas once complained to Smith that he had "an 'ell of an 'eadache". "Try a couple of aspirates," was Smith's instant reply.

According to Evelyn Waugh, who heard the story from a friend, Mr Justice Phillimore was very anxious about what sentence to pass in a sodomy trial over which he was presiding, so he consulted the Lord Chancellor. "Excuse me, my Lord," he inquired, "but could you tell me—what do you think one ought to give a man who allows himself to be buggered?" Smith replied: "Oh, thirty shillings or two pounds—anything you happen to have on you."

Smith's rise from a comfortable middle-class background in Birkenhead seemed effortless and unstoppable. As he himself put it when being installed as Rector of Glasgow University in a memorable phrase which echoes still down the years, "The world continues to offer glittering prizes to those who have stout hearts and sharp swords." No one had a stouter heart nor a sharper sword than Frederick Edwin Smith. The term he most liked to use about himself was that he was "an adventurer". He probably derived his legal ambition from his father, a well-known local estate agent who became a barrister at thirty-eight and had just been elected Mayor of Birkenhead when he died at forty-three. His son was sixteen at the time; via Birkenhead School and two years at the nascent University of Liverpool he won a scholarship to Wadham College, Oxford, along with C.B. Fry, the legendary sportsman. He soon made a name for himself at the Oxford Union with a sparkling debut speech. He had a habit of making brilliant debuts but unlike many who start well but then fall away, Smith had the ability to consolidate his position and move on to greater things. He became President of the Union, where his only rival for the title of best speaker was Hilaire Belloc. Switching from classics to law, he realised at the start of his final year that he had not done nearly enough work to get a good degree, so ditched most of his extensive social life for the life of a virtual recluse. He emerged with a First, the Vinerian Law Scholarship and a Fellowship at Merton College. The three years he spent there were to provide the underpinning of his later success at the bar; for all the high living for which he was soon to become famous, he was an excellent scholar and a conscientious teacher. He came equal first in the bar examination of June 1899 and was called to the bar at Gray's Inn.

Smith went back to his home city of Liverpool to start life at the bar. Liverpool at the turn of the century was at its liveliest and most prosperous. It was then also a deeply Conservative city and he plunged into the law and politics with equal gusto. Tall, slim, his pale, high-cheekboned face topped off with black, brilliantined hair, always stylishly dressed, Smith cut a striking figure in court and on the stump. He rapidly prospered on a diet of lucrative licensing applications, of which the thirsty city provided a steady stream, and was soon earning enough to marry Margaret Furneaux, his Oxford sweetheart, a don's daughter whom he had met at a mixed hockey match (Smith was a lifelong sports and riding enthusiast, who played a vigorous game of tennis to the end of his life). On honeymoon he happened to meet Rufus Isaacs, then among the brightest young stars in the legal firmament, for the first time. They were soon appearing on equal terms. In 1901 he made his first appearance in London, at the High Court (he always seemed to go straight to the top) before a panel headed by the Lord Chief Justice, Lord Alverstone. Smith lost the case but performed so well that Alverstone wrote him a personal note: "You argued this case admirably. I predict for you a very brilliant future."

He was not deceived. Smith's first appearance at the Old Bailey shortly afterwards was among a group of the Garrick's most glittering prize-men, including Isaacs, Edward Marshall Hall, Horace Avory and Charles Gill. F.E. was defending a Bank of Liverpool clerk who had started to commit fraud and then been sucked into greater criminality by blackmailers. He pleaded guilty, so Smith's only task was to ask for leniency and he did so with such eloquence that he was rewarded with prolonged applause from the public gallery. It did Smith's reputation no harm at all, but his client no good: he went down for ten years and died in prison.

Smith gathered more judicial plaudits back in Liverpool when he defended two young servant girls charged with murdering their employer. Again, he lost and the girls were sentenced to death but eventually reprieved. The judge wrote to Smith: "I never heard a hopeless case more ably defended." On the political front, he was selected as Conservative candidate for Liverpool Walton and proved to be an excellent campaigner, possessed of seemingly endless stamina, eloquence and humour. He won the seat at the general election of January 1906, a rare victory in the Liberal landslide, and moved to London, where his future now lay. He conquered the Commons immediately, with what is still remembered as the finest maiden speech ever delivered there, a caustic, funny and courageous attack on Liberal hypocrisy and much else besides, even daring to attack Lloyd George, then President of the Board of Trade. Lloyd George saw the funny side and congratulated Smith on a "very brilliant speech". A decade later they were to become the closest of Cabinet allies. The speech launched Smith onto the national stage in his early thirties: it was the start of a golden period when he was the rising star of the Tories who had revived party morale almost single-handed, a public speaker in demand up and down the country, a prized guest at every fashionable weekend house party, and very soon among the top rank of the bar, earning—and spending—a fortune. He took silk after only eight and a half years at the bar, just beating his brilliant Wadham contemporary John Simon, who went on to achieve equal legal and political eminence.

Smith's practice embraced the full gamut of the law: lucrative commercial cases, divorce, libel, the odd murder. His biographer John Campbell believed his greatest quality was "his exceptional clarity of mind. He had the capacity of going straight to the heart of a case." A perfect example of this was his opinion in a notable libel case involving the hugely wealthy Liverpool industrialist

W.H. Lever (later Lord Leverhulme), founder of the soap manufacturers Lever Brothers, later Unilever. Lord Northcliffe's newspapers ran a virulent campaign against the firm, accusing it of abusing its dominant market position, and eventually Lever could stand no more. The first Liverpool barrister he consulted advised against legal action but Lever would have none of it: he demanded that F.E. Smith's opinion be sought. In characteristic style, Smith took a room at the Savoy Hotel and worked through the papers overnight on a diet of champagne and oysters. His verdict was terse and to the point: "There is no answer to this action, and the damages must be enormous." He was absolutely right: although Smith did not head the Lever team in court (it was a famous triumph for Edward Carson, who did), Northcliffe settled for £50,000, then a record, after only a day.

Smith, it was said, could sway a jury more easily than he could a judge. But it was argued that he could point to no great case with which his name would always be associated, such as Carson in Oscar Wilde's first trial, or Edward Marshall Hall's performance in the Camden Town murder or his defence of Madame Fahmy. One signal victory of Smith's was when he acted for Ethel le Neve, Dr Crippen's mistress, and managed to get her acquitted of being an accomplice to murder, taking a calculated gamble by not putting her in the witness box to defend herself. In another case involving a very different sort of woman, the beautiful and formidable Victoria, Lady Sackville (mother of Vita Sackville-West), he came off decidedly worse in a court packed with many of the most fashionable women of the day who had come to see the fun. Lady Sackville had been left a fortune by her close friend Sir John Murray

Scott, formerly secretary to the widow of the founder of the Wallace Collection, but an array of disgruntled relatives challenged the will, claiming she had exerted undue influence over him to persuade him to leave her a sizeable part of his estate. Smith was among the team representing the family but could make no headway cross-examining Lady Sackville who ended up winning the case with ease. Having written to him twice before the case in a quite unethical attempt to "nobble" him, she wrote again after the case calling him "a cad", which was rubbing salt in the wound though it would not have bothered Smith in the slightest.

In a 1911 case which had echoes of the Oscar Wilde trials of two decades earlier, Smith found himself representing The Times Book Club, one of the defendants in a libel action brought by Lord Alfred Douglas, Wilde's "Bosie" and the young man at the heart of his downfall. At issue was a reappraisal of Wilde by Arthur Ransome, author of *Swallows and Amazons*, in which he criticised Douglas's role in the Wilde affair. Ransome's defence was that his book was a factual and reasonable work of literary criticism but his counsel showed no signs of grasping this, to Ransome's rising panic. Smith tapped him on the shoulder and whispered, "Never mind that old sheep. I'll put your case for you." And so he did, although Ransome was not his client (though he was a member of the Garrick), and furthermore he won it for him.

Smith's political career increasingly overshadowed his legal work, lucrative though that remained; most controversially, he backed Ulster's demand to be exempted from Home Rule, a stance that took him, alongside Carson, close to flirting with the charge of treason, but he remained an unrepentant Unionist. At the outbreak of war in 1914, he was asked to set up the Press Bureau to censor newspaper coverage of hostilities: he worked mightily to establish the office but won no plaudits for his performance in the role and was relieved to hand it over to the Solicitor-General, Sir Stanley Buckmaster, who was equally ill-equipped for the task and acquitted himself just as badly.

In 1915 Smith took over in turn from Buckmaster as Solicitor-General, and was promoted six months later to Attorney-General. His most famous task in this role was to prosecute Sir Roger Casement for treason in 1916, after he had been landed in Ireland by a German submarine. After Casement was found guilty and before being sentenced by Lord Reading, the Lord Chief Justice (formerly Sir Rufus Isaacs), Casement threw Smith's conduct over Ulster back in his face, contrasting it unfavourably with his own. At this, Smith walked out of the court with his hands in his pockets, not waiting to hear the end of Casement's speech nor Reading's delivery of the death sentence. There was a huge clamour for Casement to be allowed to appeal to the Lords (his first appeal having been dismissed), particularly from the United States, whose support the British government was desperate to retain. As Attorney-General, Smith's approval was necessary for such a move and he declined to give it. The Cabinet would not sanction a reprieve and Casement was duly hanged.

"How about the Woolsack?" said Lloyd George to Smith at the end of the war as he was putting together his first peacetime Cabinet. The suggestion came as a shock to F.E., who had resigned himself to leaving the Cabinet and returning to the more lucrative pastures of private practice, for he needed the money. Lloyd George had insisted that the Attorney-General could no longer be a member of the Cabinet, and Smith had no intention of allowing that to happen to him. He was ambivalent about the Lord Chancellorship: at forty-six he was astonishingly young for the job, but on the other hand the offer would probably never be repeated. Lloyd George gave him little time to make up his mind so Smith bit the bullet. The blameless occupant of the post, Lord Finlay, was surprised and dismayed to find himself required to resign, but go he had to.

The new Lord Birkenhead's principal achievement in office was the Law of Property Acts of 1922-5, and the Land Registration Act of 1925, which extended compulsory registration of property to the whole country, and abolished the distinction between "real" and "personal" property, ridding prospective owners of all manner of unnecessary bureaucracy which had made buying property such a burden previously. The momentum for such reforms had been growing for some time and Smith was building on the groundwork of many others but he provided the political impetus to push the bill through. He was not idle in other areas: he extended the scope of county courts, established children's courts in London and enabled some divorce cases to be heard by judges on circuit.

When Lloyd George's coalition finally disintegrated in 1922, Birkenhead's term as Lord Chancellor ended too, and he did not return when the Conservatives came back to power under Baldwin two years later. Instead, he became Secretary of State for India and a Cabinet elder statesman, much in demand up and down the country as still the most entertaining speaker the Conservatives possessed. But he was on the decline, in part due to drunkenness. He had always liked to drink, among many other pleasures, but as he grew older he became increasingly unable to handle alcohol. After he left office in 1928, he took some lucrative business positions and wrote extensively. He died in 1930, aged only fifty-eight, but long since finished as a significant public figure. The great adventure was over.

13

MORE JUDGES: FROM CHRISTMAS HUMPHREYS TO FRED LAWTON

Christmas Humphreys and Harry Leon were better known to the public in other roles. Humphreys was Britain's best-known Buddhist; while under the pen-name Henry Cecil, Leon was the best-selling author of many amusing novels and other books based on his legal experiences. Both were also long-standing members of the Garrick. There were other similarities between the two men. Both became barristers by accident and for the same reason: an older brother who was destined for the bar was killed in the First World War and they took his place. And Humphreys was almost as keen on writing as Cecil, producing a steady stream of books about Buddhism and three about the law.

Travers Christmas Humphreys (1901-1983, Garrick 1930-1964) was the son of Sir Travers Humphreys. His second name was a family tradition but he himself was known to his family and friends as Toby. He was sixteen when he was summoned to the headmaster's study at Malvern to be told that his beloved elder brother Dick had been killed by a stray shell in Belgium. Humphreys had what sounds like a breakdown shortly afterwards and in the search to forge some meaning out of a life that seemed devoid of it he chanced upon a book on Buddhism in a London bookshop which was the start of a lifelong enthusiasm. However there was another aspect to Humphreys's character, which was a deep love of British traditions and values, as epitomised by the law, institutions like the Saddlers' Company, of which he was to become Master, and the Garrick, of which he was an active member for thirty-four years. Following in his father's footsteps, he went up to Trinity Hall, Cambridge, to read law, and became President of the University Law Society at the same time as becoming a devotee of Theosophy, the philosophical creed founded by Madame Blavatsky and others which was in vogue in the 1920s and '30s, and which Humphreys followed in parallel to his Buddhist faith. "Unlike most who search for an inner way to Reality I had found what I wanted by the time I was twenty-one," he wrote, although that did not stop his ceaseless striving to learn all he could about Buddhism and to communicate his knowledge and enthusiasm to others.

His first sight of the Old Bailey, after he graduated and before he started his bar studies, could not have been more dramatic. He sat behind Sir Edward Marshall Hall (presumably invited through his family connections) as the great man defended Madame Fahmy, and thus witnessed at close quarters the dramatic denouement which was to become a bar legend. "I have heard many attempts to imitate this speech but it needed a Marshall Hall to get it over, and none, I think, would succeed with it today," he wrote more than half a century later. Humphreys embarked on his career at the bar as a criminal law specialist, like his father. At the same time he began to write: articles, reviews, his first book on Buddhism, a couple of books on crime, and a third, with a Metropolitan magistrate R.E. Drummond, on the then unfashionable subject of juvenile delinquency, which they planned over lunch at the Garrick. "It was ideally situated for me," he recalled. "I could walk there from the Temple, and lunch away from the shop talk which was the chief subject in the Old Bailey Bar Mess. The most charming feature of the club was the long table in the coffee room at which one sat where one chose. I came in early one day and sat down next to the only other person at the table. We chatted and he told me of his first visit to a film studio 'where they are doing something of mine'. I waited till the next man came in and sat beside me. 'Who's the chap on my right?' I muttered. 'He looks just like H.G. Wells.' 'He *is* H.G. Wells, you fool.'"

Through the Garrick, Humphreys came to know many actors, though some of the writers were less convivial. "Somerset Maugham was not an easy man to know, and A.A. Milne was a very silent person, but Charles Morgan enlivened any conversation."

In 1932 he was appointed junior Treasury Counsel, prosecuting on behalf of the Director of Public Prosecutions, a role he was to retain for twenty-five years, being promoted to senior Treasury Counsel in 1950. One occupational hazard was that he frequently had to appear for the Crown before his father, then the leading criminal judge at the Old Bailey. During the war, he continued working at the Old Bailey, was appointed Recorder of Deal, his first experience of sitting as a judge, and was lucky to survive unscathed when a land mine landed nearby and blew him through the front door into his Belgravia house, which was largely destroyed. In 1945 he was sent to Tokyo as a member of the British legal team forming part of the

International Tribunal dealing with Japanese atrocities, on the same lines as the Nuremberg Tribunal. He spent seven months there helping to prepare the case against the Japanese leaders and soldiers chosen to face charges, although he appears to have spent almost as much time forging links with Japanese Buddhists. Back home, he was appointed deputy chairman of Kent Quarter Sessions; on the spiritual front, his first appearance on television as a member of a panel to talk about religion was marred by his falling asleep under the heat of the studio lights, though thankfully nobody noticed.

As senior Treasury Counsel, he was involved in three of the most high-profile murder trials of the Fifties, all of which led to the execution of the accused, and were still the subject of books, films and television programmes fifty years later. Two of those executed, Timothy Evans and Derek Bentley were cleared many years later; many doubts remained about the mental state of the third, Ruth Ellis. All three trials generated huge controversy and were major factors in the growing campaign for the abolition of the death penalty for murder, which finally happened in 1965.

In the first case, that of Timothy Evans, the real murderer was later discovered to be the serial killer John Christie, who was hanged in 1953. The second was the prosecution of Christopher Craig and Derek Bentley in 1952 for the murder of a policeman, for which Bentley was hanged although he had not fired the fatal shot; Craig, who was alleged to have done so, was reprieved because he was less than eighteen at the time of the killing. Bentley was posthumously pardoned in 1998. In his memoirs, Humphreys shed no new light on the trial, which caused a public uproar, merely alluding to "the apparent injustice of hanging only the less guilty youth because the much more guilty happened to be too young for the death penalty; and the sheer drama of murder being conclusively proved by the shouting of five words, 'Let him have it, Chris', when the man who shouted was actually himself under arrest at the time." But did Bentley mean that Craig should hand over the gun?

The third major murder trial, another cause célèbre, was that of Ruth Ellis, the last woman to be hanged in Britain, for shooting her lover David Blakely in a Hampstead street. The case was tried in 1955 before Mr Justice (Sir Cecil) Havers, who was elected to the Garrick that year. It was an all-Garrick affair for Ellis's lead defence counsel was Aubrey Melford Stevenson QC, whose defence of her was later criticised as perfunctory. Humphreys asked Ellis only one question: "When you fired the revolver at close range into the body of David Blakely, what did you intend to do?" Ellis replied: "It's obvious when I shot him I intended to kill him." Humphreys sat down; Ellis had effectively convicted herself. Havers was so troubled by having to pass the death sentence that he made an annual payment for the upkeep of Ellis's young son Andy, who committed suicide in 1982. Christmas Humphreys paid for his funeral. He made no mention of either the Evans or Ellis trials in his memoirs.

In 1955, Humphreys was made Recorder of Guildford. In 1958 the Attorney-General Sir Reginald Manningham-Buller called him in to suggest that it was time he gave up his position as senior Treasury Counsel and made way for a younger man. "I was offered a choice of positions then vacant," recorded Humphreys benignly, "but being perfectly happy where I was I refused them." However the Attorney was not dubbed as Sir Reginald Bullying-Manner by Bernard Levin for nothing: he got his way by having Humphreys made a silk (traditionally, Treasury counsel relinquish the role when thus promoted). In 1960 he became a Commissioner (extra judge) at the Old Bailey, and because of the pressure of cases was soon spending most of his time on the bench. He was finally created a full-time Old Bailey judge in 1968, at the age of sixty-seven, becoming embroiled in at least one major controversy when he passed a suspended sentence on a youth convicted on two counts of rape. The newspapers went to town, the matter was raised in the Commons, and the Lord Chancellor, Lord Elwyn-Jones, asked for a report. Humphreys was supremely unconcerned by the furore, pointing out that many other judges had recently passed similar sentences for rape without attracting any adverse publicity. He was anyway within six months of retirement, which came in 1976. "I was never 'a very great criminal judge', as my father had been described when he retired twenty years before," he modestly wrote, "but I had striven to emulate some of the qualities then ascribed to him." He lived on until 1983, busying himself with writing on Buddhism, and facing the afterlife with total equanimity.

"My decision to go to the bar was made when I was fourteen," recalled Henry Cecil Leon (1902-1976, Garrick 1959-1976), always known as Harry. That was when his eldest brother Edward, who was destined for the bar, was killed in the First World War. Harry's parents asked him if he would like to go instead. "I had no idea of what going to the bar entailed," he wrote. "I just said yes ... I have never regretted my choice." He studied at Gray's Inn after reading classics and law at King's College, Cambridge, and built a successful practice, largely in civil law with only the occasional criminal case. Although he was by then in his late thirties, he joined up at the outbreak of the war in 1939. "As Walter [his brother] and I had both missed the First World War, we thought that if there were a second, we couldn't decently miss that," he wryly wrote. He had a distinguished war record, though you would never guess it from his autobiography, serving in the Western Desert under Montgomery (whom he greatly admired), at El Alamein and elsewhere, and being awarded the MC.

He returned to the bar but applied to be a judge of the County Court (which deals with civil disputes) in 1949 in order to be able to spend more time with his first wife Lettice after she contracted cancer, which rapidly proved to be terminal. He was sent to Willesden County Court in North-West London and spent his judicial career there. He also sat as a Commissioner in the Probate, Divorce and Admiralty Division of the High Court to hear divorce cases, which he disliked doing. Indeed, this led to Leon issuing a libel writ against the best-selling novelist Nicholas Monsarrat, author of *The Cruel Sea*. Monsarrat also wrote an autobiography, *Life is a Four-Letter Word*, in which he described being divorced for adultery, the judge being Harry Leon. Unfortunately Monsarrat added: "He was kind enough to take my wife out to dinner the same evening to celebrate her decree nisi." The obvious inference was that Leon had known Mrs Monsarrat when he heard the case and therefore acted improperly, so he instructed Peter Carter-Ruck, the noted divorce lawyer, and sued. Carter-Ruck engaged a young barrister called Tom Bingham, who much later went on to become Lord Chief Justice and senior law lord. Monsarrat apologised in court and Leon waived the damages to which he was undoubtedly entitled. It turned out that some time after the Monsarrats' divorce he had been present at a function at a friend's house to which Mrs Monsarrat had also been invited; that was the extent of the connection between them.

The move to the bench also afforded Leon more time for writing, which he had always enjoyed. During the war he had made up stories for the troops which he related to them in serial form on the long voyage to the Middle East via the Cape: these he wrote up after the war and with some linking material submitted to London's leading publishers. None were interested; eventually a friend put him in touch with an agent at Curtis Brown who recommended some modifications and finally secured a publisher at the seventeenth attempt. As Henry Cecil, Leon wrote several novels without making much of an impact. His writing career only took off when he decided to emulate Richard Gordon (real name Dr Gordon Ostlere, another Garrick member), who had a great success with his comic novels about hospital life. Leon was soon enjoying a similar vogue with a series of amusing novels about legal life, starting with *Brothers in Law*, which was then made into a successful film by the Boulting brothers with an all-star cast including Richard Attenborough, Ian Carmichael, Terry-Thomas, and Miles Malleson, Norman Birkett's old Cambridge friend and fellow hoaxer. He also wrote several plays which did well in the West End and wrote and lectured perceptively on legal subjects. He was incapable of writing a dull word.

In 1960 he was joined at Willesden by a new Registrar, as a County Court judge's deputy was then known. This was Stanley Prothero, a former solicitor, who became a good friend: indeed Leon and Sir William Mars-Jones later put him up for the Garrick. At the age of ninety-five, Stanley (or SP as he is usually known) is still a much-loved member, to be seen most evenings making a slow but stately progress to the club from his flat round the corner. He has many memories of Harry Leon. "He had a first-class mind, and was great fun and very generous. He once told me he had something like forty covenants but, being the wise old thing that he was, they were all tax-deductible.

"We got on very well and I very much appreciated knowing him. But having said that, he could be bloody difficult. He had been a very good barrister and was a very clever man. But he was very unpopular with some of the younger barristers who appeared before him because he made them do their stuff to the top degree. Halfway through the case, he would ask them a question and if they didn't know the answer he would be very tough on them. He very much considered he should have been a High Court judge, and that was one of the reasons he would be so hard on barristers who hadn't done their homework.

"His real love was the theatre. He was so hooked on the theatre that he would go every night when one of his plays was on in the West End, then go backstage and come up with suggestions as to improvements, much to the annoyance of the cast. I had an arrangement with him: if I came up with a plot idea, he would give me a bottle of champagne. I got several."

Leon was born Jewish but converted to Anglicanism when he met Lettice, who was a keen churchgoer, and Leon himself went on to take an active part in the activities of his local church. He had a strong social conscience and used his judicial position to improve the lot of ordinary people if he could. Concerned with what happened afterwards to those who appeared before him in court, he set up a pioneering welfare department at Willesden Court, staffed by volunteers. He also campaigned successfully for reform of the way debtors were often treated by the courts; he was appalled by the number who ended up in prison for owing trifling sums, frequently because of judges' and magistrates' ignorance of the law. Stanley Prothero remembers visiting Brixton Prison with Leon and another judge to interview a group of debtors taken there by bailiffs and incarcerated; if they had known the law, they could have applied to a judge to have their imprisonment order revoked or suspended, a simple procedure which Leon felt sure no judge would refuse. The trio's report to the Lord Chancellor's Department provoked an immediate and gratifying instruction to all the country's courts that debtors should be made aware of their rights, and the number of such imprisonments instantly halved.

On Leon's last day at Willesden, many barristers, solicitors, police officers, clerks and officials gathered to pay tribute. Leon was very touched and said how pleased he was to see so many familiar faces, but jokingly added, "The only people missing are judgment debtors," meaning those habitual debtors who had instant judgment passed on them. Unbeknown to Leon, Stanley Prothero had sent two bailiffs to collect Willesden's most consistent debtor and bring him to court, and when Leon made his little joke, he leapt up and shouted, "I'm here, m'lud!"

Leon carried on the good work in his retirement, serving on various bodies and committees dealing with prison, hospital and copyright reform. He died after suffering a stroke on the stairs up to his flat in Gray's Inn. His writings are largely forgotten today, which is a pity: he wrote with wit, flair and economy and opened up the inner workings of the law to the general public in an entertaining and informative fashion. Stanley Prothero, whom Leon called "a most able man and a cheerful companion, full of compassion and enthusiasm", went on to become a judge at Westminster County Court, in St Martin's Lane, where he served for many years, with the added benefit of being just round the corner from the Garrick.

Another judge who was frequently to be found at the Garrick was Sir Aubrey Melford Stevenson (1902-1987, Garrick 1931-1987). He was a man who divided opinions: for the Sixties generation he was the worst kind of reactionary judge who doled out harsh sentences and was particularly infamous for his conduct of the trial of fifteen Cambridge undergraduates accused of involvement in the Garden House Hotel riot in 1970. It wasn't just radicals who had a low opinion of him: Sir Robin Dunn, a professional soldier with an exemplary war record who went on to become a barrister and judge and ended up in the Appeal Court under Lord Denning, recorded that "Melford ... was, I suppose, about the worst judge who sat after the war. Not so much because of his savage sentences, but because he simply did not know how to behave himself and could not resist the admittedly often witty but unjudicial intervention."

His supporters, however, regarded Melford Stevenson as a man of forthright opinions but also a witty character who loved gossip and companionship, took his judicial duties with great seriousness and was not afraid to admit his mistakes. The leading solicitor Sir David Napley wrote: "Melford has always liked what he liked and intensely disliked what he didn't, and was none the worse for that. He has meted out in his time stern and condign punishments, but never within my recollection without cause, and on innumerable other occasions he has shown great compassion and understanding."

After education at Dulwich College, Stevenson originally trained to be a solicitor but switched to studying for the bar and was called by the Inner Temple in 1925. His practice was largely in the field of insolvency and running-down cases (actions for negligence by pedestrians against motorists who have caused them injuries) and involved little criminal work. During the war, he was a deputy judge-advocate and sat at the Hamburg war trials, an offshoot of the Nuremberg war crimes tribunal, in 1945. There he sentenced to death the captain, second-in-command and doctor of a German U-boat found guilty of murdering defenceless Greek sailors after the submarine had sunk their ship, the SS *Peleus*, off South Africa in 1944. The trio were executed by firing squad on Luneberg Heath, the only U-boat officers to suffer the ultimate penalty for wartime atrocities. "The succinctness of Stevenson's summing up perhaps foretold his subsequent conduct of criminal trials," noted Lord Roskill.

Melford Stevenson had taken silk in 1943 and after the war developed an increasingly successful practice, largely in divorce and libel and again with relatively little criminal work. According to Sir Robin Dunn, Stevenson "could be a dangerous opponent but lacked flexibility, making up his mind how he was going to run the case and refusing to be deflected." In two major criminal cases in which he did appear, the defence of Ruth Ellis and the prosecution of Dr John Bodkin Adams, accused of murdering elderly patients, he was unsuccessful and indeed criticised for his ineffectual performance.

He had to wait a long time before he was finally made a judge in 1957, initially in the Probate, Divorce and Admiralty division of the High Court, partly, it was thought, because of his loose tongue and waspish wit. "Some said that Melford was one of the great wits of his generation," noted Dunn, "and certainly some of his remarks were very funny. But they were always directed against someone else, often unkind and sometimes cruel." Napley took a more generous view: "He has a wonderful underlying sense of humour, and his repartee in conversation comes back like a whiplash."

He endured four tedious years hearing divorce cases, which perhaps influenced his bilious remark about a husband in a case before him: "He chose to live in Manchester, a wholly incomprehensible choice for any free man to make." After he was transferred to the Queen's Bench division he started to make a name for himself as a brisk, no-nonsense judge who was inclined to take a tough line with defendants. That was certainly the case with the Garden House riot students, who believed he was prejudiced against them throughout their trial at Hertford Assizes. He handed out custodial sentences of up to eighteen months to eight of them, and said they would have been even heavier "had I not been satisfied that you have been exposed to the evil influence of some senior members of the University, one or two of whom I have seen as witnesses for the defence." Six academics who had given evidence for the students wrote to *The Times* to disassociate themselves from his remarks. Forty years later, one of the jailed students called Melford Stevenson "that ridiculous man," adding: "The influence of senior members—it just didn't exist." Melford Stevenson's conduct of the case dominated the headlines at that time and was widely criticised but most of the convictions were upheld on appeal. After he had retired, he said he had imposed severe sentences as a deterrent and claimed that he had been successful because no similar student violence had erupted since, a highly arguable statement. For students of that generation his name became a byword for judicial unfairness and prejudice and nothing he said or did afterwards diminished that belief in any way. Even the fact that his home in Sussex was called Truncheons was held in evidence against him, although that had been its name when he bought it.

He had earned more approval the previous year when he sentenced the Kray brothers to long terms of imprisonment with the remark, "In my view, society has earned a rest from your activities." He later made a revealing remark, perhaps not wholly serious, about those proceedings, saying the Krays had only told the truth twice during the trial, first when Reggie called the prosecuting counsel "a fat slob" and second when Ronnie accused the judge of being biased.

His waspish tongue got him into trouble at regular intervals. When a man accused of rape was acquitted, Stevenson dismissed him with the words, "I see you come from Slough. It is a terrible place. You can go back there." That was harmless enough but when he called the Sexual Offences Act of 1967 "a buggers' charter", it drew an official rebuke from the Lord Chancellor, Lord Elwyn-Jones. He retired in 1979. "In private life he was very gregarious," noted Lord Roskill in the *Oxford Dictionary of National Biography*, "often at the centre of a group at the bar of the Garrick Club, where occasionally his witticisms trespassed across the boundary into indiscretion." But his mean side was on display at the Garrick too: he led the movement against the journalist Bernard Levin being elected to the club in 1972 after he had written a damning assessment of the legacy of the former Lord Chief Justice Lord Goddard a few days after his death. Stevenson even called a meeting of the club's lawyer members to rally support for his campaign. He got his way: Levin was blackballed but the ensuing bad publicity (and accusations of anti-Semitism) did the club's reputation no good at all. That was not an outcome that would have bothered Melford Stevenson in the slightest.

Another judge who was regularly in the news before and after his retirement was Sir Frederick Lawton (1911-2001, Garrick 1954-2001). He had the reputation of being a stern judge who conducted his trials briskly and efficiently and was a tough sentencer, but this was not the whole story. He took a softer line with non-violent young offenders for whom he was an advocate of non-custodial options such as probation. And he was a pioneering proponent of sentencing guidelines for judges when most of the bench was against any interference in their independence in the matter, an issue still keenly debated today.

But as far as certain sections of the press were concerned he was never allowed to forget his pre-war flirtation with fascism. The son of a London prison governor, he was a bright grammar school boy who went to Cambridge, where he studied law. A keen admirer of Sir Oswald Mosley, he founded the university Fascist Association and as a young barrister defended Mosley supporters charged with public order offences. His interest in fascism did not survive the outbreak of war. He developed a thriving practice at the criminal bar: among his pupils were Margaret Thatcher and Robin Day, a subsequent pillar of the Garrick along with Lawton.

David Napley frequently briefed him and became a close personal friend. He recalled a long fraud trial at Oxford in which Lawton led for the defence against Ryder Richardson QC. In his final speech Lawton likened the proceedings to a cricket match, with the judge as umpire and the barristers as bowlers. "So, members of the jury," he concluded, "let us look at some of the balls which has come down from my learned friend Mr Ryder Richardson." Afterwards Napley congratulated him and told him how funny he thought his speech had been. Lawton was horrified. "Gosh," he exclaimed, "did I say that?"

He was appointed a High Court judge in 1961 and in 1965 sentenced the East End gang leader Charlie Richardson to twenty-five years in prison, in response to which Richardson ironically dedicated his autobiography to Lawton. He also presided over the Kray brothers' third trial for murder; they were acquitted. His geographical jokes could be as ill-chosen as Melford Stevenson's: he once caused offence from the bench by remarking: "Wife beating may be socially acceptable in Sheffield but it is a different matter in Cheltenham."

He went to the Appeal Court in 1972 and retired in 1986. But he was by no means done: his views had hardened again by then, and, while always available for broadcasters who needed a conservative voice, he became a prolific correspondent to the newspapers, denouncing society's declining mores, the stupidity of jurors and, in particular, what he saw as the pernicious influence of the civil liberties lobby. The arguments over such issues rage on unabated today.

14

POLITICAL LAWYERS:
HARTLEY SHAWCROSS,
DAVID MAXWELL FYFE AND
GERALD GARDINER

In March 1953 the *Sunday Express* announced a forthcoming series of articles under the headline, "Man or Superman?" The man in question was the lawyer and Labour MP Sir Hartley Shawcross (1902-2003, Garrick 1952-1966, 1989-2003), and the series was to be written by another Labour MP Woodrow Wyatt. The trailer for the series could not have been more fulsome: "Admired by the Tories and Socialists alike, feared—and dismissed—as counsel in the courts, Hartley Shawcross has stepped into the stream of great lawyer-politicians. In the steps of F.E. Smith, Carson, and [Lord] Simon, he has risen in stature at the Bar and Westminster ... Where is he going, this glittering, brilliant barrister, still only 51?" (Shawcross was persuaded by an eminent fellow QC that the series would be very damaging, and got Winston Churchill to ask Lord Beaverbrook, proprietor of the *Sunday Express*, to kill it. Afterwards, Shawcross, who did not have a low opinion of himself, rather regretted that he had allowed himself to be talked into suppressing it.)

The comparison with F.E. Smith in particular was an accurate one. They may have been on opposing sides of the political spectrum (although by the end of his long life Shawcross's beliefs were indistinguishable from those of most Conservatives) but there were many more similarities: both came from respectable middle-class Lancashire backgrounds (Smith's father was Mayor of Birkenhead, Shawcross's grandfather was Mayor of Rochdale), both rose from the Liverpool bar to become brilliant lawyers, both were picked out for political advancement relatively young and swiftly became highly influential government law officers, both were fine public speakers much in demand all round the country, both were eminent international statesmen, both loved the good things in life and enjoyed living in style, both displayed a certain arrogance and recklessness in public life—and oddly, given that they were born thirty years apart, both were close friends of and advisers to Winston Churchill. And of course both were members of the Garrick Club, Shawcross for a total of twenty-eight years. One thing they did not share was longevity: Smith died, burnt-out, at fifty-eight, while Shawcross lived to be a hundred and one, and well into his eighties still had his fingers in all sorts of pies at the highest levels of government and society.

Shawcross in fact met F.E. (by then Lord Birkenhead) when he was a young and impecunious barrister at Gray's Inn in the 1920s and spoke on behalf of the Inn's students to drink a toast to the great man at a dinner to celebrate his earldom. Young Shawcross compared Birkenhead to Francis Bacon and referred to him as a jurist. Birkenhead replied that he had never been so insulted in his life, Bacon having been a bankrupt and jurists being foreigners who knew nothing about the law. Birkenhead took to Shawcross (perhaps he saw something of himself in the young man) and recommended him to Christ Church, Oxford, to teach law. In the event, Shawcross opted for a part-time lectureship at Liverpool University (where Smith had studied before Oxford) while he tried to establish himself on the Northern circuit, having found it impossible to make a living in London.

Shawcross had passed up a place at Oxford to study for a profession (at first he thought it would be medicine), a decision he regretted for the rest of his life. His father was an unworldly German scholar, and his upbringing was unorthodox: he did not attend school until he passed the Common Entrance for Dulwich College, and he was more interested in Labour politics than his studies. After nine months at the University of Geneva, he met the Labour politician Herbert Morrison (grandfather of Peter Mandelson), who was part of a delegation to a Socialist conference. Morrison recommended that he study law if he wanted to go into politics, and Shawcross promptly ditched all thoughts of medicine. He was to be a Cabinet colleague of Morrison in Attlee's Labour government of 1945-51; indeed, his friendship with Morrison (with whom he had very little in common) dissuaded him from any thought of standing for the Labour leadership when Attlee retired in 1955, although he had influential backers in the party. In the event, Morrison came a humiliating third behind Hugh Gaitskell and Aneurin Bevan, and for the rest of his life Shawcross would periodically be asked whether he regretted his decision; he always said he did not, but it is an intriguing thought that had he done so, he might well have become Prime Minister in 1964 instead of Harold Wilson, who much later expressed his surprise that Shawcross had not seized his opportunity in 1955.

In Liverpool Shawcross joined the small chambers headed by David Maxwell Fyfe (later the Earl of Kilmuir), whom he had known in Gray's Inn. Fyfe was the polar opposite of Shawcross, an earnest Conservative dedicated to his work ("the nearest thing, to death in life, is David Patrick Maxwell Fyfe", as a widely-circulated witticism had it) but the two got on amiably enough, and their careers ran in parallel lines thereafter, intersecting at various crucial junctures. Shawcross's practice slowly built up, encompassing all manner of briefs, from licensing applications to murder. He never lacked a sense of style. "On Saturday mornings, accompanied by a vast St Bernard, he would appear in his Liverpool chambers dressed in a canary pullover, light-brown tweeds and — then a startling novelty — suede shoes," according to one account. He was prosecution junior to J.C. Jackson KC and Maxwell Fyfe at the trial in 1936 of Dr Buck Ruxton, one of the most notorious murder trials of the Thirties. Ruxton, who was accused of murdering and dismembering his wife and a maid, was defended by Norman Birkett, whose performance excited Shawcross's admiration, though Ruxton went to the gallows and admitted his guilt to a national newspaper. (Shawcross, Birkett and Maxwell Fyfe were all to play major roles in the Nuremberg war crimes trials a decade later.) Soon after he had formed his own set of chambers in Manchester, Shawcross's big break came, as so often seems to happen in the law, when a senior barrister dropped out of a case, the government inquiry into the explosion at Gresford Colliery, in North Wales, in 1934, in which 265 miners died. The leading commercial silk hired by the colliery owners decided he was not right for the case and the mining company left it with his junior, Shawcross. Up against Stafford Cripps (another Labour notable) representing the miners' union, Shawcross did well enough to limit the company's liability to a derisory fine. It shocked public opinion but did Shawcross's career no harm at all.

He took silk in 1939 and, like Smith before him, had to move to London. Although he quickly acquired some lucrative briefs, he was called away to chair the tribunal examining aliens in order to root out suspected enemy agents; as most of them were German Jews fleeing Hitler, none were detected. Shawcross was then appointed legal adviser to the regional commissioner for South-Eastern England, a job he could remember little about, for as he put it in his delightfully concise and informative memoirs, published when he was ninety-three, "Legal niceties were not our main concern in the South-East just then." But he did remember the young female driver assigned to him, Joan Mather: she became his second wife later in the war after his first wife, an invalid with multiple sclerosis, took an overdose of sleeping pills in 1942. Just as Birkenhead had tried to promote his professional advancement, the widow of another great lawyer was a great comfort to him after her death. This was Stella, Lady Reading, widow of Lord Reading, formerly Sir Rufus Isaacs, who urged him to marry again. He never regretted taking her advice. To his surprise, he was promoted to be regional commissioner of the North-West region, and was also adopted as Labour candidate for St Helens in Lancashire. It was a safe Labour seat and he was elected in the Labour landslide of 1945. Although a political novice, he was appointed Attorney-

General in succession to Maxwell Fyfe because he was, he said, "the only obvious candidate at the time".

Rarely can an Attorney-General have faced such a demanding agenda, dealing with the legal aftermath of the war. His first task was to lead for the prosecution in the treason trial of William Joyce, "Lord Haw-Haw", which was a highly controversial affair, for Joyce was born in the United States, although he lived there only for the first two years of his life before his parents moved first to Ireland, then England. He held a British passport, which was the basis of Shawcross's case. In the colourful phrase he used in his opening speech, "Joyce had wrapped himself in the Union Jack." Joyce was found guilty and his appeals to the Appeal Court and the Lords were unsuccessful, so he was hanged. But far from savouring a convincing victory, Shawcross felt that his conduct of the case had not been a success and the outcome was probably wrong. He believed that most lawyers and the majority of the public felt that Joyce's conviction was unfair, and he blamed himself for not winning over either constituency. "I fear the prosecution—which in this context means me—failed to give to the public a simple, straightforward legal basis on which to rest a capital charge," he wrote.

It is for his role as chief British prosecutor at Nuremberg that Shawcross will probably be best remembered. The International Tribunal was set up with extraordinary speed, given the appalling logistical problems caused by the war in Europe and the fact that the Americans, British, French and Russians (the latter of whom were in favour of altogether more peremptory justice) had to agree on its format and procedures. Shawcross was intimately involved and because of his massive workload in London suggested that Maxwell Fyfe be his deputy in day-to-day charge of the British end of the proceedings. "Although I did not have the highest opinion of him intellectually," he wrote, "he was obviously a capable criminal advocate and had been fully involved in the preparatory work. Moreover, I felt it would be a good thing to demonstrate that this trial had no party political implications." It was an excellent decision: Maxwell Fyfe had been appointed Solicitor-General by Churchill in 1942 and in that capacity had been deeply involved in the Allies' planning for an international legal response to Germany's waging war, its campaign of genocide against the Jews and other racial minorities and the numberless atrocities its forces committed. Shawcross himself delivered the opening and closing speeches, and was in overall charge of the British case but left its day-to-day conduct to Maxwell Fyfe. He was the ideal choice for he had an extraordinary capacity for hard work and the historian's ability to place the Germans' activities in their historical context. History was a living force for Maxwell Fyfe: he was at Nuremberg for a year, with only a couple of visits from his wife Sylvia (sister of the actor and longstanding Garrick member Rex Harrison), and spent many of his free Sundays tramping on his own around the countryside near his villa in Zirndorf, site of the Battle of the Alte Veste in 1632, trying to work out how Wallenstein had defeated the Swedish king Gustavus Adolphus on behalf of the Holy Roman Emperor, Ferdinand II.

Shawcross's opening speech was an eloquent argument that the International Tribunal was not   some kangaroo court set up to impose "victors' justice" but a court administering the rules of international law to which Germany had been a willing party for many years before the war. Many years later, Shawcross was highly critical of himself when he came to consider his performance, realising that "I lack the gift of being incisive. My speeches [were] all too long-winded … Alas, it is a lesson I have learned too late in life." He was being too hard on himself. The general verdict was that he had performed an historic task with great distinction.

Maxwell Fyfe has a fair claim to having rescued the Nuremberg proceedings from disaster after the American prosecutor Robert Jackson botched the first cross-examination of Goering. Norman Birkett, Britain's alternate judge, noted in his diary that within ten minutes Goering "was the complete master of Mr Justice Jackson". Jackson lost his temper and "for a few hours the fate of the Nuremberg Trials trembled in the balance", wrote Maxwell Fyfe two decades later. He stepped into the breach, well aware how high the stakes were. "Without question, Goering was the most formidable witness I have ever cross-examined … When I took over from the discomfited Jackson, Goering's confidence was overweening. 'I have destroyed Jackson,' his eyes seemed to say as I approached him; 'I am going to enjoy dealing with you'." That was not how he felt after five hours of Maxwell Fyfe's well-prepared, clinical and, above all, calm cross-examination, honed at the English bar. "Ignoring his jibes and insolence, which often produced laughter from the packed court, I led him firmly on to the dangerous ground where I knew my case was invincible … After a few hours of this ding-dong duel, I noticed a new look of wariness coming into Goering's cold eyes."

On the domestic legal front, Shawcross's principal achievement was to pilot through the Commons the Legal

Aid and Advice Act, making legal aid available to both defendants and plaintiffs (except for libel), subject to a means test. It was to have enormous repercussions and extended the right to legal representation to a huge number of people who had hitherto not enjoyed it. Shawcross was never in doubt about the fundamental principle underpinning legal aid but he came to fear that it was yet another massive and open-ended drain on the public finances. He was a consistent opponent of the death penalty (which had added to his unease about the Joyce verdict and even about Nuremberg) and came close to resigning from the government when the Lords rejected a five-year moratorium on hangings. His reputation was enhanced by his cross-examination of witnesses summoned by the Lynskey Tribunal inquiring into corruption in public life. It even drew a private word of praise from the taciturn Attlee.

This was just as well, because Shawcross had a habit of getting into trouble with throwaway remarks, partly caused by a certain arrogance, partly by political naivety. The most notorious was his Commons speech in which he allegedly said of the Labour government, "We are the masters now." It was taken down and used in evidence against him for the rest of his political life, and he accepted that it was a major gaffe but like most such sayings that haunt politicians for evermore it wasn't quite what he said, or meant. He had been quoting from Humpty Dumpty in Lewis Carroll's *Through The Looking-Glass* ("The question is, which is to be the master—that is all") and comparing Churchill to him. He went on: "We are the masters *at the moment* [author's italics]. And not only at the moment but for a very long time to come." It was widely taken to be an expression of supreme, almost totalitarian, arrogance, which was not at all what Shawcross stood for, then or later. But it is the one phrase for which he will always be remembered.

In 1949 he led for the prosecution of the serial killer John George Haigh, following the long tradition that the Attorney-General prosecutes all cases involving poison. It was a headline-grabbing case in which Maxwell Fyfe defended and the judge was Sir Travers Humphreys. The jury were not persuaded that Haigh was insane, and he went to the gallows.

Shawcross always took a keen interest in foreign affairs, having many memorable battles with the Russians at the United Nations General Assembly, to which he was a British delegate, and he harboured hopes of becoming Foreign Secretary. He was also sounded out about becoming Lord Chief Justice or Master of the Rolls but preferred to stay where he was. However, after Labour were returned to office with a tiny majority in 1950, he had a brief stint as President of the Board of Trade. The following year Churchill and the Conservatives were back in office and Shawcross returned to the bar. He was immediately back in the fray at the highest level. The day after the election the Labour-supporting *Daily Mirror* published the front-page headline "Whose Finger on the Trigger?", accompanied by a picture of a revolver. The clear implication was that Churchill could not be trusted with Britain's nuclear armoury. Shawcross recounted how within a few minutes of him returning to his chambers both the *Mirror's* and Churchill's lawyers wanted to hire him to represent them in the inevitable libel proceedings that would ensue. Shawcross had to accept the first retainer, from the *Mirror*, whom he advised to settle. The newspaper eventually agreed. But Shawcross went on to advise Churchill privately, particularly over an alleged libel in Volume Four of his *History of the Second World War*, published in 1951. The matter required especially delicate handling as Shawcross was one of the few people in London who knew how incapacitated Churchill was by illness in 1953; indeed, he was present at the dinner party at which the Prime Minister suffered his second stroke.

Shawcross rarely appeared in the Commons any more; it was partly the pressure of his legal career but also he did not enjoy the confrontational style in which party politics was increasingly conducted. He was also increasingly out of sympathy with Labour policy, such as wholesale nationalisation and high taxation, and many thought he would join the Conservatives, among whose ranks he had many friends. Indeed, the columnist Bernard Levin memorably renamed him "Sir Shortly Floorcross", but Shawcross disclaimed any such intention and remained a Labour member, at least until he effectively left politics. (Much later, he would become a firm admirer of Margaret Thatcher.) In the 1950s Shawcross was the best-known and probably the highest-paid silk in Britain, a fact not lost on the Lord Chief Justice Lord Goddard when Shawcross appeared before him on behalf of an accountant prosecuted by the Inland Revenue for his part in covering up a fraud by a client. In mitigation, Shawcross said the accountant had repaid all the fees involved and was now penniless. "Well," said Lord Goddard, "he does not seem to have exercised any notable economy in his defence," a sally which occasioned "roars of laughter in court", Shawcross later ruefully recalled. But the ruinously high level of marginal taxation then in force (as high as 98 per cent on unearned income) meant that Shawcross kept very little of what he earned, and certainly not enough to sustain the high standard of living which he enjoyed. In 1956 Hugh Gaitskell, Labour's new leader, told him (in the Garrick) that he wanted him to be his Lord Chancellor if he won the next election. "This was not a job I coveted at all," recorded Shawcross. So he resigned from the Commons, left the bar (although he retained the chairmanship of the Bar Council for a while longer) and took up various lucrative directorships, notably of Ford and Shell, as well as helping to found the legal pressure group Justice.

In 1959 he was created a life peer and from then on accumulated a vast number of "great and good" jobs. He chaired the Royal Commission on the Press from 1961-2 which, predictably, found that Fleet Street was vastly overstaffed. Equally predictably, the print unions resisted any notion of change for a further quarter of a century before a combination of new technology, new trades union laws and Rupert Murdoch drove the final nail in their coffin, to the regret of few and certainly not of Lord Shawcross. A new Press Council also emerged as a result, and Shawcross was its first chairman. (It has now developed into the Press Complaints Commission.) He remained a force in the land until late in his long life. He resigned from the Garrick in 1966 after fourteen years as a member in protest at the blackballing of his friend and candidate Harold (later Lord) Lever, the former Labour Minister and economic adviser to Harold Wilson. It was a characteristic act of principle. Was Lever blackballed because he was Jewish? Perhaps it was a precursor of the

Bernard Levin affair in 1972. Shawcross was re-elected in 1989 and remained a member until his death in 2003.

David Maxwell Fyfe (1900-1967, Garrick 1942-1949) enjoyed a curiously parallel career to Shawcross, both political and legal, after their paths diverged in Liverpool. He took silk at thirty-four; prematurely bald and with a swarthy, almost Levantine look, he enjoyed the advantage of looking much older than he really was. He became a Conservative MP in 1935, Solicitor-General in 1942 and briefly Attorney-General in 1945, before going to Nuremberg. His ferocious appetite for hard work was never more apparent than when he returned to London and resumed his career at the bar and in Parliament. Like Shawcross (and many others in the ruined post-war continent) he was a keen supporter of European integration. Indeed, he was a key figure in drafting the European Convention of Human Rights in 1949-50 and was intensely proud of his achievement. He would doubtless have been astonished to learn that six decades later it is a subject of bitter controversy because of its wholesale incorporation into the legal systems of the United Kingdom.

When the Conservatives returned to power in 1951, he was appointed Home Secretary; but where Shawcross was a liberal by instinct, Maxwell Fyfe was an old-fashioned law-and-order conservative, as he showed when refusing clemency for Derek Bentley, sentenced to death in 1953 for his part in the shooting of a policeman. (Bentley was not posthumously pardoned until 1998.) Like Shawcross, he was increasingly spoken of as a possible leader as his colleagues jockeyed for position in the run-up to the battle to succeed an ageing leader. But Maxwell Fyfe acknowledged that Anthony Eden was bound to take over from Churchill and settled for Lord Chancellor in 1954, taking the title of Viscount (later the Earl of) Kilmuir. He held the post for seven years, the longest period since Halsbury. He is not remembered as a great reformer but he was a keen moderniser. He overhauled the county courts, the divorce laws, restrictive practices in industry and the tribunal system, and introduced an age limit of seventy-five for judges. He was also heavily involved in developing and establishing new constitutions for the many Commonwealth colonies which became independent in the 1950s and early 1960s. Along with Lord Salisbury, the Leader of the Lords, he played a key role in selecting a new Prime Minister in 1957 after Sir Anthony Eden resigned, destroyed by Suez: the two men interviewed all the members of Eden's Cabinet to find out if they backed Rab Butler or Harold Macmillan to succeed. ("Wab or Hawold?" as Salisbury tersely put it.) They then reported to the Queen that Macmillan was the choice of the overwhelming majority. Macmillan asked Kilmuir to stay on, which he did, continuing to perform his duties diligently and competently for five more years, before being summarily and unexpectedly sacked in 1962 in the Night of the Long Knives, when Macmillan dismissed half his Cabinet ("the wrong half," Harold Wilson wittily remarked). It was a sad and rather undignified end to a long and distinguished political and legal career, and it left Kilmuir angry and hurt at his treatment. Ironically, it was he who had coined the memorable phrase "Loyalty is the Tories' secret weapon." He cut his links with both the law and the Conservative Party, and, like Shawcross, headed for the City, becoming chairman of Plessey. He died in 1967.

Gerald Gardiner (1900-1990, Garrick 1925-1990) was the epitome of the liberal lawyer, associated with all the great libertarian causes of the twentieth century: the fight to abolish capital punishment, the battle against the use of torture at home and abroad, and the campaigns to reform the law on divorce, homosexuality, and theatrical and literary censorship. Unlike many such campaigners, he found himself in a position to do something about his passion for justice: in 1964 he was appointed Lord Chancellor by Harold Wilson and in the six years he served in that post earned the reputation of being one of the great legal reformers of the century.

Gardiner was a member of the Garrick for sixty-five years. He was elected in the footsteps of his father, Robert Septimus Gardiner, who became a member in 1895. At the age of eighty he was granted life membership on the same day as Laurence Olivier and John Gielgud. Indeed, had he followed his first inclination he might well have been the third actor so honoured that day, for at Oxford he seemed destined for a career on the stage, although he was nominally studying law. Tall, good-looking and the possessor of a beautiful voice, he acted in several productions for the Oxford University Dramatic Society with such contemporaries as Tyrone Guthrie, Robert Speight and Emlyn Williams, and while still an undergraduate did well enough to be invited by Gerald du Maurier to appear opposite Tallulah Bankhead in a play he was shortly to produce in the West End. His father had dabbled in the entertainment business himself before going on to make a fortune from shipping and coal but he swiftly put a stop to his son's theatrical ambitions. So Gerald turned the offer down and confined himself to acting and producing for OUDS, of which he became President in 1922. He was also a fine debater and became President of the Union too, and in the same term achieved notoriety by being sent down: he gallantly took responsibility for an article in *Isis*, the student magazine, attacking the university for its antiquated restrictions on female undergraduates. The article was the work of Dilys Powell, later the *Sunday Times*'s long-serving film critic, but Gardiner agreed to take the rap and was sent down, although he had by then acquired his degree, albeit only in the fourth class. Unperturbed, he immediately set about studying for the bar, and was called in 1925.

Throughout his life he was noted for his dedication to his work and his meticulous preparation of cases, and he developed a good all-round practice. "Gerald always reckoned to know more about any case he was working on than his opposite number," wrote his second wife, the noted film producer Muriel Box. "This involved an enormous amount of preparatory work, often calling for the most precise and detailed knowledge of all aspects of everyday life." He also began to earn a reputation in the field of libel and slander: the first big libel case in which he was briefed was Sir Oswald Mosley's action against the *Star* newspaper in 1933, in which he was junior to Patrick Hastings, successfully representing Mosley. Norman Birkett acted for the newspaper and Gardiner frequently worked under him too so he learnt his trade at the feet of two of the great masters. Indeed, he found himself, while still a junior, appearing in the House of Lords instead of Birkett in the final act of a highly publicised breach of contract suit brought by Baron Victor de Stempel, a Russian aristocrat, against his former employer and father-in-law. De Stempel could not afford to continue with Birkett's services so Gardiner, who had been Birkett's junior in the two previous rounds, stood in, and won the case.

Gardiner had become a socialist, like so many other middle-class young men and women of the 1920s and '30s, because of their deep concern about the poverty and inequality that divided Britain. His hatred of the death penalty dated from this period too. He became active in the Haldane Society, an organisation of radical lawyers, but broke with it after the war because of Communist infiltration, and helped to found the Society of Labour Lawyers, which was to become an influential pressure group for legal reform. Gardiner was a conscientious objector and during the war volunteered for the Friends Ambulance Service, in which he rose to take a senior leadership role. He crossed to France soon after D-Day and distinguished himself by his courage and selflessness. He arrived at Belsen soon after it was liberated and helped to organise desperately needed extra medical aid for the survivors.

Gardiner took silk in 1948 and stood for Labour at Croydon West in 1951 but by then the great enthusiasm for Labour of the 1945 landslide had evaporated and he was not elected. He did not try for the Commons again, instead concentrating on his career at the bar and on a wide range of reform-minded campaigns and committees. He travelled the country tirelessly to speak against capital punishment at meetings which were often sparsely attended, and also travelled to South Africa in 1956 to attend as an observer the preliminary hearing of the historic so-called Treason Trials of a hundred and fifty-one opponents of apartheid.

Back in London, he was soon embroiled in a much less serious—indeed richly comic—business, a libel action brought by Evelyn Waugh against Lord Beaverbrook's *Daily Express* over an article by the writer Nancy Spain making what Waugh believed to be misleading (and malicious) statements about his sales. Like many libel actions, it seems extraordinarily pointless in retrospect, but it made plenty of column inches at the time, perhaps unsurprisingly given the dramatis personae. Gardiner represented Waugh, while Sir Hartley Shawcross acted for the newspaper, then at the zenith of its circulation and influence. Shawcross was giving Waugh a tough time in the witness box when he was suddenly called away. Waugh described his view of the proceedings in a letter to Nancy Mitford:

> I had taken the precaution of telling the Dursley Parish Priest that he should have 10 per cent of the damages. His prayers were answered in dramatic Old Testament form. A series of Egyptian plagues fell on Sir Hartley Shawcross from the moment he took up the case, culminating in a well-nigh fatal motor-accident to his mother-in-law at the very moment when he had me under cross-examination and was making me feel rather an ass. He had to chuck the case and leave it to an understrapper whose heart was in the Court next door, where a Bolivian millionaire was suing Lord Kemsley for saying he buggered his wife (the Bolivian's wife, not Lady Kemsley).

In his speech to the jury, Gardiner demonstrated his icy wit by appearing to go out of his way not to attack Nancy Spain: "Her articles are most cleverly written and most amusing and it may well be that as a result of this case she will receive a higher post in the Beaverbrook organisation.

She has certainly followed in her master's footsteps..." He reserved his criticism for the *Express*, and the jury awarded Waugh £2,000 damages and his costs. "So Father Collins got £200," wrote Waugh, "and a lot of chaps at White's got pop."

But even this trial could never begin to match another libel action for colour and controversy. In 1959, Gardiner acted for the *Daily Mirror,* which was defending itself against the pianist and entertainer Liberace in a case which went into legal and showbusiness folklore and is still remembered today. The flamboyant Liberace was the world's highest-paid entertainer at the time and in 1956 made his debut in London to great popular acclaim, which disgusted the *Mirror*'s grizzled old columnist Cassandra (William Connor). His verdict on Liberace can still raise an eyebrow today—"this deadly, winking, sniggering, snuggling, chromium-plated, scent-impregnated, luminous, quivering, giggling, fruit-flavoured, mincing, ice-covered heap of mother-love"— and Liberace sued for libel, claiming the article implied that he was homosexual; he took particular exception to the word "fruit-flavoured". Cross-examining Liberace, Gardiner described the word as "just a reference to your sugary manner" but Liberace was having none of it. In six hours of cross-examination he completely won over the jury while Connor made a poor impression, and the entertainer won £8,000 damages, a considerable sum in those days. No wonder the title of his autobiography was *Crying All The Way To The Bank*. Much later, of course, after Liberace's death in 1987 of an Aids-related illness, the full story of his homosexuality was revealed: it turned out he had perjured himself all the way to the court.

Another case that still resonates today was the *Lady Chatterley's Lover* trial in 1960, when Gardiner represented Penguin Books, charged with publishing "an obscene article" in the shape of D.H. Lawrence's long-banned novel. It was a test case of the new Obscene Publications Act, which had reached the statute book the previous year, and which laid down a new definition of obscenity, as tending "to deprave and corrupt persons ... having regard to all relevant circumstances". Gardiner's conduct of the defence was exemplary: he called thirty-five expert witnesses, ranging from academics to a bishop, and announced that he had another fifty up his sleeve should the need arise. By the end of his roll-call of the liberal great and the good, the defence, led by Mervyn Griffith-Jones QC, had given up bothering to cross-examine them, a fact which Gardiner emphasised in his final speech to the jury. "Mr Gardiner's speech was a masterly performance," wrote H. Montgomery Hyde, the noted legal biographer in his introduction to a book on the trial, "and has been considered as one of the best, if not the best, that he made at the bar." It was indeed a superb speech, which repays reading today, but it may have had no effect at all on the jury. One juryman, interviewed after they had acquitted Penguin, revealed that they had already made up their minds after reading the book, as they were required to do by the judge, Mr Justice Byrne, at the start of proceedings, that it was not obscene. The trial was, in any event, a watershed in British publishing history.

The 1961 High Court action against the Electrical Trades Union (ETU) was another watershed, this time in trades union history, and once again Gardiner was on the winning side, leading the case against the union's

Communist leaders for rigging its internal elections to maintain themselves in control of its affairs. It was an epic struggle and it had profound repercussions for the union movement in Britain.

In 1963, Harold Wilson invited Gardiner to become a life peer and intimated that he would ask him to be Lord Chancellor if and when Labour returned to power after the long period of Conservative government that appeared to be drawing to a close. So it proved. In 1964 Gardiner became Lord Chancellor and set about instituting or encouraging the many reforms for which he had long campaigned. The biggest structural innovation was the creation in 1965 of the Law Commission "to keep the law under review and recommend reform where it is needed", a task it has been successfully carrying out ever since. The list of reforms carried out by or under the Labour government of 1964-70 is a long one and Gardiner was at the heart of the process. The one that gave him the greatest satisfaction was the abolition of the death penalty for murder in 1965. The law on homosexuality was liberalised, theatre censorship ended, new rights for divorced wives introduced, the office of Ombudsman created, and training for judges and magistrates extended and improved. Gardiner also set up a Royal Commission chaired by Lord Beeching to overhaul the court system, which had not been properly reformed for a century. Gardiner had left office before the Commission's proposed reforms could be implemented but his Conservative successor, Lord Hailsham, oversaw the process and the courts were successfully modernised and streamlined.

Perhaps the greatest tribute to Gardiner's moral authority came, again after he had left office, when he was asked in

1972 to join two other senior political and legal figures on a committee of inquiry into allegations of alleged torture by the British authorities interrogating terrorist suspects in Northern Ireland. The Prime Minister, Edward Heath, accepted Gardiner's heavily critical minority report rather than the majority report produced by his colleagues. In the same year he had the rather more agreeable task of becoming the second Chancellor of another Labour innovation, the Open University. In his typically thorough way, he insisted he could only do the job properly if he became an OU student himself and embarked on a social sciences degree course. He was awarded his degree in 1977, and three years later his eightieth birthday party was celebrated at the Garrick, featuring a speech by Lord Elwyn-Jones, who had followed him as Labour Lord Chancellor.

15
HIGH-PROFILE SOLICITORS:
DAVID NAPLEY AND PETER CARTER-RUCK

Readers may complain, with some justification, that this book has concentrated almost exclusively on barristers and judges to the exclusion of solicitors. There are good reasons for this bias: there have been far more of the former group than the latter in the ranks of the Garrick, and their professional lives tend to be more interesting. But two solicitors of recent vintage deserve mention because they became nationally known figures, for very different reasons: Sir David Napley was an active President of the Law Society and came to public attention when he chose to defend the politician Jeremy Thorpe himself in committal proceedings rather than entrust the task to a barrister as would normally have been the case. Peter Carter-Ruck, on the other hand, never sought the limelight in court, but behind the scenes he was a hugely influential figure in the field of libel and could justifiably be called the most hated—certainly feared—man in Fleet Street.

David Napley (1915-1994, Garrick 1976-94) was born David Naphtali of Jewish parents in the East End of London, and anglicised his name as a young man for fear of the anti-Semitism prevalent in England in the 1930s, though you will look in vain for any reference to his Jewish roots in his lengthy memoir *Not Without Prejudice*, published the year before he died. As a boy he was a keen reader (one of his favourite authors was the now forgotten nineteenth-century Garrick lawyer-writer Harrison Ainsworth) but his father, an insurance broker, saw no reason to pay for him to go to university, a decision David regretted all his life. Instead, he went to a local school and then to a crammer to prepare him for the law, and at the age of sixteen joined a firm of solicitors in Bloomsbury, run by a friend of his father, as an articled clerk. When he had qualified as a solicitor, a friend, Sidney Kingsley, who was a year ahead of him, invited Napley to go into business with him, and within a few months made him a partner in Kingsley Napley which they would turn into one of London's best-known firms of solicitors. After war service, in which he was invalided home with a greatly enlarged spleen which the doctors thought would soon kill him, a wealthy uncle offered to lend him £500 to enable him to set up his practice again. Napley, never a man to duck the truth, said he could not accept a loan as he could not guarantee repaying it but he would take the money as a gift. Within a few months business was good enough for him to be able to invite his uncle to the Savoy for lunch and give him a cheque for £500. But Napley loved courtroom advocacy and decided to switch to the bar. He began the process, which involved a course of study and retraining, but at the last moment decided to seek the advice of a barrister whom he had often briefed, John Maude, later a well-known judge. Maude recommended against the uncertainties of life at the bar and Napley decided to stay a solicitor. He claimed that he did not really regret his decision but although he went on to great fame and fortune there is little doubt that he was always a barrister manqué.

The proof of this was that he relished representing clients in criminal committal proceedings, at which magistrates used to decide whether there was a case to answer in a higher court. Napley believed strongly that a good solicitor who had done his homework was better suited to the role than a barrister brought in solely for the role. He argued that the role of the solicitor-advocate at the committal stage was to tease out lines of defence which would be useful at the next stage, if he could not get the case dismissed altogether. He did not dispute that barristers were in general better fitted to handle cases at higher levels although he also believed that some solicitors (and himself in particular) could do the job just as well. His campaigning was instrumental in solicitors eventually gaining the right of audience in the higher courts.

Napley was not merely dogged in pursuit of greater rights for solicitors: he was always a determined campaigner for his clients' rights as he demonstrated in the case of three young working-class Londoners charged in 1959 with possessing offensive weapons. They claimed the weapons had been planted by the police officers who had arrested them, but were duly convicted and fined £10 each. They continued insisting on their innocence and Napley became convinced of the justness of their case. Their appeals were dismissed but Napley continued working on their behalf, and four and a half years later a public inquiry, under William Mars-Jones, later a distinguished High Court judge, was set up to investigate the allegations of police corruption in this and another case. Napley was the only solicitor-advocate among a string of top barristers to appear before the inquiry. Mars-Jones's report was damning, and led to pardons and compensation for all three of Napley's clients six year after they were first arrested.

He fought just as tenaciously, but without success, for Michael Luvaglio, who with Dennis Stafford was found guilty of murdering Angus Sibbett in 1967 in what came to be known as "the one-armed bandit murder" and which was the inspiration of the cult North-East gangster film *Get Carter*. The two men were sentenced to life imprisonment but were released on licence after serving twelve years. Napley always believed in Luvaglio's innocence and his former client was still involved in proceedings to try to clear his name in 2008, without success. There was little Napley could do, either, for another client, Harry Roberts, a ruthless career criminal charged with murdering three policemen near Wormwood Scrubs in 1966, an incident which shocked the nation. Roberts and his two associates got life, with a minimum of thirty years in prison before parole could be considered; at the time of writing, Roberts was still in jail and thought unlikely ever to be released.

A case in which Napley was involved in 1972 was to have a profound effect on the career of a Manchester-based barrister then hardly known in London, George Carman. Napley represented a consulting engineer charged with the manslaughter of five children killed when the Big Dipper rollercoaster at Battersea Fun Fair was derailed; Carman defended the funfair manager. Both were acquitted, and Napley was so impressed by Carman's final address to the jury that he made a note to start using his services. (Incidentally, the stipendiary magistrate hearing the committal proceedings was Ted Robey, son of the great comedian Sir George Robey, and Napley was to lunch with him at the Garrick almost daily after his retirement from the bench.)

In 1977 Napley had recently completed his one-year term as a very high-profile President of the Law Society when he was asked by Michael Havers, then shadow Attorney-General, to go to South Africa to attend as an observer the inquest into the death of the student leader Steve Biko, who had died of appalling head injuries after being arrested for his political activities. The case aroused worldwide anger and though the inquest was conducted fairly and a huge amount of damning evidence was revealed, the magistrate's verdict, which took a mere eighty seconds to deliver, was a ludicrous whitewash. Napley was so outraged that he raced back to his hotel and dictated a long report of his own which was published in *The Times* and other newspapers around the world and firmly pinned the blame on the security forces. It was a bold and courageous act.

So indeed, in rather a different way, was his decision personally to represent the former Liberal leader Jeremy Thorpe in committal proceedings at Minehead magistrates' court in Somerset. Thorpe and three other men were charged with conspiracy to murder, the alleged target being Norman Scott, who claimed to be Thorpe's former lover. The normal procedure in such a high-profile case would have been to brief a leading barrister; the prosecution was led by Peter Taylor QC, later Lord Chief Justice. Napley's decision to do it himself raised eyebrows and was criticised in the press and, naturally, at the bar. He was accused of craving the limelight and not being up to the job. It was said to be unprecedented for a solicitor to act in such a way. As Napley was at pains to point out in his own defence, he had been appearing at committal proceedings in magistrates' courts for more than forty years and reckoned he was pretty good at it by now. "The conduct of committal proceedings involves a technique of its own," he wrote later. "It is necessary to be able to test the veracity of witnesses, to lay the foundation for their ultimate destruction as witnesses without going for the kill. It is necessary to be able to search around for leads which can show the way for further factual research by the solicitor before the trial itself, without unduly alerting one's opponents. It is something to which the training of a solicitor is far more suited than is that of a barrister. It is a wholly different technique from that involved in the trial itself."

Realising that the magistrates would inevitably commit Thorpe and his co-defendants for trial, he gave a good deal of thought as to which barristers he should brief to defend the politician, and decided on George Carman, still little known outside Manchester. He was part of the defence team at Minehead but did not speak. The committal proceedings inevitably aroused enormous public interest and Napley was on the front pages throughout. Despite his two-and-a-half-hour final speech submitting there was no case to answer, the accused were all sent for trial at the Crown Court. The former Lord Chancellor Lord Dilhorne (formerly Sir Reginald Manningham-Buller) was overheard to say with delight: "Good, good. Now they will never again allow a solicitor to conduct committal proceedings." Napley was, of course, vindicated: Thorpe was acquitted after a brilliant performance by George Carman which made his name. He was to go on to become England's most celebrated courtroom advocate, along with

Jeremy Thorpe one of the many clients and colleagues who had reason to be grateful for the perspicacity of David Napley.

To this day, if you hear the words "Carter-Ruck" you immediately think there's a libel action pending. It is the greatest possible tribute to the life and work of Peter Carter-Ruck (1914-2003, Garrick 1975-2003), the London solicitor and libel specialist who was at the heart of many major actions for defamation from the 1950s until the end of the twentieth century. As his fame and influence grew, he became a more and more controversial figure, whose fearsome reputation was at odds with his quiet, reserved and polite demeanour. There was no doubt about his effectiveness: he usually got what he wanted for his client and generally by settling out of court, which he claimed he always tried to do. But as the years rolled on he increasingly fell out with his colleagues (including his daughter) and acquired the reputation of overcharging for his services.

Carter-Ruck came from a comfortable middle-class background and showed an early aptitude for mathematics but after his schooling at St Edward's, Oxford, he decided against accountancy because he felt "it would not provide the human interest I wanted." So he turned to the law instead. His progress was very like that of David Napley at much the same time: he did not go to university, in Carter-Ruck's case of his own volition because he wanted to get started in the law. Like Napley, he regretted it ever after. He also joined a London firm of solicitors owned by a friend of his father, although before he did so he spent three months in Germany and attended a rally in Freiburg addressed by Hitler. After qualifying as a solicitor he was headhunted by the firm Oswald Hickson, where he was to stay for many years. In 1938 he was driving his first motor, a Wolseley sports car bought for £49, down Park Lane when he collided with a large limousine, whose back-seat passenger blamed him for the accident, saying he must have been in a hurry. The man tore in half an invitation he was clutching and wrote his name on it: it was David Maxwell Fyfe, then a rising young KC, but Carter-Ruck shrewdly had the better of the incident. He noticed the invitation was for a dinner starting at 7 pm; as the accident happened at 7.10 pm, he was able to convince the insurers that the limousine, not he, had been speeding.

He served as a gunner in the war and, again like Napley, he was allowed to return to civilian life early, but not in his case through illness: the founding partner of his firm, Oswald Hickson, was dying and asked him to take it over. The firm was well known in the field of libel, copyright and related areas of law, and Carter-Ruck built on this reputation until he and it were pre-eminent in the field. The list of the famous libel cases in which Carter-Ruck and his firm were involved would fill a chapter on its own. His first big case came in 1948 when he defended the *Bolton Evening News* against a libel writ from the amply-proportioned Labour MP Bessie Braddock after the newspaper reported that she had "danced a jig" of triumph and sat in Winston Churchill's seat after most Conservative MPs had quit the Commons chamber in protest at a Labour guillotine motion. The newspaper won. The case had been heard by a special jury, consisting of merchants, bankers or well-to-do landowners; as a result of the Braddock case, special juries were abolished in 1949.

Carter-Ruck's favourite client was probably Sir Winston Churchill's son Randolph, a rumbustious writer and journalist who enjoyed dishing out criticism and took plenty of flak himself in return but did not hesitate to take to the courts if he felt attacks on himself went too far. Reading some of the transcripts of his evidence, one is tempted to conclude that he enjoyed himself tremendously under cross-examination and felt he was getting his money's worth whatever the outcome. The press certainly lapped it up. In 1956 he and Carter-Ruck won hefty damages against *The People* newspaper, which had called him a "paid hack" among other insults, and against the flamboyantly moustachioed Conservative MP Sir Gerald Nabarro in 1960 for calling him a coward (I can still vividly remember reading the daily newspaper reports of the trial as a twelve-year-old schoolboy, because the main characters sounded so fascinating and exotic). Churchill also won the first successful libel action against the new satirical magazine *Private Eye* in 1963. The magazine was to become a persistent critic of Carter-Ruck and a constant thorn in his side. To this day, it carries on a running battle against the firm that still bears his name.

Another libel action whose repercussions were still rumbling on thirty years later was the case brought in 1957 by three Labour politicians—Aneurin Bevan, Richard Crossman and Morgan Phillips, then General Secretary of the Labour Party—against *The Spectator*, which had carried an article reporting that the trio were constantly drunk during an Italian Socialist Party congress in Venice. Carter-Ruck was briefed by the magazine, which briefly considered bringing over some of the many employees of the Hotel Luna who could attest to the sobriety or otherwise of the British politicians. But the lawyers concluded that the word of a few Italian waiters would not be believed against that of three major public figures. After a favourable (to them) summing-up by the Lord Chief Justice, Lord Goddard, the Labour trio were awarded £2,500 each but doubts always persisted about their veracity. Crossman himself admitted at a *Private Eye* lunch in 1972 that he and Bevan had been "as pissed as newts" and then in the last volume of his *Diaries* that Phillips had been drunk the whole time they were in Venice. There have of course been other examples in recent times of politicians perjuring themselves in libel actions they themselves have brought, but then having been caught out and sent to prison as a result. Crossman and Co were luckier.

In 1972 Carter-Ruck helped to secure what was then the second highest award made by a libel jury, £50,000 plus costs, which went to Captain Edward Prchal, the Czech pilot of the Liberator aircraft which crashed just after taking off from Gibraltar in 1943, killing the Polish leader in exile, General Sikorski. Prchal was the sole survivor. He sued the German playwright Rolf Hochhuth, who had claimed in his play *The Soldiers*, produced at the National Theatre, that the accident had been ordered by Churchill to get rid of Sikorski. Another triumph for Carter-Ruck, which cost half of Fleet Street dear in 1975, was the case of Princess Elizabeth of Toro, a Ugandan exile who had been Idi Amin's Foreign Minister before falling foul of the dictator and fleeing to Britain. To blacken her name, Amin claimed she had posed in the nude and also made love to a European diplomat in a public lavatory at Orly airport, Paris. The allegations were repeated by a string of national newspapers, which one by one had to apologise and pay the princess substantial damages.

Carter-Ruck also had a walk-on role in the Jeremy Thorpe affair, when he represented the Bahamas-based millionaire businessman and philanthropist Jack Hayward, known as "Union Jack", who claimed that the *Sunday Telegraph* had effectively accused him of helping to pay for the alleged plot to murder Norman Scott. Hayward won £50,000 in damages but the case went all the way to the House of Lords before the award was confirmed, a process which took three-and-a-half years.

By the 1980s Carter-Ruck dominated the field of libel. He had started out largely defending newspapers, magazines and publishers against libel accusations but his practice had developed into representing individuals who believed they had been libelled. This change led to him being regarded with some trepidation and distaste in Fleet Street, egged on by *Private Eye*, which wasted no opportunity to poke fun at him. They had plenty to feast on in 1984 with the libel action brought by the then editor of the *Daily Express*, Derek Jameson, against the BBC over an item in a satirical radio show which described him as "the archetypal East End boy made bad", a man "uncluttered with faith or talent", a "nitty-gritty titivation tout" and plenty more in similar vein. It was written in a mock-tabloid style and Jameson would have been well advised to ignore it. Such things are usually forgotten within minutes, and as a general rule journalists should be the last people to sue anybody. Not untypically for a libel case in those days, the case dragged on for four years before it came to court, and Jameson lost: the jury decided the item was defamatory but fair comment and without malice. It then emerged that David Eady QC, the barrister retained by Carter-Ruck (later to become a well-known libel judge), had had doubts before the case that it would succeed, informed Carter-Ruck of his fears and advised that Jameson accept the £10 the BBC had paid into court, a derisory sum perhaps but one that would have limited his exposure to costs. Carter-Ruck persuaded him he was wrong, but neglected to inform Jameson of Eady's doubts. Jameson was outraged. Carter-Ruck described events in a typically purse-lipped fashion: "This led to a rift in my good relations with Derek Jameson and to a number of untenable statements being made by that small minority of newspapers ready to engage in negative journalism." He did not, however, sue them for libel. By Carter-Ruck's own account, the case cost Jameson £35,950 in fees ("excluding VAT"), of which Carter-Ruck's share was £24,000.

There was increasing disquiet about the scale of his charges. He certainly did well for himself, owning homes in Hertfordshire, London, Marbella and the Scottish Highlands, a Rolls-Royce (like Napley), and a series of yachts each called *Fair Judgment* in which he indulged his passion for sailing and ocean racing. By 1977, his firm, Oswald Hickson Collier, had grown to be a large practice with more than twenty partners. But most of them had come to disapprove of Carter-Ruck's way of doing things and in December of that year, they informed him that unless he retired within a week and became a consultant, they would quit instead. Litigation followed and the row dragged on for four years until he departed with a handful of partners, including his daughter Julie, and set up his own firm, Peter Carter-Ruck and Partners, on a different floor of the same building. The atmosphere at the new firm was no happier and the other founding partners had moved on again within a few years. Now simply called Carter-Ruck, the firm is still a leading player in the ever-growing field of media law. Oswald Hickson Collier, by then Crockers Oswald Hickson, merged with Farrer & Co in 2001.

Peter Carter-Ruck continued working until his late seventies, when he was Britain's oldest practising solicitor. On his death in 2003, the knives came out. The leading defamation solicitor, David Hooper, a fellow Garrick member who had once worked for him, wrote in *The Guardian*: "He was a chancer, out for the maximum fee. And he did for freedom of speech what the Boston Strangler did for door-to-door salesmen."

16
GARRICK FAMILIES

Legal dynasties run through the history of the Garrick, providing a tangible link with the past: the names Russell, Humphreys and Havers, for example, crop up from generation to generation. No other profession can match the law in this respect.

Sir Travers Humphreys and his son Christmas Humphreys were members of the club for fifty-five years and are dealt with elsewhere in this book. The Russells take some beating, both for legal distinction and their long involvement with the affairs of the Garrick. Charles Russell (1863-1928, Garrick 1896-1928) and his younger brother Frank (1867-1946, Garrick 1893-1946) had a head start: their father, Charles Arthur, Lord Russell of Killowen (1832-1900), was twice Gladstone's Attorney-General and then Lord Chief Justice for six years, dying in office. Charles was his second son and he became one of the most distinguished solicitors in London, founding the firm which still bears his name and still prospers. He was educated at the Roman Catholic school Beaumont College, Windsor, went straight into articles with a City solicitors' firm and founded Charles Russell & Co in 1891.

Russell was the first solicitor to instruct Edward Carson when he came to London from Dublin in 1893 and was yet another Garrick name to be involved in the Oscar Wilde trials in 1895, by virtue of his diligence. The Marquess of Queensberry, father of Wilde's friend Lord Alfred Douglas, at first approached Sir George Lewis, but he declined to take the case on. The furious Queensberry went looking for a replacement, but it was Saturday when few solicitors were at work in the City. The first one he came across was the young Charles Russell, hard at work, and he took the case on with alacrity. He was instrumental in meticulously compiling the evidence about Wilde's relationships with young men that led to the collapse of his action against Queensberry under Carson's relentless cross-examination. The case made both Carson's and Russell's names. Russell was discreet, worldly and wise, and advised many of the great names of the era, keeping many cases out of court and the glare of publicity. Charles Russell & Co were the Garrick's solicitors for many years and Russell himself handled the club's legal affairs. A Liberal, he twice stood for Parliament, losing narrowly on each occasion, and was deeply committed to public affairs, particularly as they affected his fellow Roman Catholics. He campaigned hard for Catholic schools, sought to increase Catholic involvement in local politics and was active in Catholic and other charities, such as the British Red Cross. He was created a baronet in 1916.

His brother Francis, always known as Frank, was the first Lord Russell's fourth son. He was a brilliant student, following his brother to Beaumont College and going on to Oriel College, Oxford, where he made a name as a fine speaker at the Union and got a first in jurisprudence. He was called to the Bar at Lincoln's Inn and developed a thriving Chancery practice, with a steady stream of briefs from his older brother (a case of self-interest, not nepotism). He took silk in 1908. Like his father and brother, he was a devout Roman Catholic and in a landmark case in 1919 he persuaded the House of Lords to accept that a bequest for masses for the dead was a valid charitable bequest and not a superstitious gift. The Lord Chancellor, Lord Birkenhead, was presiding and was so taken with Russell's performance that he gave him the next vacancy on the High Court bench the same year, where he managed to decline the customary knighthood. He went to the Court of Appeal in 1928 and the following year went to the House of Lords, taking the same title as his late father. He was noted for the brevity and precision of his judgments but he was undoubtedly of a conservative hue, informed by his religious faith. His verdict on divorce (which was difficult to obtain in those days) was typical and memorable: "What was once a holy estate enduring for the joint lives of the spouses is steadily assuming the characteristics of a contract of a tenancy at will." He was a keen golfer, a noted and witty after-dinner speaker and Chairman of the Garrick trustees.

Frank's only son and youngest child (of four), Charles Ritchie Russell, later the third Lord Russell of Killowen, (1908-1986, Garrick 1939-1986) followed in his footsteps with almost startling fidelity. He too went to Beaumont and Oriel, where, however, he was a far less diligent student, preferring golf and the cinema to law, and left with a third. He too was called at Lincoln's Inn and joined the Chancery bar. He had a gallant war, flying a glider into France on D-Day and being wounded in another glider flight over the Rhine. After the war he resumed his successful Chancery practice, taking silk in 1948. Lord Templeman wrote of him: "Russell was handsome, tall, slim and elegant; he was dark with expressive eyes and a sensitive, sometimes sardonic expression. He was possessed of a warm melodious voice which made his well structured arguments almost irresistible." In 1960 he was promoted to the Chancery bench and only two years later to the Appeal Court, hearing mainly commercial and property cases. "His judgments were models of analysis and lucidity," noted Templeman. Off the bench, Russell was a keen golfer and village cricketer, and perhaps rather too keen on a drink. In the year he became a judge he was convicted of drink-driving, fined and banned from driving for a year. The consequence was that he served thirteen years in the Appeal Court before finally being appointed a Law Lord, taking the same title as his father and grandfather. Like his father he was Treasurer of Lincoln's Inn, an active member of the Garrick and a Trustee of the club.

The Russell tradition at the Garrick was carried on by the third baronet, Sir Charles Ian Russell (1918-1997, Garrick 1950-1997), a partner in the family law firm and grandson of the founder. An affable man known to all as Tim, he was the club's solicitor for many years and chairman of the House Committee, which runs the club's affairs.

The Havers family almost equals the Russells in Garrick longevity. The dynasty was headed by Sir Cecil Havers (1889-1977, Garrick 1955-1977). He was educated at Norwich Grammar School and Corpus Christi, Cambridge, where he was a classical scholar, played tennis for the university, and went on to take his LLB. After distinguished service in the First World War he was called to the bar at the Inner Temple in 1920. "At the Bar, his success ... revealed his qualities," noted a colleague. "There was always thoroughness, patience, courtesy, alertness." He became a High Court judge in 1951 and presided over the trial in 1955 of Ruth Ellis, the last woman to be hanged for murder in Britain. He was obliged to pass the death sentence but wrote privately to the Home Secretary, Sir David Maxwell Fyfe, to request mercy. Maxwell Fyfe turned him down, and resisted the intense pressure from all quarters to commute the sentence. "He was an admirable judge," wrote an additional obituarist in *The Times*. "Never seeking the limelight or the spectacular, reticent in utterance, never deflecting from the quest for truth, always firm and resolute to uphold right standards."

His son, Sir Michael Havers (1923-1992, Garrick 1954-1992), was Mrs Thatcher's Attorney-General for eight years, the longest tenure of the office since the eighteenth century, briefly Lord Chancellor, and an affable, colourful and somewhat controversial member of the club. He was a regular luncher at the Garrick while in office and like most members enjoyed a drink or two before going down to the Coffee Room to eat. The head barman, Harry Soekarni, would always have a glass of white wine and a cigar ready on the bar by the time Havers reached it. Havers was a delightfully indiscreet man with a voice that carried and many journalist members of the club would crowd round him in the Cocktail Bar to be treated to a running report on the political issues of the day. It was better than a press conference as far as some leading political correspondents and columnists were concerned. Unwritten "Garrick Rules" apply within and without the walls of the club, meaning that members are not supposed to pass on any confidences picked up while in the club. However, various stories that could be traced back to Havers trickled into the national newspapers, causing himself and the government occasional embarrassment.

Michael Havers was educated at Westminster, then went into the Royal Navy in 1941, aged only eighteen. He served for six years, and had his ship sunk beneath him three times. He followed his father to Corpus Christi for a shortened post-war degree and was called to the bar in 1948. He built a substantial civil and criminal practice on the South-Eastern circuit and took silk in 1963. One famous client was Mick Jagger, who was sentenced to three months' imprisonment in 1967 for possession of four pep pills, a verdict swiftly overturned on appeal after the Editor of *The Times* William Rees-Mogg (a Garrick stalwart) wrote a famous leader on behalf of Jagger beneath the headline "Who Breaks a Butterfly on a Wheel?" Havers was elected Conservative MP for Wimbledon in 1970 and achieved rapid advancement, being appointed Solicitor-General only two years later, a position he held until the fall of the Heath government in 1974.

Having shadowed the role for five years, he became Attorney-General when Mrs Thatcher was elected in 1979, and his period in office was full of incident from start to finish. He was deeply involved in all the major policies and crises of the Thatcher years: the legislation to curb the power of the unions, the Falklands war, the miners' strike, and the Westland affair, where his robust stance on seeking a key "leaker" led to the resignation of the Trade and Industry Secretary, Leon Brittan. His naval experience was invaluable during the Falklands conflict, when he was a member of the inner war cabinet and he had to be continually vigilant to make sure his hawkish Prime Minister did not overstep international law. "Two British ships had been sunk in our territorial waters around the Falklands," Lady Thatcher wrote in her memoirs. "Perhaps we should send our submarines to sink Argentine ships in theirs? But the Attorney-General, Michael Havers, would not have this." There was no such opposition to sinking the battle cruiser *General Belgrano*.

Amid the great political events of the decade, there were criminal matters to attend to. Havers led for the prosecution in the trial of Peter Sutcliffe, the Yorkshire Ripper, at the Old Bailey, initially accepting Sutcliffe's pleas of guilty to manslaughter by virtue of diminished responsibility. Mr Justice Boreham, however, refused to entertain them and Sutcliffe's trial on thirteen murder charges went ahead. Havers also successfully prosecuted the MI6 officer Michael Bettany, the GCHQ employee Geoffrey Prime and the Canadian Professor Hugh Hambleton on espionage charges, and was closely involved in the unmasking by Mrs Thatcher of Sir Anthony Blunt as a former Soviet spy. As a former prosecutor of the Birmingham Six and the Guildford Four, alleged republican terrorists who were cleared many years later on appeal, Havers was a prime target for the IRA, who bombed his Wimbledon flat when he and his wife were, luckily, away on holiday.

Havers was appointed Lord Chancellor in succession to Lord Hailsham in 1987 but he had undergone serious heart surgery in 1985 and his health did not allow him to serve in the post for more than a few months before resigning and returning to private life. The Havers legal dynasty at the Garrick continues in the person of his elder son Philip Havers QC; his younger son, the actor Nigel Havers, is also a member.

The Rougiers, father and son, added colour to the club. Ronald Rougier QC (1900-1976, Garrick 1955-1976) came to the bar late; he was previously a mining engineer. He married Georgette Heyer, the best-selling historical novelist, and their son Richard Rougier (1932-2007, Garrick 1963-2007) was a well-known High Court judge, a forthright and outspoken character who featured in a number of high-profile trials and regularly made headlines. He could not conceal his astonishment at the end of a Welsh murder trial when the jury found Jonathan Jones guilty of murdering his girlfriend's parents at their remote farmhouse. Rougier wrote privately to the Home Secretary, Michael Howard, to express his concern at the verdict which, he said, "caused me some surprise" because of "significant doubt" about the evidence against Jones. He was vindicated a year later when the Appeal Court freed Jones in a unanimous judgment. Rougier was never afraid to speak his mind, once denouncing the "me" generation and "dirt and squalor and the rat race". As one of his contemporaries put it, "on a good day, he turned out a damned amusing judgment".

17
GREAT MODERN ADVOCATES:
GEORGE CARMAN AND DICK FERGUSON

The two finest courtroom advocates of the modern era were probably George Carman and Richard Ferguson. They were both members of the Garrick, but no two men could have been more dissimilar. Carman was a gambler, in and out of court, a troubled individual with a rackety private life, a lawyer who frequently sailed close to the wind and liked to produce the odd rabbit out of a hat at the climax of a trial. He was feared by every opponent as a brilliant legal mind and lethal cross-examiner. Dick Ferguson shared those two qualities in equal measure, but he was a quiet, modest, reflective man who relished taking on the most unpopular cases and was famous for his integrity and innate decency.

Few people outside the legal profession and the nightclubs of Manchester had heard of George Carman QC (1929-2001, Garrick 1982-2001) before 1979. That was the year of the Jeremy Thorpe trial and Carman was Sir David Napley's surprise choice to lead for the defence when the former Liberal leader went before a jury at the Old Bailey on a charge of conspiracy to murder. Napley did not know of Carman either before he watched him in action defending the manager of the Battersea Park funfair, on trial for manslaughter after his Big Dipper ride had crashed, killing five children in 1972. Napley was very impressed by Carman's final speech to the jury. "It seemed to me that the jury were mesmerised," he wrote. "George's client was duly acquitted. As I left the court I remarked to my partner, Christopher Murray, that a silk who could thus perform was worth retaining and we should start to brief him." Carman's brilliant defence of Thorpe (who, on Carman's insistence, did not give evidence on his own behalf) captured the attention of the press, who were delighted to find a new legal star. They dubbed him "Gorgeous George", a sobriquet Carman did not mind in the least. He moved to London from Manchester, where he had been based since 1953, to capitalise on his new-found fame and never looked back. He successfully defended a string of famous figures against criminal charges, then moved into the lucrative world of libel and rapidly established a glittering reputation in a series of high-profile cases, eagerly reported in the newspapers, burnishing Carman's image further.

But the truth about the man behind the public image did not emerge until after his death from cancer in 2001, only a few months after he had abruptly announced his retirement from the bar. His only child, Dominic, published an extraordinarily intimate biography of his father, *No Ordinary Man*, in 2002, which revealed his alcoholism, his addiction to gambling, his appalling treatment of his three wives (all his marriages ended in divorce), and the full sordid details of his disorganised and unstable lifestyle. But the book also provides just as many insights into what made George Carman such a great advocate: his brilliant mind, his meticulous preparation (of big cases, at any rate), and his "feel" for a jury which enabled him to pitch his final speeches at just the right level.

If the portrait of him left by his son has the ring of authenticity, it was George Carman's own fault. When his second marriage, to Dominic's mother Celia Sparrow, ended, Carman demanded custody of the boy, then aged eleven, and threatened to take her through "every court in the land" unless she agreed. Desperate to get out of the marriage, she agreed and thenceforth saw Dominic only once a year. But George insisted that the boy be his constant companion, taking him along on his frequent forays to public houses, drinking clubs, casinos and nightclubs, a sort of teenage Boswell to an often drunk and dissolute Johnson, who witnessed his father in all manner of undignified situations, gambling away his week's earnings, chatting up escort girls and bringing home gangs of hangers-on to continue carousing into the small hours. The wonder is that Carman senior managed to perform so well in court but he did. Dominic Carman related that one Manchester solicitor who regularly instructed him said: "Many thought George actually performed better in court when he was drunk." Dominic described how George would use him as a sounding board for ideas about handling a big case, pacing up and down, chain-smoking, going through all the options, rehearsing possible lines and quotes. "When involved in a big trial, which was most of the time, everything else in George's world ceased to exist," he wrote. "Sifting through a mass of evidence helped him to filter the important detail in his mind. Key points were then distilled. Listening to your responses and reactions assisted in deciding what might work with a jury."

Their intimate relationship continued after George moved to London and Dominic's own first marriage broke down. After a day in court, George liked to frequent Fleet Street wine bars like El Vino in Fleet Street, where a frequent fellow imbiber was James Crespi QC, and the Wine Press, from which he was banned for bad behaviour. When he went back and tried to buy a drink, the barman asked him to leave. Carman famously remarked, "If you tell me why you are banning me, I will sue you for slander." Then he would often move on to the Garrick, where he would dine with Sir Robin Day, who had been at Oxford with Carman in the 1950s and was a fellow barrister before moving into television. Dominic describes how one evening after dinner at the club they rehearsed how Carman might handle the National Union of Mineworkers leader Arthur Scargill whom he was due to cross-examine after Scargill had sued the Chief Constable of South Yorkshire for false imprisonment following an alleged speeding incident. Day played the part of Scargill brilliantly and the session was invaluable; Scargill lost his case. But his son thought his father never really felt comfortable at the Garrick. "The rich food, cerebral company and faded elegance of the Garrick were not always to George's liking," he wrote. "He found a number of members 'too stuffy'. Inherited privilege, understated charm and old money—part of the club's fabric—made him feel ill at ease." Dominic thought this was unfair. "Most Garrick members are meritocratic in outlook," he wrote. "The reality was that broader conversation could discomfit George. He had no real interest in, or knowledge of, the arts or politics beyond superficial chitchat." He felt much more at home in

Mayfair drinking clubs, topless bars, and gambling clubs like Aspinall's.

It was a long way from the respectable middle-class world of 1930s Blackpool in which George Carman grew up. His father was a furniture auctioneer, his mother ran a ladies' dress shop (there must be a PhD thesis to be written about great advocates—Carman, Birkett, Hewart—whose parents ran clothes shops in North-West England). George was small (he never grew taller than 5ft 3in) but determined: he was educated at St Joseph's College, Blackpool, a Roman Catholic school, with a two-year stint at Upholland Seminary, near Wigan, before he discovered he did not have a vocation to be a Catholic priest and returned to St Joseph's to complete his secondary education. He was a voracious reader and devoured biographies of or articles about the great advocates of the day, such as Marshall Hall, Hastings, Carson and F.E. Smith, who was his particular hero. Their example inspired him to determine on a career at the bar. He went up to Balliol, where he took an unvivaed First in Law, an achievement he was justly proud of for the rest of his life. (A young man called Jeremy Thorpe got a Third at the same time.) Then after qualifying for the bar in London it was back to the North-West to start his career in Manchester, where he gradually built a reputation as a clever young advocate with an extravagant lifestyle. Nobody minded as long as he got results, which he did particularly in the field of personal injury. He took silk in 1971 but turned down the chance of a move to London. That was to be delayed until the Thorpe trial eight years later, which changed his life.

His demolition of Peter Bessell and Norman Scott, the alleged target of the so-called murder conspiracy, and his moving final speech to the jury—"Mr Thorpe has spent twenty years in British politics and obtained thousands and thousands of votes. Now the most precious twelve votes of all come from you"—helped, it must be said, by Mr Justice Cantley's extraordinary summing-up, saw Thorpe acquitted.

Installed in London, Carman enjoyed two decades as one of the highest-earning silks in the country and certainly the most quotable. His client list seemed to come from the pages of *Variety*, with one or two notable exceptions: he once said the result he was proudest of was securing the acquittal of Dr Leonard Arthur, a consultant paediatrician charged with the attempted murder of a Down's Syndrome baby boy for whom he prescribed "nursing care only" after the parents expressed a wish that the child not survive. Carman had a gift for boiling down complicated concepts into simple language which a jury could understand. "He could, like Pontius Pilate, have washed his hands of the matter," he said in his final speech to the Arthur jury. "He did not, because good doctors do not turn away ... Are we to condemn him because he cared?"

When the comedian Ken Dodd was charged in 1988 with defrauding the Inland Revenue of massive sums, he insisted on retaining Carman. It was a wise choice. Carman secured his acquittal at Liverpool Crown Court by painting Dodd as a decent man who was old-fashioned, naive and completely chaotic in handling his money, and who had no idea that he had to pay tax on the interest accruing from the many offshore bank accounts he had set up. "Some accountants are comedians, but comedians are never accountants," Carman memorably remarked. Dodd's acquittal revived his career and gave a further boost to Carman's.

It was in the 1990s that Carman acquired the reputation as "the king of libel", from a standing start. The libel bar was not exactly a closed shop but it was confined to a relatively small group of specialists. Carman broke into this charmed circle with a series of bravura performances and spectacular damages awards for a string of celebrities or successful defences of media organisations. It was an era of increasingly massive awards made by juries so the stakes were high, which is how Carman, the obsessive gambler, liked it. Many of them made marvellous copy for Fleet Street, often because of a memorable phrase of Carman's or passages in his cross-examination. When a South African journalist, Jani Allen, sued Channel 4 for reporting that she had had an affair with the white supremacist leader Eugene Terre Blanche, Carman made great play with the evidence of a former flatmate of Allen's who claimed to have witnessed Allen in bed with Terre Blanche through the keyhole of her bedroom door. Carman elicited a description of a white bottom going up and down between Allen's knees. Allen had earlier said under cross-examination from Carman, "Whatever award is given for libel, being cross-examined by you would not make it enough money," a sentiment doubtless echoed by many other people subjected to his merciless questioning. In the event, Allen got nothing except a £300,000 bill for costs.

A similar fate befell the *EastEnders* actress Gillian Taylforth who unwisely sued the *Sun*, represented by Carman, for reporting she had taken part in a "sex romp" in a car parked in a lay-by. But one of his most famous remarks, about the then Conservative Minister David Mellor, was not his own. In a libel action brought by a friend of Mellor, Mona Bauwens, against the *People* newspaper, Carman said: "If a politician goes there [Marbella], and in the honest view of some, behaves like an ostrich and puts his head in the sand, thereby exposing his thinking parts, it may be that a newspaper is entitled to say so." In fact, Carman had first heard the phrase as far back as 1950, from Sir David Maxwell Fyfe in a speech at the Oxford Union, and doubtless squirreled it away to await the opportunity to deliver it himself.

In several major cases, Carman found himself up against fellow Garrick members. In the Bauwens trial, it was Richard Hartley QC; in the hugely important case of Richard Branson against an American businessman Guy Snowden and the US lottery operator G-Tech, it was Richard Ferguson. Branson and Carman won and the case went to the Appeal Court, where another Garrick member, Gordon Pollock QC, took over from Ferguson. Carman won there too. Mellor was not the only British politician with little reason to love him: he successfully defended the *Guardian* against the former Conservative Minister Jonathan Aitken, who later went to prison for perjury in the case, and Mohammed Al Fayed against Neil Hamilton, the former Conservative MP, over allegations of corruption. As the latter case neared its end, Carman's fellow silk and Garrick member Bob Marshall-Andrews recalls walking down Fleet Street after dining at Gray's Inn. A dishevelled figure in a dark overcoat, dragging wheezily on a cigarette clutched between thumb and middle finger, emerged from a doorway and made his unsteady way towards him. Marshall-Andrews fumbled in his pocket for a few coins to give to the man before realising it was not a vagrant but George Carman, very much the worse for wear. "Hello, George," he said. Carman replied, "How do you think I'm doing?", referring to the Hamilton case. "I've no idea," said Marshall-Andrews. "Oh, I thought I saw you in the corridor," said Carman, dragging deeply on his cigarette. "Yes, I'm appearing in the court next door," explained Marshall-Andrews. Evidently disappointed, Carman lurched off into the night, "probably to Annabel's," laughed Marshall-Andrews. "But next morning, he was in court at 10.30 and he won the case."

Like every lawyer, Carman had his share of libel losses; indeed, one of his most famous victories, acting for the Pakistani cricketer Imran Khan against the England players Ian Botham and Allan Lamb over ball-tampering allegations, came after a run of four big defeats. It was rather like his activities at the gaming tables: a series of big losses would be followed by a big win, and Carman would be off again. His reputation was certainly dented after his death by the revelations about his personal life in his son's biography: particularly damaging were the accounts by all three of his wives of how he repeatedly beat them. But something went out of British public life when George Carman died. He was one of the few advocates in the modern era who could justly be compared with the giants of the past, whose flamboyant and exciting style had set the boy from Blackpool on the path to the bar in the first place.

Richard Ferguson QC (1935-2009, Garrick 2001-2009) vied with George Carman for the title of top criminal silk of his generation. They occasionally appeared opposite each other, had a magical way with a jury and a healthy mutual respect. The quality Ferguson, universally known as Dick, possessed above all others was courage: as well as creating a name for himself in Ulster as the finest advocate since Carson, he went into politics as an Ulster Unionist member of Stormont, the Northern Ireland parliament. His loyalty to the Unionist cause never deflected him from taking on the most unpopular cases, such as defending one of the men charged with involvement in the republican bombing of the La Mon House restaurant in 1978, in which twelve people died, an incident that caused outrage throughout the Protestant community and beyond. His reward for opposing sectarianism was to be bombed out of his own home by terrorists. Ferguson took great pride in the fact it could have been either side, republican or loyalist, who carried out the attack. It drove him out of politics, for the sake of his family, but did not deter him from continuing to take on the toughest cases in court.

He represented both alleged IRA men and officers of the Royal Ulster Constabulary and the British Army in both Belfast and Dublin, where like Carson he had taken his first degree at Trinity College; he returned to Belfast to take his LLB. He was the son of a police officer in County Fermanagh and he was inspired to become a barrister by seeing the film of Terence Rattigan's play *The Winslow Boy*, based on one of Carson's most famous triumphs. Ferguson's other great hero was Marshall Hall.

He honed his skills in the courts of his native province. "Northern Ireland is a tremendous stomping ground for advocates," said his widow Roma Ferguson, a barrister and Ulsterwoman herself. "Juries like their literary references." He took silk in Northern Ireland in 1973 and moved to London for health and personal reasons in 1984, making an immediate impact. His first brief was to represent a young man accused of murdering a security guard at a Tube station in North London who was shot during a robbery. The man had sacked his previous lawyers, attempted to represent himself, and then sought a new barrister. Ferguson took the brief at 24 hours' notice. He swiftly won over the jury, who found his client guilty of manslaughter instead. It was the first but by no means the last English jury to be persuaded by Ferguson, aided considerably by his mellifluous Ulster accent.

"He had plenty of natural charm," agreed his chambers colleague and fellow Garrick member Bob Marshall-Andrews, "but his accent helped tremendously." However, it nearly cost him a lucrative fraud brief in Hong Kong, Marshall-Andrews recalled. "There was a beauty parade, and it came down to Dick and me. Then the solicitor rang me, of all people, to ask me if I thought a Chinese jury would understand Dick's accent. It was one of those moments of high moral struggle, but I had to say that no jury in the world would misunderstand Dick Ferguson, whatever language they spoke."

His close friend Lord Falconer, the former Lord Chancellor, said: "Dick had great understanding, insight and objectivity but he was so intensely committed. That drove his advocacy not into implausible overstatement but into always being rigorous about what he could say for his clients. He was always aware that his job was to persuade; hyperbole was not very sensible. Instead, 'Here are five reasons why my client is innocent'.

"He had a very understated style. He thought very carefully about what he wanted to say. It was conversational advocacy, not high-flown advocacy. His conversational style made it appear as if it was his first thoughts until you listened to what he was saying and you realised it was a powerful, well-crafted argument. He was a very clever man, straightforward and committed.

"From time to time he would get into scrapes with judges. In one case in Hong Kong, he became convinced that the judge was unfair in his summing-up to the jury. He made representations in the absence of the jury, without success. Eventually Dick intervened in front of the jury and made the complaint that he was putting the case unfairly. The judge got angry and tried to get other judges to intimidate Dick, but he was repulsed by Dick's bar colleagues.

"Representing an IRA man, which was incredibly unpopular, he made it clear to the prison officers that if any harm came to him while he was on remand they would have to answer to Dick."

"A lot of the judges here in England thought of Dick as a staunch Republican," commented Roma Ferguson. "Nothing could have been further from the truth. He was a great believer in the rule of law, but he had this great belief too in an individual's right to freedom and justice."

Bob Marshall-Andrews added: "He would chew over cases and judges because he wasn't universally liked on the bench. There was a raft of judges who could see a relationship growing between him and juries, and they didn't like it. Juries could see the polarisation between the defence counsel and the judge, which would often redound to the defender's advantage. There was that Rumpolian aspect to it. He had a great affinity with the common man."

Ferguson successfully defended many well-known clients, including the boxer Terry Marsh, who was accused of the attempted murder of the promoter Frank Warren, and the guitarist Peter Buck, of the rock band REM, who was acquitted of various "air-rage" incidents on a British Airways transatlantic flight which he claimed were the result of the unfortunate mixture of alcohol and his sleeping medication. "He loved doing that case as he didn't know who anybody was," said Roma. "Bono arrived to give evidence on Buck's behalf. Dick said you can't call yourself a stupid name like that, what's your real name? He gave evidence as Paul Hewson."

Ferguson was less successful defending the Brighton hotel bomber, Patrick Magee, who nearly assassinated Mrs Thatcher. But the case for which Dick Ferguson was best known to the general public was that of Rose West, wife of Fred West, the Gloucester mass murderer who committed suicide before he could be brought to trial, leaving Rose to face the music, and to absorb all the public hatred of her husband which was now channelled towards her alone. "Dick always felt that Fred had killed before he met her," said Roma. "He believed she was being tried by the media, something he couldn't bear. He felt she had been involved in a lot of nasty stuff but there were elements of mitigation. He believed she was a hate victim."

During West's trial at Winchester Crown Court, the police called at the Fergusons' North London home to say they would like to escort their young son Patrick to school every day because of anonymous threats. Ferguson declined the offer. He himself was used to getting hostile mail because of the sort of cases he fought. "He got the most revolting letters for representing Ernest Saunders in the Guinness trial," said Roma. "He wasn't affected because of growing up in Northern Ireland and being used to bullets in the post."

All his friends agreed that the Rose West trial took a considerable toll on Ferguson. Charlie Falconer commented: "The passion and intensity of that case was very high. Dick was locked over a period of months into a bleak and horrible world." Bob Marshall-Andrews added: "The Rose West case took a lot out of him. Indeed, all of his cases took a lot out of him. He had this languor about him but it was deceptive. He was a worrier."

Not the least of Ferguson's achievements was to take over a moribund set of criminal chambers, formerly headed by the colourful Billy Rees-Davies MP, and turn them into the powerhouse set which is now Carmelite Chambers, of which he was head for 25 years. He died while still at the top of the tree after unsuccessful heart surgery. "He had a very unbarristerial personality," said Charlie Falconer. "He loved the bar and was highly committed to the integrity of the process. He had all the qualities that you would want in a barrister." I am one of the many who still miss seeing his cheerful face across the centre table at the Garrick and hearing him expatiate on the latest legal lunacy in his inimitable Ulster brogue.

18
A MODERN MEDLEY:
JAMES CRESPI TO JOHN MORTIMER

C lubmen are liable to lament the lack of "characters"
these days, although a bit of research into club
history tends to make one think that clubs might
not have been as full of them as people today think.
However, in the case of the Garrick, an exception must
honourably be made for James Crespi QC (1928-1992,
Garrick 1976-1992). He was a genuine eccentric, vastly
corpulent, a brilliant lawyer and conversationalist for
whom the Garrick was a second home. His great friend at
the club, the author Brian Masters, provides an affectionate
and insightful portrait of Crespi in his memoir *Getting
Personal*, from which I have drawn liberally. Physically, he
was an extraordinary figure, as Masters describes:

> He was, to start with, bulky, his body spherical, sloping
> majestically out from beneath a cushioned chin to a
> waistline which was longer in circumference than the
> totality of his height, a rolling tank, a big sombre presence
> ... His head was like an egg, balding at the front, two large
> black eyes, a generous mouth which pouted in repose and
> in reflection, and spread wide agape in loud laughter...

Crespi's lifestyle was extraordinary too. He breakfasted
at the Connaught Hotel, munching his way through the
entire menu while he read the newspapers. He would take

a taxi to court (he went everywhere by taxi, whether to the shop round the corner or some distant provincial city), have a second breakfast, then lunch in the lawyers' mess, and when the court, usually the Old Bailey, had risen would take a huge tea at the Waldorf Hotel on Aldwych. From there, it was on to El Vino wine bar in Fleet Street, haunt of lawyers and journalists until the latter were dispatched to Canary Wharf and other distant parts in the 1990s. He would then make his way to the Garrick for dinner. One of his drinking friends at El Vino was George Carman, who frequently had his son Dominic in tow. Dominic wrote: "Crespi was an eccentric, highly intelligent and humorous man whose bulky frame and gout-inspired lifestyle (copious nightly port at the Garrick dinner table) made him the embodiment of a Rowlandson caricature." Carman junior noted that Crespi was "reputed to have inspired Sir John Mortimer in conceiving the Rumpole character". This was widely believed to be true, but Brian Masters claims that Mortimer himself always denied it, adding however: "I should not be surprised if some little of James went into the cocktail, for they had the same love of the law and mischievous respect for those who got round it." This sounds about right: Crespi had a brilliant legal mind, had obtained a Double First at Cambridge and taken silk. The whole point about Rumpole is that he isn't a silk but the eternal junior who gets landed time and again with the dregs of the criminal classes in their usually unavailing attempts to stay out of prison. And of course he went home every evening to She Who Must Be Obeyed. Crespi was the bachelor incarnate, although he had once been married to a nightclub hostess who left him shortly afterwards, or possibly even straight after the register office wedding. Masters described visiting him once, with the entire set of the *Encylopaedia Britannica*, which Crespi had expressed a desire to read, possibly to aid his research into an unfinished History of the Second Punic War, written in his neat but almost illegible handwriting. He offered his guest a cup of tea (he had twelve pots, which he used successively until the cleaning lady arrived to wash them out). When he opened his enormous refrigerator in search of milk, the only thing it contained was a John Buchan novel. He claimed, however, to be able to boil an egg satisfactorily by playing a section from the Overture to *Tannhauser* which lasted precisely four-and-a-half minutes.

Caesar James Crespi was the son of the second resident conductor at La Scala, Milan; his mother came to England around the time of his birth, and he was brought up in modest circumstances in south London. He went to City of London School and after Cambridge went straight into the law. He achieved national fame in the most unexpected way in 1972 when he was caught by the blast of a bomb planted at the Old Bailey by Irish republicans. He explained that a policeman had told him to run, "so I ran, but unfortunately towards the bomb". The photograph of him being led away, covered in blood, by the rescue services made all the front pages, and became an instant symbol of English phlegm under the latest terrorist onslaught. He was memorably quoted as saying: "I perceived the danger to the state and considered it my duty to place myself between the building and the bomb." He also claimed that his doctors told him he had been saved by his enormous bulk: a thinner man would undoubtedly have had vital arteries severed by the shrapnel which merely lodged in Crespi's copious fatty tissue.

He was by all accounts a memorable figure to watch in action in court. He disdained notes, relying instead on his formidable memory and intellect in cross-examination. Leonard Krikler, later a judge, recalled defending a client whom he advised not to give evidence on his own behalf. Crespi was the prosecuting counsel and the accused watched with growing dismay as he demolished a defence witness. Krikler asked him if he wanted to change his mind about giving evidence. "What, and be run over by a steamroller?" he retorted.

After dinner at the Garrick Crespi would hold forth, fortified by Green Chartreuse, under the stairs, where members gather for a post-prandial drink or two. There, wrote Sir Michael Davies in a memoir of Crespi, "he would entertain fellow members with his stories, often repeated with embellishments, so that there was always something new". Davies went on:

> Typical was the incident which he described alternatively as "my finest hour" and "the moment I realised I would not be Lord Chancellor". As junior counsel for the Crown in the notorious Kray trial he called the first witness, a sixteen-stone barman, arms liberally adorned with tattoos, from the Blind Beggar public house. James's first question before a packed court began: "Are you a barmaid....?"

Crespi sat as a part-time Recorder and many thought he had all the qualities to be an excellent judge. But it was believed that the Lord Chancellor thought his private life rendered him unfit for judicial office. This was unfair: Crespi was eccentric but, as Davies put it, "never guilty of discreditable behaviour, in or out of court". It was an opportunity missed: His Honour Judge Crespi would probably have become a national treasure.

One of Crespi's Garrick companions when he was staying in London was Peter Taylor, the future Lord Chief Justice, whose family home was in Newcastle. His son Louis recalls that he would call home afterwards and explain that he had been "under the stairs with Crespi". The phrase "under the stairs with Crespi" became part of the Taylor family folklore.

Peter Taylor (1930-1997, Garrick 1979-1997) had to choose between music and the law for his career. He was a talented pianist and after leaving the Royal Grammar School in his home city of Newcastle-upon-Tyne had places at the Royal Academy of Music and Pembroke College, Cambridge, to study law. His friend, fellow Pembroke man and Garrick member Sir Alan Ward, a Lord Justice of Appeal, relates how Peter's Jewish mother advised against a musical career, saying he would live out of a suitcase for the rest of his life. "He often remembered this when he was living out of a suitcase as a barrister on the North-Eastern Circuit," Sir Alan recalled.

Taylor rose to become a hugely respected Lord Chief Justice but he never forgot his North-Eastern roots and looked back on his circuit days with great fondness. "He loved those early days in Newcastle, doing different things every day, from undefended divorces to a shipyard worker suffering burns to a miner losing a finger in an accident," his son Louis, also a Garrick member, remembers.

Although Peter Taylor had opted for the law as a career, music remained a great solace. He gave several recitals at the Garrick to raise money for the staff Christmas Fund, and did the same for legal charities. Indeed, he said he would only play for charities because nobody would ask for their money back. When he chaired the public inquiry into the Hillsborough football stadium disaster in which ninety-six people were killed, he was greatly affected by the harrowing stories that he heard and by the sight of senior police officers breaking down in tears as they gave evidence, according to Louis Taylor. "During the inquiry, he stayed at the judges' lodgings in Leeds, which fortunately possessed a grand piano. He would often play it in the evening to help him relax."

Taylor, by then in the Appeal Court, was the ideal man to head the inquiry as in addition to his outstanding judicial qualities he had been a fine sportsman in his youth, winning a Rugby Blue at Cambridge; he was also a keen supporter of Newcastle United Football Club, and had spent many afternoons on the terraces of St James's Park watching his team in its glory days. His influence can still be seen at every Premiership football match played in England. Where before Hillsborough every big stadium had terraces where the fans could stand, Taylor demanded that stadiums should be converted to seating only, as they had been for decades elsewhere in the world. It was a huge culture change for British football followers and many of them still find it difficult to stay seated to this day. But Taylor's reforms ushered in a new era in sporting safety; no event like Hillsborough has occurred since, and many football clubs took the opportunity to demolish their old stadiums and build new ones incorporating all Taylor's recommendations as a matter of course.

Taylor first came to public notice as prosecuting counsel in various trials involving the activities of the corrupt architect John Poulson, whose tentacles reached throughout the North-East. Poulson and local politicians

T. Dan Smith and Andrew Cunningham all went to jail. But Taylor was less successful as prosecutor of the former Liberal leader Jeremy Thorpe, accused of conspiracy to murder, who was defended by George Carman. Taylor disclosed privately to Carman that the prosecution had plenty of evidence of Thorpe's homosexuality. Cross-examining Norman Scott, the alleged murder target, Carman referred to Thorpe's "homosexual tendencies." Because of this, Taylor did not introduce further evidence of them. Dominic Carman wrote: "Taylor's honourable gesture reflected his strong commitment to fairness and objectivity. Many prosecutors in his position would not have done the same."

Taylor was appointed a High Court judge in 1980, a Lord Justice of Appeal in 1988 and Lord Chief Justice in 1992 in succession to Lord Lane. His tenure as Lord Chief Justice was notable for its openness and reforming initiatives. He held a press conference soon after taking over, appeared on *Desert Island Discs* and gave the Dimbleby Lecture on BBC Television in 1992, calling for more judges to be appointed to handle the growing backlog of cases. He was deeply concerned about miscarriages of justice, having been part of the prosecution team in at least two major examples. The first was the case of Stephen Kiszko, who was wrongly convicted of the murder and rape of a young girl in 1976 and served sixteen years before he was eventually freed on appeal, the day before Taylor was appointed Lord Chief Justice. He lived for only a year afterwards. The second was the imprisonment of Judith Ward in 1974 for her alleged part in the M62 coach bombing in which twelve soldiers and family members were killed; she served seventeen years in prison before she too was acquitted.

Taylor would have been happy for judges and barristers to dispense with wigs, and allowed women barristers to wear trousers in court. And he was not afraid to criticise the then Home Secretary Michael Howard, who wanted to introduce mandatory sentences for repeat offenders; Taylor fought for the right of judges to decide on sentencing. His period in office was sadly cut short by a brain tumour; he resigned in 1996 and died in 1997. "He was a man of immense charisma and strength," is the verdict of the former Lord Chancellor Lord Falconer. "He was not at all rude or aggressive on the bench but he bristled with authority. He was a man made to be Lord Chief Justice."

Peter Taylor's love of music and the law is carried on by his family and combined in a body which does immense good work today. His wife Irene predeceased him in 1995 and the Taylor family set up a trust in her name which organises music projects in prisons throughout Britain. Their daughter Deborah sits as a circuit judge dealing with criminal cases. Roderick Young, a close friend of Deborah since their Oxford days, recalled how after he decided he could not bear another Christmas at home with his mother, whose main interest was hunting, the Taylor family came to his rescue: "Every Christmas for about six years I went up to Newcastle. Those trips are amongst the happiest memories of my life. Irene and Peter always hosted a large family lunch on Christmas Day. Being a Jewish family, it was of course a secular Christmas lunch—a fantastic excuse for the extended family to be together. Peter was a wonderful pianist and he would sit down at the piano and play carols for a raucous sing-along. He was also a great host and I had never experienced such a warm and fun family get-together in my life.

"I was very intrigued by Peter and Irene's Jewishness. They explained to me that they were definitely culturally Jewish but that practising the religion held little interest to them. They were nominally members of the Orthodox synagogue in Gosforth, but never went now the children were grown. During those Christmas visits Peter was a lively, amusing and interested conversationalist. I was in awe of him and at the same time felt incredibly comfortable with him. He and Irene were tremendously welcoming and made me feel like one of the family. One Christmas I remember Peter saying something to wind Deb up. She gave her father a reproving look. As soon as she had left the room Peter turned to me and said: 'Did you know that my daughter glares for England?'"

The story of Anthony Babington (1920-2004, Garrick 1964-2004) is one of extraordinary courage and valour. He was wounded on active service in 1944, suffering the most appalling brain damage and paralysis, yet through sheer willpower and perseverance recovered sufficiently to continue his law studies, qualify and practise as a barrister, become a stipendiary magistrate and finally be appointed a circuit judge. He was the son of a talented but alcoholic Irish engineer who died when Anthony was about ten, leaving his widow and four children in much reduced circumstances. She managed to scrape together enough money to send Anthony to Reading School, where he excelled at sport. He wanted to study for the bar but he had to finance himself so he took a job as a telephonist with the Press Association, accompanying reporters on stories and telephoning over their reports. An enterprising and always positive young man, he also wrote features and articles for magazines in his spare time as well as playing rugby for London Irish.

Babington had just enrolled to study at the Middle Temple when war broke out and he was called up. He suffered his near-fatal injuries serving as an infantry captain with 231 Brigade which was involved in heavy fighting with the retreating Germans after the Arnhem debacle in the waterlogged region of the Netherlands between the Lower Rhine and the Waal. A shell exploded nearby, causing severe brain injuries and paralysing him down the right side. He was to regain the partial use of his right leg but not of his right arm so he had to learn to write after a fashion with his left hand. His speech function was destroyed and he had to learn to speak again, from scratch. For the rest of his life he suffered from dyslexia and dysgraphia but he refused to give in to his handicaps. Despite the army doctors' scepticism, Babington was determined to pursue his ambition of becoming a barrister and when he had recovered sufficiently he started studying by correspondence course, funded by the government's Further Education and Training Scheme for demobilised ex-servicemen and his invalidity pension. The bar bent over backwards to help; the Council of Legal Education provided an amanuensis to whom he dictated his bar examination answers, and although he found the experience extremely gruelling he passed with flying colours. No sooner had he been called than he had to return to hospital with tuberculosis but after another prolonged convalescence he was offered a tenancy in Gerald Howard's chambers. Within a month he was back in hospital suffering from pleurisy and had half a lung removed. It was a year and a half before he could return to work. After a tour of the

North as marshal to Mr Justice Streatfeild, he went back to Howard's chambers and gradually acquired a respectable practice on the South-Eastern Circuit. He also published his first book, *No Memorial*, an account of his wartime injuries and long recovery.

Babington was appointed second prosecuting counsel to the Post Office, succeeding Michael Havers, but his doctors were concerned about the dangers to his health from such a busy life involving a lot of travel, so he applied to be a metropolitan stipendiary magistrate, and after a lengthy and anxious pause was appointed to serve at Bow Street. Because of his courageous fight against his disabilities the story made the front pages. So did a case he tried in his first summer as a "stipe", a long hot one in which "going topless" was suddenly all the rage for young women, or at least those seeking some cheap publicity via the popular newspapers. Three appeared (clothed) before Babington, charged with indecency in a test case which few took seriously, and certainly not the press. He gave them all conditional discharges, provoking a national debate involving the top newspaper columnists of the day such as Bernard Levin (who condemned Babington as a prude) and T.E. Utley (who defended him).

It was during this period that Babington was elected to the Garrick, a membership he cherished for the rest of his life. Bow Street is just a stone's throw from the club so he was able to lunch there regularly with the likes of the actors Donald Wolfit and Kenneth More. "My excitement at belonging to the club, and my devotion to it, have never lessened," he wrote in his autobiography *An Uncertain Voyage*, published in 2000. "Most of the members feel the same way as I do. Somebody sitting next to me at dinner on one occasion remarked, 'If one could be sure that the after-life would have the same ambience as the Garrick, it would help to take the sting out of death.'" He movingly described how he had fallen in love with a beautiful young Wren during the war but she had broken off their engagement when she heard of his terrible injuries and could not bring herself to see him although she had gone to Oxford, where he lay at death's door, to do so. Institutions like the Garrick and the Middle Temple, in whose activities he was deeply involved, helped to fill the gap she left in his life although he had a close relationship with the children's author Josephine Pullein-Thompson which lasted until his death.

It was a drink at the Garrick with his fellow stipendiary Frank Milton that was the first step towards Babington's promotion to the Bench. The ancient Assizes and Quarter Sessions were about to be abolished and replaced by Crown Courts and a new breed of all-rounders called circuit judges created, hearing criminal, civil and matrimonial cases. Babington thought he had been away from the latter two categories for too long so did not bother to apply. Over their drink Milton told him he was surprised he hadn't and told him it wasn't too late. Babington's appointment to sit on the South-Eastern Circuit followed soon afterwards. He eventually, and happily, fetched up at the new Knightsbridge Crown Court, round the corner from Harrods. He sat as a circuit judge for sixteen years, being noted for his tolerance, decency and good humour. Somehow he found the time to write ten books on legal and military themes, the best-known being *For The Sake of Example*, a study of the unfortunate men shot for desertion in the First World War. He was closely involved with the activities of the authors' organisation PEN International and often travelled with Josephine Pullein-Thompson to its overseas conferences. He retired in 1988, although he continued to sit as a part-time deputy judge for a further five years despite finding it increasingly difficult to do so because of his disabilities. He finished his autobiography with the moving words: "If grave misfortune befalls you in your earlier years, it need not be the end of your life—in many ways it can be a new beginning." No man ever dealt with grave misfortune more courageously than Anthony Babington.

One of the defining facts about Michael Davies (1921-2006, Garrick member 1969-2006) was that he was a Midlander, from his accent to his attitudes. He came from Stourbridge, on the edge of the Black Country, went to school and university in Birmingham, lived thereafter near Kidderminster and was Leader of the Midland Circuit. He prized plain speaking and had something of the "I know what I like" manner of a provincial mayor or football club chairman. But he was at heart a kind and thoughtful man who adored the Garrick and steeped himself in its history. As a High Court judge, he was for a time head of the libel court and was felt to be anti-newspaper by many journalists. He was, however, known to go easy on any editors who appeared in the witness box wearing the Garrick tie.

In retirement, he became a regular radio and television broadcaster on legal matters. He was not at all shy about expressing his opinions in a forthright manner and he was constantly in demand to be interviewed. News producers rapidly realised that he provided good value for money. Only a few weeks before he died at the age of eighty-five, he complained to a Garrick friend that he had to turn down three television interviews and five radio broadcasts because of his increasing infirmity. He also devoted a lot of time to delving into the archives of the club in search of material for a series of profiles of past "Garrick Personalities", as he called them, to be published in the club's quarterly newsletter, which he had been instrumental in setting up in 2002. The last to appear was number 20, and he planned it to appear after his death, which came in September 2006. He began: "Providence has decreed that this is the last of the series, at least by its creator," and concluded: "May *The Garrick* [newsletter] continue to prosper. Please arrange for it to be delivered to me every quarter to wherever I may be."

The name of Horace Rumpole is scattered through these pages, evidence of the powerful hold on the public imagination exercised by John Mortimer's immortal fictional barrister. John Mortimer (1923-2009, Garrick 1960-2009) was a throwback to those early Garrick members who managed to combine successful legal and artistic careers; he was in addition a lifelong political radical, although he maintained a deep affection for traditional English institutions and customs such as hunting and indeed the Garrick.

He had always wanted to be a writer but was dissuaded by his father, Clifford Mortimer, a blind divorce barrister whom he immortalised in his play *A Voyage Round My Father*. Instead, after Oxford John followed him into the law, and indeed the same speciality: he became an expert at handling "undefendeds"—uncontested divorce cases— in the dark days before the divorce laws were eased in 1969. Understandably bored by the tedium and hypocrisy of divorce work, he switched to a mainly criminal practice after he took silk, and started tilling the fertile ground that was to provide the raw material for Rumpole. He enjoyed the change. "In the end I achieved a far greater admiration for our criminal law than for the peculiar simplifications and superstitions which governed matters of love and marriage," he wrote. "I also found, to my surprise, that alleged criminals were the most pleasant type of client, often being less malevolent than divorced wives in pursuit of their husbands' property, and a great deal less grasping than beneficiaries in will cases." It is the true voice of Rumpole.

As Mortimer's writing career boomed, he changed direction once again in his legal life, to concentrate increasingly on representing authors and publishers whose work was in danger of being censored or banned, starting with the defence of the novel *Last Exit to Brooklyn* by Hubert Selby Junior, "a powerfully written work," as Mortimer put it, "if conspicuously short on the jokes." Full of graphic accounts of drug abuse and homosexual prostitution, the book was banned in a lower court but Mortimer won in the Appeal Court. "I was led into a new department of law which I, in my more elevated moments, called arguments about free speech," he recalled, "but most of the friendly hacks in the robing-room call 'dirty-book cases'." His stylish and witty performances in a stream of such cases brought him to the attention of the wider public as an advocate, matching his increasing fame as a playwright and novelist.

He was an acutely perceptive observer of the law and its practitioners, great and humble, in his fiction and his other writing. "There is no art more transient than that of the advocate, and no life more curious," he mused. In his writing life, he came to know Peter Sellers, who could imitate anybody but somehow lacked substance himself. "In his way, Peter Sellers was like the late Sir Edward Marshall Hall, a man who stood empty, waiting to be inhabited by other people."

Mortimer loved the Garrick, and described it in his novel *Paradise Postponed*, thinly disguised as the Sheridan Club, its members "the sort of Englishman who has never totally recovered from an emotional relationship with his nanny". He was often to be seen at the Garrick until the very end of his long and productive life, beaming beneficently at one and all as he tottered into the Coffee Room for dinner, barely able to walk but determined to enjoy a good evening.

19
GHOSTS AND CONTEMPORARIES

Many ghosts stalk the corridors and dining rooms of the Garrick Club. In the case of the great actors of recent decades, their portraits look down from the walls on today's members. Of the club's departed lawyers, few such memorials survive; they remain alive only in the memory of older members. Some played a significant role in the club's affairs, such as Viscount Bledisloe QC (1899-1979, Garrick 1936-1979), a chairman of the House and General Committees and a senior Trustee, whose son Christopher, the third viscount (1934-2009), was also an active member of the club; Judge William "Billy" Hughes (1915-1990, Garrick 1954-1990), also a Trustee; and Sir Charles Fletcher-Cooke QC (1914-2001, Garrick 1951-2001), once a Conservative MP, who was obliged to resign from his junior government post in 1963 after a louche young man was stopped by the police driving Fletcher-Cooke's limousine along the Commercial Road; Fletcher-Cooke was active in the Garrick and played a key role in promoting the legislation which removed the limits on the number of partners that solicitors' firms could have, paving the way for today's giant partnerships. Conversely, Lord Alexander QC (1936-2005, Garrick 1984-2005) was seen little in the club outside the private dining rooms; he was unquestionably one of the country's leading advocates, who won £500,000 in libel damages for Jeffrey Archer against *The Star* newspaper, which did not look such an admirable achievement when Archer was sent down for perjury some years later. He was also President of the MCC, and instrumental in changing the face of cricket for ever when he successfully represented Kerry Packer and three England cricketers who claimed restraint of trade against the International Cricket Council and the Test and County Cricket Board. A no less keen cricket lover, if not on such an exalted scale, was Judge Michael Hyam (1938-2004, Garrick 1985-2004), who was the Recorder of London (the senior Old Bailey judge), and a modest and delightful centre table companion.

Few members of recent vintage were more widely mourned than Sir Nicholas Pumfrey (1951-2007, Garrick 2003-2007), who dined at the club two or three times a week and was greatly liked. He was a somewhat shambling, portly figure with a genial face topped off by a shock of white hair who was once greatly amused to be mistaken in the Garrick bar for the actor Richard Griffiths. He was a brilliant legal figure, an expert in intellectual property who was appointed a High Court judge at the early age of forty-six and had just been promoted to the Appeal Court at fifty-six at the time of his premature death. He wore his learning lightly and enjoyed riding his motor-bike to court and to his house in the South of France, where he produced his own honey and liked to entertain his many friends.

Still, if you sit down at the centre table of the Garrick you are still liable to find yourself in conversation with some of the leading movers and shakers in the legal world. It might be Ken Clarke, the Justice Secretary; Lord

Neuberger, the Master of the Rolls (Head of the Appeal Court); Lord Irvine, the former Lord Chancellor; or the combative commercial silk Gordon Pollock. It might be one of Lord Neuberger's predecessors, Tony Clarke, now the Supreme Court Justice Lord Clarke of Stone-cum-Ebony, as he is most unlikely to refer to himself, or the Supreme Court's first President, Lord Phillips of Worth Matravers, a member of recent vintage. From the Appeal Court, you are very likely to run into Sir John Laws, Sir Alan Ward or Sir Stephen Tomlinson. From the High Court, one often sees Sir Andrew McFarlane or Sir John Mitting. Tony Butcher QC, a former Chairman of the Trustees, and Joe Harper QC, who looks a bit like Leo McKern as Rumpole but operates at a much more elevated level of the bar, are Garrick institutions. You will almost certainly meet Jonathan Acton Davis QC, an urbane commercial silk and the club's current chairman. William Clegg QC, who has righted a series of miscarriages of justice, is often to be seen there, as is Sir Hugh Bennett, one of whose last tasks before retiring from the High Court was to decide how much Heather Mills should receive from Paul McCartney as a divorce settlement (and see her tip a jug of water over McCartney's lawyer Fiona Shackleton). It all makes for good conversation, as does any encounter with Bob Marshall-Andrews QC, the epitome of the bolshie backbencher when he was a Labour MP, who has inherited John Mortimer's wig and Dick Ferguson's lectern in the hope, he says, of something rubbing off.

One of the club's oldest and most popular members is George Dobry, now ninety-two, who came to Edinburgh as a student from his native Poland in 1936, and was awarded a war degree in 1940. Meanwhile he had volunteered for the Polish army and served through the war in the Polish parachute brigade and air force under British command. As a friend of General Anders, he could not return to Poland after the war so settled in London to study law. He was called to the bar in 1946 and enjoyed a successful career at the planning bar and as a circuit judge. He was finally able to return to Poland in 1989 after an absence of exactly fifty years. You can check him out on his own website. The great tradition of Garrick lawyers continues.

BIBLIOGRAPHY

F.W. Ashley: *My Sixty Years in the Law*. John Lane The Bodley Head, 1936.

William (Mr Serjeant) Ballantine: *Some Experiences of a Barrister's Life*, Vols 1 and 2. Richard Bentley & Son, 1882.

The Old World and the New, Richard Bentley & Son, 1884.

George Pleydell Bancroft: *Stage and Bar*. Faber, 1939.

The Rev R.H. Barham: *The Garrick Club: Notices of One Hundred and Thirty-Five of its Former Members*. 1896.

The Earl of Birkenhead: *Fourteen English Judges*. Cassell, 1926

Law, Life and Letters. Hodder and Stoughton, 1927.

Lord Birkett: *Six Great Advocates*. Penguin Books, 1961

Augustine Birrell: *Sir Frank Lockwood, A Biographical Sketch*. Smith, Elder & Co, 1898.

A.W. Bowker: *A Lifetime with the Law*. W.H. Allen, 1961.

Muriel Box: *Rebel Advocate, A Biography of Gerald Gardiner*. Victor Gollancz, 1983.

Baron Brampton: *The Reminiscences of Sir Henry Hawkins, Baron Brampton*, Vols 1 and 2, edited by Richard Harris KC. Edward Arnold, London, 1904.

Douglas G. Browne: *Sir Travers Humphreys, A Biography*. George G. Harrap & Co, 1960.

John Campbell: *F.E. Smith, First Earl of Birkenhead*. Jonathan Cape, 1983.

Peter Carter-Ruck: *Memoirs of a Libel Lawyer*. Weidenfeld and Nicolson, 1990.

Henry Cecil: *Just Within the Law*. Hutchinson, 1975.

Sir Edward Clarke: *The Story of my Life*. John Murray, 1918.

Sir Charles Gavan Duffy: *The League of North and South*. Chapman & Hall, 1886.

Robin Dunn: *Sword and Wig: Memoirs of a Lord Justice*. Quiller Press, 1993.

Valerie Grove: *A Voyage Round John Mortimer*. Viking, 2007.

Sir Patrick Hastings: *Autobiography*. Heinemann, 1948.

R.F.V. Heuston: *Lives of the Lord Chancellors, 1885-1940*. Clarendon Press, Oxford, 1964.

Lives of the Lord Chancellors, 1940-1970. Clarendon Press, Oxford, 1987.

Christmas Humphreys: *Both Sides of the Circle*. George Allen & Unwin, 1978.

Travers Humphreys: *Criminal Days*. Hodder & Stoughton, 1946.

H. Montgomery Hyde: *Carson: The Life of Sir Edward Carson, Lord Carson of Duncairn*. Heinemann, 1953;

Sir Patrick Hastings, His Life and Cases. Heinemann, 1960.

Lord Reading: The Life of Rufus Isaacs, First Marquess of Reading. Heinemann, 1967.

Norman Birkett: The Life of Lord Birkett of Ulverston. Hamish Hamilton, 1964.

(Editor): *The Lady Chatterley's Lover Trial*. The Bodley Head, 1990.

Robert Jackson: *Case for the Prosecution: A Biography of Sir Archibald Bodkin*. Arthur Barker, 1962.

The Chief: The biography of Gordon Hewart, Lord Chief Justice of England 1922-40. George G. Harrap & Co, 1959.

Roy Jenkins: *Gladstone*. Macmillan, 1995.

The Earl of Kilmuir: *Political Adventure*. Weidenfeld & Nicolson, 1964.

Gordon Lang: *Mr Justice Avory*. Herbert Jenkins, 1935.

Edgar Lustgarten: *Verdict in Dispute*. Wingate, 1949.

Defender's Triumph. Wingate, 1951.

Edward Marjoribanks: *The Life of Sir Edward Marshall Hall*. Gollancz, 1929.

Brian Masters: *Getting Personal*. Constable, 2002.

John Mortimer: *Clinging to the Wreckage*. Weidenfeld and Nicolson, 1982.

Sir David Napley: *Not Without Prejudice*. Harrap, 1982.

Benjamin Coulson (Mr Serjeant) Robinson: *Bench and Bar*. Hurst & Blackett, 1891.

Lord Shawcross: *Life Sentence*. Constable, 1995.

Leslie Stephen: *The Life of Sir James Fitzjames Stephen*. Smith, Elder & Co, 1895.

Derek Walker-Smith and Edward Clarke: *The Life of Sir Edward Clarke*. Thornton Butterworth, 1939.

Montagu Williams QC: *Leaves of a Life*, Vols 1 & 2. Macmillan & Co, 1890.

Later Leaves, Macmillan, 1891.

Geoffrey Wansell: *The Garrick Club: A History*. The Garrick Club, 2004.

NOTES

I have used the online version of the *Oxford Dictionary of National Biography*, so I have not included the relevant dates when referring to the *ODNB*.

Chapter One

Sir Joseph Littledale: *ODNB*, *The Times*, 20 June 1842.
Sir James Wigram, Edmund Phipps: *ODNB*. Sir Thomas
Noon Talfourd: *ODNB*; *Law Magazine*, Vol 51, 1854. Sir
John Adolphus: *ODNB*; Benjamin Coulson (Mr Serjeant)
Robinson, *Bench and Bar*, p66-67; William (Mr Serjeant)
Ballantine: *Some Experiences of a Barrister's Life*, Vol 1, p83-
85; The Rev R.H. Barham: *The Garrick Club: Notices of One
Hundred and Thirty-Five of its Former Members*, p2; Cecil
Roth, *History of the Great Synagogue*, Chapter XII (The
Susser Archive). Robert Cutlar Fergusson: *ODNB*; *Express
& Evening Chronicle*, Maidstone, 12 April, 1798.

Chapter Two

William Ballantine: Anthony Trollope, *Orley Farm*, Oxford
World's Classics, p166, p342; Sir Edward Clarke: *The
Story of my Life*, p81-82; Montagu Williams, *Leaves of a
Life*, Vol 1, p86; William Ballantine: *Some Experiences*, Vol
1: Childhood: p5-11; legal studies, p11-14; Early years in
law, p37-51; Garrick Club: p219-228; Thackeray: p133-
137; Dickens: p138-140; Crimea victims, p319-320; Vol 2:

Arrested with Cockburn, p30-32; Antiquated legal system:
p257-258; Tichborne Claimant trial, p161-186; Gaekwar
of Baroda trial: p207-256; Williams, *Leaves*, Vol 2, p217;
Ballantine: *The Old World and the New*: US tour, p92-111;
Trollope, Reade, p206-208; Jewish witness, Williams,
Leaves, Vol 1, p95-97; Financial difficulties, F.W. Ashley:
My Sixty Years in the Law, p31, Williams, *Leaves*, Vol 2,
p217; Last years, Ashley, p37-38, Williams, *Leaves* Vol 2,
p219.

Chapter Three
Serjeant Parry: Ballantine, *Some Experiences*, p82,
Williams, *Leaves of A Life*, Vol 1, p249-250; *ODNB*; Ashley,
My Sixty Years, p32-33. Montagu Williams: *Leaves*, Vol 1:
Army and acting, p29-55, reflections on defending, p77,
typical day, p296, Garrick Club p308-309; *Later Leaves*,
stipendiary magistrate, p241-411; *ODNB*. Sir Harry Bodkin
Poland: Physique: Ashley, p19; holidays, p25; *ODNB*. Sir
Charles Willie Mathews: Edward Marjoribanks: *The Life
of Sir Edward Marshall Hall*, p90-91; Travers Humphreys:
Criminal Days, p68-70; Edgar Lustgarten: *Defender's
Triumph*, p105-106; *ODNB*.

Chapter Four
William Harrison Ainsworth: *ODNB*; Ballantine, *Some
Confessions*, p331. Tom Taylor: *ODNB*. Francis Stack
Murphy: Robinson: *Bench and Bar*, p234-238; Sir Charles
Gavan Duffy: *The League of North and South*, p211, p229.
Sir John Huddleston, Walter Coulson, Sir Edward
Creasey, Sir James Bacon: *ODNB*. Sir John Rolt: *ODNB*;
Ballantine, *Some Experiences*, p106. Frank Fladgate: T.H.S.
Escott: *Anthony Trollope, His Work, Associates and Originals*,

p146; Ballantine, Vol 1, p227. Edwin James: *ODNB*; *Law Magazine*, February 1862, p263-286; *Illustrated London News*, 13 October 1860, p330; D.J.Taylor, *Thackeray*, p267, p410, p412; *The Reminiscences of Sir Henry Hawkins, Baron Brampton*, Vol 2, p129-133; *The Times*, 7 March 1882.

Chapter Five
Sir John Holker: *ODNB; The Times* 25 May 1882; *Law Magazine*, 26 May 1882; Sir Edward Clarke, *The Story of My Life*, p127; Montagu Williams, *Leaves of A Life*, Vol 2, p44; Ballantine, *Some Experiences*, p455-457. Sir Henry James: *ODNB*, Roy Jenkins: Gladstone, p542. Lord Halsbury: The Earl of Birkenhead: *Fourteen English Judges*, p327-361, Clarke, *My Life*, p82, Williams, *Leaves*, Vol 1, pp273-274, p279. Earl Loreburn: *ODNB*; R.F.V.Heuston: *Lives of the Lord Chancellors, 1885-1940*, p133-180. Sir Frank Lockwood: Augustine Birrell: *Sir Frank Lockwood, A Biographical Sketch*, p3, p27-36, p41-46, p56-57, p80-82, p108-109, p201-202, p209, p213-215; *Pall Mall Gazette*, 10 January, 1898; Lord Finlay: *ODNB*; Heuston, pp313-347; Lord Buckmaster: *ODNB*, Heuston, pp243-308.

Chapter Six
Sir Edward Clarke: Main sources: Derek Walker-Smith and Edward Clarke: *The Life of Sir Edward Clarke*; Sir Edward Clarke: *The Story of my Life*; Lord Birkett: *Six Great Advocates*, p38-39, Edgar Lustgarten: *Defender's Triumph*, p12.

Chapter Seven
Sir James Fitzjames Stephen: Main source: Leslie Stephen: *The Life of Sir James Fitzjames Stephen*; Birkenhead: *Fourteen English Judges*, p304; Edgar Lustgarten: *Verdict in Dispute*, p39-40.

Chapter Eight
Sir Henry Hawkins (Lord Brampton): The *Reminiscences of Sir Henry Hawkins, Baron Brampton*, Vol 1, p3-4, p308-311; Vol 2, p49-64; Travers Humphreys: *Criminal Days*, p149, p155, F.W. Ashley: *My Sixty Years in the Law*, p34, p177-178, p180. Sir Horace Avory: Ashley, p57-58, p 101-102, p110-111, p267, p302; Gordon Lang: *Mr Justice Avory*, p40-46; Henry Cecil: *Just Within the Law*, p64; George Pleydell Bancroft: *Stage and Bar*, p181. Sir Travers Humphreys: Main sources: Douglas G. Browne, *Sir Travers Humphreys, A Biography*, and Sir Travers Humphreys: *Criminal Days*; Christmas Humphreys *Both Sides of the Circle*, p62. Lord Hewart: Main source: Robert Jackson: *The Chief*, p13-14, p36-39, p161-162, p183-184, p197, p199-205, p213-216, p336; Henry Cecil: *Just Within the Law*, p61-62.

Chapter Nine
Edward Carson: Chief source: H. Montgomery Hyde: *The Life of Sir Edward Carson*; Douglas G. Browne: *Sir Travers Humphreys*, p34; *Dictionary of Irish Biography* (online); Humphreys: *Criminal Days*, p92-93; Marjoribanks, *Marshall Hall*, p113-115. Lord Reading: Main source: H. Montgomery Hyde: *Lord Reading: The Life of Rufus Isaacs*; Lord Birkett: *Six Great Advocates*, p58.

Chapter Ten
Sir Archibald Bodkin: Main source: Robert Jackson: *Case for the Prosecution: A Biography of Sir Archibald Bodkin*; Sir Patrick Hastings: Main source: H. Montgomery Hyde: *Sir Patrick Hastings, His Life and Cases*; Hastings, *Autobiography*, p246. Birkett quote: Hyde, Foreword, xiii-xiv.

Chapter Eleven
Sir Edward Marshall Hall: Main source: Edward Marjoribanks: *The Life of Sir Edward Marshall Hall*; Birkenhead: *Law, Life and Letters*, p286, p289-291, p294-296; Birkett, *Six Great Advocates*, p16; Lustgarten, *Defender's Triumph*, p81-144; Bancroft: *Stage and Bar*, p240; Hastings, *Autobiography*, p132. Lord Birkett: Main source: H. Montgomery Hyde: *Norman Birkett: The Life of Lord Birkett of Ulverston*; A.W. Bowker: *A Lifetime with the Law*, p69-70; Lustgarten, *Defender's Triumph*, p200, 201, p211; *Political Adventure: The Memoirs of the Earl of Kilmuir*, p100.

Chapter Twelve
Lord Birkenhead: Main source: John Campbell: *F.E. Smith, First Earl of Birkenhead*; Evelyn Waugh, *Diaries*, 11 July 1924.

Chapter Thirteen
Christmas Humphreys: Main source: *Both Sides of the Circle: The Autobiography of Christmas Humphreys*. Harry Leon: Main source: Henry Cecil: *Just Within the Law*; Author interview, Stanley Prothero, February 2011. Sir Aubrey Melford Stevenson: *ODNB*; Robin Dunn: *Sword*

and Wig, p142; Napley, p223; *Cam Magazine*, Michaelmas Term, 2010; Geoffrey Wansell: *The Garrick Club*, p113. Sir Frederick Lawton: *ODNB*; Napley, p134; *Daily Telegraph*, 6 February 2001.

Chapter Fourteen
Lord Shawcross: Main source: *Life Sentence: The Memoirs of Lord Shawcross*; *Daily Telegraph*, 11 July 2003. Lord Kilmuir: Main source: *Political Adventure: The Memoirs of the Earl of Kilmuir*. Lord Gardiner: Main source: Muriel Box: *Rebel Advocate, A Biography of Gerald Gardiner*; H. Montgomery Hyde (Editor): *The Lady Chatterley's Lover Trial*, p1-48.

Chapter Fifteen
Main sources: Sir David Napley: *Not Without Prejudice*; Peter Carter-Ruck: *Memoirs of a Libel Lawyer*; *The Guardian*, 23 December, 2003.

Chapter Sixteen
Russell family: *ODNB*; Sir Cecil Havers: *The Times*, 11 May 1977; Sir Michael Havers: *ODNB*; Margaret Thatcher, *The Downing Street Years*, p228; Sir Richard Rougier: *Daily Telegraph*, 27 July 2007.

Chapter Seventeen

George Carman: Main source: Dominic Carman: *No Ordinary Man*; Napley, *Not Without Prejudice*, p342-343; *Daily Telegraph*, 3 January, 2011; Author interview, Robert Marshall-Andrews, March 2011. Richard Ferguson: Author interviews, Roma Ferguson, Lord Falconer, Robert Marshall-Andrews, March 2011; *The Times*, 30 July 2009; *The Independent*, 31 July 2009; *Daily Telegraph*, 10 August 2009; *The Guardian*, 11 August 2009.

Chapter Eighteen

James Crespi: Brian Masters, *Getting Personal*, p283-288; Carman, p16; Author interview, Leonard Krikler, February 2011; Sir Michael Davies, *The Garrick,* No 9, February 2004. Lord Taylor: *ODNB*; Author interviews, Sir Alan Ward, Hon Louis Taylor, Lord Falconer, March 2011; Carman, p97; Rabbi Roderick Young, personal memoir, March 2011. Anthony Babington: Main source: Anthony Babington: *An Uncertain Voyage*; *Daily Telegraph*, 25 May 2004. Sir Michael Davies: *The Garrick*, No 20, November 2006. John Mortimer: Main sources: Mortimer, *Clinging to the Wreckage*, Valerie Grove, *A Voyage Round John Mortimer*.

APPENDIX

LAWYER MEMBERS OF THE GARRICK CLUB 1831-2011
NAME AND DATES OF BIRTH & DEATH (WHEN KNOWN)
WITH YEARS OF MEMBERSHIP

A
—

John Thomas Abdy (1822-1899) 1865-1893
Gilbert Abbott à Beckett (1811-1856) 1843-1850
William J.A. Abington *Elected in* 1837
Anthony Claud Walter Abrahams (1923-2011) 1965-2011
Harold Maurice Abrahams (1899-1978) 1953-1978
Sir Edward Acton (1865-1945) 1921-1939
Jonathan Acton Davis, Q.C. (b.1953) *Elected in* 1992
Captain John Roland Adams 1940-1969
John Adolphus (1768-1845) *Original member*-1834
Philip L. Agnew (1863-1938) 1899-1938
Robert Albert *Elected in* 1977
Michael James Albery, Q.C. (d.1975) 1953-1975
Lt. Colonel Fredcric Bower Alcock 1958-1967
David R.J. Alexander, Q.C. (b.1964) *Elected in* 2003
Robert Scott Alexander, Baron Alexander, Q.C. (1936-2005) 1984-2005
Archibald John Allen 1904-1914
Robert Allen (d.1854) 1853-1854
Peter Henry Bruce Allsop 1964-2010
Anthony J. Anderson, Q.C. (b.1938) *Elected in* 1981
Sir Francis Robert Anderton (d.1950) 1879-1917; 1931-1946
William P. Andreae-Jones, Q.C. (b.1942) 1994-2004
Biggs Andrews, Q.C. (1795-1880) 1831-1834
Charles Appleyard (d.1882) 1853-1882
Richard Arabin (d.1865) 1847-1865
Francis Kendray Archer, K.C. 1935-1937
John G. Archibald 1948-1962

Joseph Arden (1799-1879) 1834-1879
Percy Arden (d.1909) 1883-1909
Major Ronald Owen Lloyd Armstrong-Jones, Q.C. (1899-1966) 1953-1966
Francis R. Armytage (d.1907) 1878-1907
A.W. Arnold (d.1889) 1847-1889
Sir Joseph Arnould (1813-1886) 1863-1869; 1875-1886
Edward Gibson, 1st Baron Ashbourne (1837-1913) 1876-1893
Lionel Robert Ashburner (1827-1907) 1867-1895
Hon. (Anthony) Evelyn Ashley (1836-1907) 1864-1871
Arthur Ashton, K.C. (d.1925) 1889-1920
G.R. Askwith (d.1904) 1890-1904
Sir Algernon Edward Aspinall (1871-1952) 1903-1926; 1928-1933
Butler Aspinall, K.C. (1861-1935) 1927-1930
Sir John Meir Astbury (1860-1939) 1920-1939
Percy Harland Atkin (d.1938) 1895-1938
Sir Edward Hale Tindal Atkinson (1878-1957) 1906-1929
George Atkinson 1842-1857
John Atkinston, Baron Atkinson (1844-1932) 1889-1903
James Beresford Atlay (1860-1912) 1901-1912
David Aukin (b.1942) 1986-1996
Ian Hamilton Shearer, Baron Avonside (1914-1996) 1953-1983
Sir Horace Edmund Avory (1851-1935) 1897-1935
Thomas Ayscough *Elected and resigned in* 1831

B
—

Anthony Patrick Babington (1920-2004) 1964-2004

Patrick Back, Q.C. (1917-2003) 1975-2003

Francis Bacon 1835-1868

Francis Henry Bacon (d.1911) 1877-1911

George Bacon 1844-1852

Henry Bacon *Elected in* 1837

Sir James Bacon (1798-1895) 1834-1870

Peter Badge (1931-1997) 1993-1997

Thomas S. Badger 1850-c.1865

Sir Arthur Bagnall (d.1976) 1952-1976

Frederic G. Bagshawe 1890-1908

Robert Bailey-King, 1973-2010

Donald Charles Bain, M.C. (d.1956) 1948-1956

Sir John Forster Baird (d.1882) 1870-1882

Sir (Alfred) John Balcombe (1925-2000) 1975-2000

David J. Balcombe, Q.C. (b.1958) *Elected in* 1994

Tony Baldry (b.1950) *Elected in* 2006

Andrew Baldwin (b.1943) *Elected in* 1984

William Ballantine (1812-1887) 1850-1881

Robert H. Balloch 1907-1927

George Pleydell Bancroft (1868-1956) 1890-1931; 1943-1953

John W. Bankes 1967-2002

Ralph Vincent Bankes 1893-1898

Clement Milton Barber (d.1942) 1916-1942

Arthur P. Barlow 1846-1860

Francis Barlow, Q.C. (b.1938) *Elected in* 1990

Adrian Barnes, C.V.O. (b.1943) *Elected in* 2004

Sir Frederic Gorell Barnes (1856-1939) 1887-1921

Richard Vaughan Barnewall (1799/80-1842) 1832-1836

David Barr (b.1925) *Elected in* 1976

Sir Fiennes Barrett-Leonard, 5th Bt. (1880-1963) 1914-1932

Thomas Irwin Barstow (d.1889) *Elected and died in* 1889

Ronald D. Bartle *Elected in* 1982

Sir Dunbar Plunket Barton, K.C. (1853-1937) 1924-1937

John Bass (d.1954) 1951-1954

Nigel Fox Bassett (1929-2008) 1983-1987

Stewart Bates, Q.C. (d.1999) 1975-1999

Andrew Bateson, Q.C. 1973-1988

Sir Dingwall Latham Bateson, M.C. (1898-1967) 1926-1939

Bathurst, *see also* Bledisloe

Algernon Bathurst 1912-1931

Sir Maurice Bathurst, Q.C. (d.2004) 1967-2004

Lauriston Batten K.C. (1863-1934) 1889-1934

Charles Beal (d.1921) 1896-1921

Sir William Phipson Beale, Q.C. (1839-1922) 1891-1914

William Hastings Beckett (d.1906) 1882-1906

George Bedford *Original member*-1833

John Beechey (b.1952) *Elected in* 2008

Thomas L. Behan (d.1869) 1850-1869

George W. Bell 1889-1906

Sir Christopher Bellamy, Q.C. (b.1946) *Elected in* 2001

Archibald Bence-Jones (1856-1937) 1894-1903

Sir Charles Wilfrid Bennett, 2nd Bt. (1898-1952) 1947-1952

Sir Hugh Bennett (b.1943) *Elected in* 2006

Nigel B. Bennett (b.1945) *Elected in* 2006

Ralph A. Benson 1859-1866

Augustus Fitzhardinge Maurice Berkeley (d.1991) 1955-1991

Rowland Thomas Mortimer Berkeley (1867-1924) 1904-1924

Henry Berners (d.1900) 1873-1900

Adrian L. Berrill-Cox (b.1964) *Elected in* 1992

His Hon. Montague Berryman, K.C. (d.1974) 1947-1974

Frederick Ponsonby, 6th Earl of Bessborough (1815-1895) 1860-1895

Oscar Beuselinck (d.1997) 1981-1997

Edward Julian Bevan, Q.C. (b.1940) 1976-2010

Peter James Stuart Bevan 1962-1967

William Bevan 1840-1857

John Roger Bickford-Smith (d.1996) 1972-1996

Stephen W. Bickford-Smith (b.1949) *Elected in* 2002

Claud Bicknell (1910-2002) 1972-2002

Charles Oliver Bigg (d.1917) 1891-1917

Geoffrey Bindman (b.1933) 1981-1983

Ernest E. Bird (d.1945) 1912-1945

Ellis Birk (d.2004) 1977-2004

F.E. Smith, 1st Earl of Birkenhead (1872-1930) 1921-1930

(William) Norman Birkett, 1st Baron Birkett (1883-1962) 1942-1948

Richard Birnie 1837-1846

Sir Chartres Biron (1863-1940) 1906-1940

Hon. Sir William A. Blackburne (b.1944) *Elected in* 2002

His Hon. Andrew J. Blackett-Ord *Elected in* 1966

Robert Blackmore 1831-1839

Sir Ernley Blackwell (1868-1941) 1906-1925; 1930-1938

His Hon. John Basil Blagden (d.1964) 1952-1964

Anthony Bland (d.1989) 1954-1989

Sir Robert Younger, Baron Blanesburgh (1861-1946) 1920-1940

Benjamin Bathurst, 2nd Viscount Bledisloe (1899-1979) 1936-1979

Christopher Bathurst, 3rd Viscount Bledisloe (1934-2009) 1959-2009

His Hon. Frank Blennerhassett, Q.C. (1916-1993) 1975-1978

Lionel Bloch (d.1998) 1981-1998

His Hon. L.K.A. Block, D.S.C. 1966-1967

Frederick W. Blunt 1877-1886

His Hon. (John) Graham Boal, Q.C. (b.1943) *Elected in* 1974

John Symonds Bockett (d.1884) 1874-1884

Sir Archibald Henry Bodkin (1862-1957) 1889-1957

William P. Bolland *Elected in* 1846

Thomas Henry Bolton (1841-1916) 1882-1916

His Hon. Guy Boney, Q.C. (b.1944) *Elected in* 2001

Gordon Borrie, Baron Borrie QC (b. 1931) *Elected in 1988*

Percy D. Botterell 1928-1946

George Boulton 1881-1897

Hon. Robert Bourke, *later* 1st Baron Connemara (1827-1902) 1850-1853

Sir (John) Wilfrid Bourne (1922-1999) 1956-1974

Martin Bowdery, Q.C. (b.1956) *Elected in* 2007

Michael Bowers (d.2000) 1986-2000

Henry P. Bowie (d.1920) 1910-1920

Martin Richard Bowley, Q.C. (b.1936) *Elected in* 2007

Edward Charles Percy Boyd 1916-1934

Percy Boyd 1854-1857

Peter Boydell, Q.C. (1920-2001) 1951-2001

Sir Edward Boyle, 2nd Bt. (1878-1945) 1909-1931; 1936-1945

Sir Derek Bradbeer (b.1931) *Elected in* 2001

William Laurence Bradbury 1890-1919

Paul Braddon 1936-1941

John M. Bradshaw (b.1938) *Elected in* 2009

Sir Francis William Brady, 2nd Bt., Q.C. (1824-1909) 1876-1909

Henry Hawkins, Baron Brampton (1817-1907) 1855-1886

George Bramwell, 1st Baron Bramwell (1808-1892) 1850-1856

George Daubeney Brandreth (d.1982) 1959-1982

Hon. Sir Nicolas D. Bratza (b.1945) *Elected in* 1981

Daniel Brennan, Baron Brennan, Q.C. (b.1942) *Elected in* 2003

Nicolas Bridges-Adams (d.1998) 1966-1998

Edward Bright 1856-1884

Frank Pudey Brindley (d.1965) 1954-1958; 1962-1965

Peter H.R. Bristow 1938-1950

William John Broderip (1789-1859) 1836-c.1840

William Broderip 1847-1866

Michael G. Bromley-Martin, Q.C. (b.1955) *Elected in* 2002

John Austin Brown (d.1996) 1959-1996

Frederick William Brown (d.1933) 1904-1933

Michael J. Brown 1982-1993

Simon Brown, Baron Brown of Eaton-under-Heywood (b.1937) *Elected in* 1999

Rt.Hon. Sir Stephen Brown (b.1924) *Elected in* 1972

His Hon. Nicholas Browne, Q.C. (b.1947) *Elected in* 2011

Sir Patrick Browne (1907-1996) 1935-1996

Nicholas Browne-Wilkinson, Baron Browne-Wilkinson (b.1930) 1986-1989; *re-elected in* 2008

Derek Walker-Smith, Baron Broxbourne, Q.C. (1910-1992) 1983-1992

John Wyndham Bruce (1809-1868) 1842-1860

A.G. Bryant, M.C. (d.1967) 1930-1967

Guy James McLean Buckley (b.1936) *Elected in* 1978

John Maclean Buckley (d.1972) 1938-1972

Thomas George McLean Buckley (1932-2011) 1966-1973

Stanley Owen Buckmaster, 1st Viscount Buckmaster (1861-1934) 1909-1934

William Perkins Bull, K.C. (1870-1948) 1919-1948

James E. Bullen (b.1943) 1989-2006

Thomas Borrow Burcham (d.1869) 1857-1866

James Charles Burge 1953-1967

Peter Burke (1811-1881) 1868-1881

Sir Richard Frank Burnand (1887-1969) 1927-1966

Clive Stuart Saxon Burt (1900-1981) 1951-1981

Frederick Edwin Bushell (d.1928) 1893-1928

Anthony J. Butcher, Q.C. (b.1934) *Elected in* 1975

His Hon. Gerald Butler, Q.C. (1930-2010) 1997-2010

Richard Butler (d.1965) 1964-1965

Simon D. Butler (b.1971) *Elected in* 2003

Woodfin Lee Butte (1908-1981) 1959-1981

Wilfrid Allen Button 1944-1953

C
—

Benjamin Bond Cabbell (1782-1874) 1847-1874

Peter Cadbury (1918-2006) 1950-1969

Hon. Edward Cadogan (b.1880) 1908-1909

Thomas Inskip, 1st Viscount Caldecote (1876-1947)

George Caldwell 1833-1834

His Hon. Clive V. Callman (b.1927) *Elected in* 2000

Jeremy D. Callman (b.1969) *Elected in* 2006

Sir R.F. Graham Campbell (d.1946) 1899-1946

Brian Capstick, Q.C. (1927-2005) 1980-2005

Hugh B.H. Carlisle, Q.C. (b.1937) *Elected in* 1984

Mark Carlisle, Baron Carlisle of Bucklow, Q.C. (1929-2005) 1975-2005

George Carman, Q.C. (1929-2001) 1982-2001

Sir Robert Carnwath, Q.C. (b.1945) 1985-1996

Sir Edward Carson, Baron Carson (1854-1935) 1896-1921

Peter Carter-Ruck (1914-2003) 1975-2003

Michael Cartwright-Sharp 1968-1977

Joseph Cary (d.1875) 1845-1875

William N.P. Cash, M.P. (b.1940) *Elected in 2002*

Sir Harold Cassel, 3rd Bt. (1916-2001) 1960-1966

Timothy F.H. Cassel, Q.C. (b.1942) *Elected in 1981*

Sir James Dales Cassels (1877-1972) 1925-1928

Henry Casson (1830-1902) 1874-1902

Philip J.B. Cayford, Q.C. (b.1952) *Elected in 2009*

Sir Edward Cazalet, Q.C. (b.1936) *Elected in 1981*

Deiniol J. Cellan Jones (b.1965) *Elected in 1999*

Sir Charles E.H. Chadwyck-Healey, 1st Bt. (1845-1919) 1882-1919

Henry William Challis (d.1898) 1892-1898

Richard Chamberlain 1966-1997

Montague Chambers, Q.C. (1799-1885) 1860-1885

His Hon. Nicholas M. Chambers, Q.C. (b.1944) *Elected in 1981*

Sir Thomas Chambers (1814-1891) 1842-1852

Edgar Charles Chancellor 1945-1948

Sir Arthur Charles (b.1840) 1864-1892

Henry E. Chilton 1834-1835

His Hon. Michael W.M. Chism (b.1931) *Elected in 1999*

Edward Chitty (d.1920) 1873-1920

J.H. Christie 1835-c.1840

Francis Chronnell *Elected in 1994*

Henry B. Churchill (d.1881) 1841-1881

Louis Claiborne (1927-1999) 1976-1999

His Hon. Paul Clark (1940-2008) 1989-2008

Anthony Clarke, Baron Clarke of Stone-cum-Ebony (b.1943) *Elected in 1999*

Sir Edward George Clarke, Q.C. (1841-1931) 1884-1931

His Hon. Edward Clarke, Q.C. (d.1989) 1943-1989

Rt. Hon. Kenneth Clarke, Q.C., M.P. (b.1940) *Elected in 1993*

His Hon. Sir Jonathan Clarke (b.1930) *Elected in 1999*

Sir (Edward) Percival Clarke (1872-1936) 1894-1936

Peter W. Clarke, Q.C. (b.1950) *Elected in 1984*

Robert George Clarke 1842-1850

Thomas Clarke 1831-1838; 1840-c.1845

Frederick Clarkson 1854-1860

Haviland Clayton (d.1876) 1851-1876

Sir Walter Clegg (1920-1994) 1978-1993

William Clegg, Q.C. (b.1949) *Elected in 1998*

Robert Clinton, C.V.O. (b.1948) *Elected in 2005*

Christopher Clogg (b.1936) 1990-2006

Philip G. Clough *Elected in 1968*

John Francis Scott Cobb, Q.C. 1975-1976

John F. Cobbett *Elected and resigned in 1909*

John Morgan Cobbett (1800-1877) 1856-1874

Charles Moss Cockle 1886-1901

George Cockle (d.1900) 1884-1900

Sir James Cockle (1819-1895) 1880-1895

David J. Cocks, Q.C. (b.1935) *Elected in 1986.*

Sir Benjamin Arthur Cohen, K.C. (1862-1942) 1934-1942

Jonathan L. Cohen, Q.C. (b.1951) *Elected in 2000*

Lionel Cohen, K.C., *later* Baron Cohen (1888-1973) 1931-1946

Sir Arthur Colefax (1866-1936) 1917-1936

Henry Collinson *Elected in 1845*

Timothy J. Comyn (b.1951) *Elected in 2002*

Sir Michael B. Connell (b.1939) *Elected in 2000*

Peter Coni, Q.C. (b.1935) 1977-1992

His Hon. Jeremy G. Connor (b.1938) *Elected in 1982*

Sir John Coode-Adams (1859-1934) 1905-1934

Geoffrey Coode-Adams (b.1899) 1926-1962

Edward Cooke 1855-1861

George Wingrove Cooke (1814-1865) *Elected and died in 1865*

Stephen Cooke (b.1946) *Elected in 2005*

His Hon. Michael Coombe (1930-2007) 2002-2007

Gilead Cooper, Q.C. (b.1955) *Elected in 2011*

Major Richard Philip Cooper (1902-1966) 1937-1966

Colonel Charles Copeman 1919-1938

James Corbett, Q.C. (b.1952) *Elected in 2009*

His Hon Michael Corkery, Q.C. (b.1926) *Elected in 2003*

His Hon. Professor Eugene Cotran (b.1938) 1985-1991

C. Ronald L. Coubrough *Elected in 1977*

Walter Coulson, Q.C. (1795-1860) 1832-1833; 1844-1860

Edward Cousins (b.1943) *Elected in 2011*

His Hon. Peter R. Cowell (b.1942) *Elected in 1999*

Hugh Cowie, Q.C. (1829-1886) 1870-1885

Neill D. Cox 1957-1964

Eric E. Crabtree (1913-1995) 1981-1995

Norman Craig 1907-1910

Lucius Fairchild Crane 1930-1939

Leslie E. Cranfield (d.1962) 1958-1962

George Morland Crawford (1812-1885) 1840-1850

His Hon. Peter Crawford, Q.C. (b.1929) 1990-1996

S. Creaser 1838-1841

Sir Edward Shepherd Creasy (1812-1878) 1837-1838

Richard D. Creed (b.1939) 1977-1981

James Crespi, Q.C. (1928-1992) 1976-1992

Francis Henry Cripps-Day 1917-1936

J. Hugh Crisp (b.1958) *Elected in* 1999

Commander Leonard Critchley 1971-1995; *re-elected in* 2000

Alistair C. Croft (b.1977) *Elected in* 2009

Lewis Crombie *Elected in* 1831

Sir David Croom-Johnson, D.S.C. (1914-2000) 1943-2000

Sir Reginald Croom-Johnson (1879-1957) 1922-1957

Max Cullinan (d.1884) 1871-1884

William F. Cullinan 1879-1893

Sir John Robert Ellis Cunliffe 1920-1939

Sir Joseph Herbert Cunliffe 1925-1939

Robert Cunliffe (d.1903) 1882-1903

David J.C. Cunningham (b.1945) *Elected in* 2001

James Currie 1831-1832

Peter Curry, Q.C. 1979-1980

Sir Richard H. Curtis (b.1933) *Elected in* 1997

Derek Curtis-Bennett (*c.*1904-1956) 1938-1950

Sir Henry Curtis-Bennett (1879-1936) 1919-1936

Sir Ralph Vincent Cusack (1916-1978) 1966-1978

D
—

Sir Harold Otto Danckwerts (1888-1978) 1909-1931

W.O. Danckwerts (d.1914) 1883-1914

John Stuart Daniel, Q.C. (d.1977) 1963-1977

John P.C. Danny 1978-1997

Paul Darling, Q.C. (b.1960) *Elected in* 2009

Joseph Henry Dart (1817-1887) 1864-1887

Alan Herbert Davidson (d.1919) 1902-1919

James Bridge Davidson (1824-1885) *Elected in* 1846

Nigel G. Davidson 1908-1913

Sir Michael Davies (1921-2006) 1969-2006

William L.M. Davies, Q.C. 1977-1995

Major Arthur Henry Davis, D.S.O. (d.1932) 1928-1932

F.M. Drummond Davis 1862-1863

Sir Henry Davison (d.1860) 1850-1860

Douglas Day, Q.C. (b.1943) *Elected in* 2001

Joseph Jolyon Dean, Q.C. (1921-2010) 1955-1975; 1993-2010

Martin Dean *Elected in 1966*

Stephen Richard Dean 1943-1980

Charles Deane (d.1865) *Elected in* 1854 & 1858-1865

Richard de Lacy, Q.C. (b.1954) *Elected in* 2011

André L. De Moller (b.1942) *Elected in* 1979

Simon N. Denison, Q.C. (b.1961) *Elected in* 2007

His Hon. W. Neil Denison, Q.C. (b.1929) *Elected in* 1979

John David Michael Denny 1959-1964

Alan De Piro, Q.C. 1955-1973

Sir Henry Fielding Dickens, K.C. (1849-1933) 1875-1876

James Dickinson, K.C. (d.1933) 1927-1933

John Henry Dillon 1856-1869

John Dixon (d.1918) 1866-1918

His Hon. George Dobry, C.B.E., Q.C. (b.1918) *Elected in* 1980

J. Hume Dodgson (d.1891) 1875-1891

John Doherty 1861-1871

Joseph Douglas (d.1852) 1831-1852

Ian W. Dove, Q.C. (b.1963) *Elected in* 2006

George Morley Dowdeswell, Q.C. (d.1893) 1839-1893

Dominic M. Dowley, Q.C. (b.1958) *Elected in* 2000

Edward Dowling 1835-*c.*1845

William Dowling 1843-1868

Richard Vigors Doyne (1824-1897) 1869-1897

Sir William Richard Drake (1817-1890) 1869-1890

Warwick Draper (d.1926) 1925-1926

Sir John M. Drinkwater, Q.C. (b. 1925) *Elected in 1966*

Douglas James W. Dryburgh (d.1987) 1948-1987

A. Gordon Duff 1879-1884

Harry Duff 1882-1894

Duke, *see* Merrivale

Sir Robert Ernest Dummett (1872-1941) 1921-1941

Anthony Dumont (d.1979) 1975-1979

John Dunbar 1871-*c.*1878

Patrick Butler, Baron Dunboyne (1917-2004) 1955-1964

Sir Laurence Rivers Dunne, M.C. (1893-1970) 1938-1970

Joseph William Dunning (1833-1897) 1862-1897

Lewis Duval (1774-1844) 1838-1844

Professor Ronald Dworkin (b.1931) *Elected in* 1976

J.J. Dykes 1946-1983

E

Sir Michael Eastham (1920-1993) 1980-1993
J.T. Edgerley 1947-1966
Thomas Ker Edie 1961-1969
Andrew Edwards (d.2003) 1975-2003
Anthony W.C. Edwards (b.1946) *Elected in* 2004
Brian Ernest Edwards 1968-1999
Christopher D.K. Edwards (b.1953) *Elected in* 1992
E. Watkin Edwards 1845-c.1868
John Michael Edwards, Q.C. (d.2007) 1968-2007
Commander Patrick Harrington Edwards, D.S.O. (d.1945) 1930-1945
Richard Lionel Edwards, Q.C. (1907-1984) 1930-1966
Charles Cuthbert Eley (c.1873-1960) 1901-1917
Frederick Boileau Elliott (d.1881) 1866-1881
John Elliott 1856-c.1865
Charles Ellis *Original member* 1836
His Hon. Christopher Elwen (b.1944) *Elected in* 2006
Robert M. Englehart, Q.C. (b.1943) *Elected in* 1993
Sir William Erle, Q.C. (1793-1880) 1854-1871
Erleigh, Viscount *see* Reading, 2nd Marquess of
David C.L. Etherington, Q.C. (b.1953) *Elected in* 2009
Charles Seddon Evans (d.1956) 1933-1956
H. Nicholas Evans (b.1945) *Elected in* 2003
Jack Evans 1964-1984
James Evans, C.B.E. (b. 1932) *Elected in 1967*
John Field Evans, Q.C. 1975-1978
Sir Samuel Evans (1859-1918) 1912-1918
Sir Edward Eveleigh (b.1917) 1975-2008
John Michael Evelyn (1916-1992) 1960-1992
William Everett 1832-1835
Raymond Evershed, K.C., 1st Baron Evershed (1899-1966) 1931-1948; 1952-1966

F

Frederick Arthur Greer, 1st Baron Fairfield (1863-1945) 1919-1926
Robert George Cecil Fane (1796-1864) 1831-1832
Francis Edwin Essington Farebrother 1897-1925
Frank Farrer 1891-1915
George Farrer 1864-1882
Henry L. Farrer 1890-1920
Sir George Farwell (1845-1915) 1882-1915
John Joseph Faulkner (d.1910) 1898-1910
Edward Faulks, Baron Faulks, Q.C. (b.1950) *Elected in 1982*
Henry Fellows (d.1910) 1889-1910

Thomas Howard Fellows (1822-1878) 1845-1852
Richard Ferguson, Q.C. (1935-2009) 2001-2009
Thomas Benyon Ferguson (1836-1875) 1861-1873
Robert Cutlar Fergusson (1768-1838) 1831-1834
Jonathan M. Ferris (b.1955) *Elected in* 1993
His Hon. Sir Richard A. Field (b.1947) *Elected in* 1994
St John Field (d.1949) 1912-1949
Lieutenant Colonel George Fladgate Finch (d.1983) 1919-1983
George William Finch (d.1937) 1892-1937
Sir Robert Finch (b.1944) *Elected in* 2006
David M. Fingleton (1941-2006) 1982-2006
His Hon. Peter Fingret (b.1934) *Elected in* 1994
Sir Robert Bannatyne Finlay, 1st Viscount Finlay (1842-1929) 1871-1919
Bruce A. Fireman (b.1944) *Elected in* 1998
Gerald Fitzgibbon, Q.C. (1837-1909) 1877-1909
Francis Fladgate (d.1892) 1832-1892
Sir William Francis Fladgate (d.1937) 1878-1937
William Mark Fladgate (1806-1888) 1865-1888
John Woulfe Flanagan 1887-1910
Sir Julian M. Flaux (b.1955) *Elected in* 2002
John Brett Fletcher (d.1993) 1970-1993
Sir Charles Fletcher-Cooke, Q.C. (1914-2001) 1951-2001
F. Stuart Fleuret (d.1945) 1930-1945
Michael F. Flint (b.1932) *Elected in* 2007
Wickham Flower (d.1904) 1894-1904
William Flower *Elected in* 1831
Sir Christopher D. Floyd (b.1952) *Elected in* 1995
Edgar Foà 1932-1940
Sir Dingle Mackintosh Foot, Q.C. (1905-1978) 1953-1978
Sir Thayne Forbes (b.1938) *Elected in* 2006
Edward W. Fordham (d.1956) 1946-1956
His Hon. Jeremy Fordham *Elected in* 1982
Wilfrid Gurney Fordham, Q.C. 1965-1984
Arthur Francis Forster (d.1932) 1908-1932
John Henry Forster 1869-1904
Ralph W.E. Forster (d.1879) 1869-1879
William Langford Foulkes (d.1887) 1857-1887
Bertram M. Fournier (1922-1992) 1977-1992
Sir Michael Fox (1921-2007) 1978-2002
Nigel Fox Bassett (1929-2008) 1983-2008
Walter Frampton 1947-1959
Ian Fraser, Baron Fraser of Tullybelton (1911-1989) 1979-1985
William Fraser 1832-1834
Sir Christopher James Saunders French (1925-2003) 1962-2002
John William Corrie Frere (d.1918) 1908-1918
Philip B. Frere, M.C. 1934-1938

W.E. Frere (d.1900) 1879-1900
Hon. Sir Adrian Fulford (b.1953) *Elected in* 2006
Peter S. Fullerton (b.1943) *Elected in* 2004
Grenville Richard Fulton 1913-1920
Sir David Maxwell Fyfe, K.C. (1900-1967), *later*
1ˢᵗ Earl of Kilmuir 1942-1949

G
—

William Edward Louis Gaine (d.1907) 1906-1907
Michael Gale, Q.C. (b.1932) *Elected in* 2005
Gerald Austin Gardiner, Baron Gardiner (1900-1990) 1925-1990
Sir Edward Gardner, Q.C. (1912-2001) 1955-2001
Nicholas Garrett (b.1936) 1978-1995
Dr. Curt Walter Gasteyger (b.1929) 1966-2006
Major Vernon R.M. Gattie (1885-1966) 1915-1939
Charles R. George, Q.C. (b.1945) *Elected in* 2006
Denis Gerrard, Q.C. 1947-1956
Gibson, *see* Ashbourne
Sir Ralph Gibson (1922-2003) 1986-1999
Giffard, *see* Halsbury
Michael Francis Gilbert (1912-2006) 1956-2006
Arthur Edmund Gill 1890-1931
Sir Charles Frederick Gill, Q.C. (d.1923) 1888-1923
Ian Hedworth Gilmour, *later* Baron Gilmour (1926-2007) 1955-1964
Il Duca Lorenzo Giovene di Girasole (b.1936) *Elected in* 1978
Henry Paterson Gisborne (d.1953) 1937-1953
David John Gladwell *Elected in* 1976
Edwin John Glasgow, Q.C. (b.1945) *Elected in* 2007
Anthony T. Glass, Q.C. (b. 1940) *Elected in* 1993
John Inglis, Baron Glencorse (1810-1891) 1856-1860
Ian B. Glick, Q.C. (b.1948) *Elected in* 2010
Rt.Hon. Sir Iain Glidewell, Q.C. (b.1924) *Elected in* 1976
Clayton Louis Glyn (1857-1915) 1902-1913
John F. Goble (b.1925) *Elected in* 1978
Rayner Goddard, Baron Goddard (1877-1971) *Elected and resigned in* 1930
Hugh Charles Godfray (d.1918) 1912-1918
Hugh Marshall Godfray (d.1924) 1919-1924
Joseph Silvester Godfrey (d.1893) 1879-1893
Laszlo Gombos 1955-1991
Douglas Goodbody 1942-1992
Edward Wallace Goodlake 1854-1881
Martin A.F. Goodwin (b.1949) *Elected in* 2011
Francis C. Gore 1874-1888
Charles Frederick Goss (d.1893) 1888-1893

Gerald W. Gouriet, Q.C. (b.1947) *Elected in* 1982
Anthony Grabiner, Baron Grabiner, Q.C. (b.1945) *Elected in* 1978
Percy R. Grace 1868-1870
Wing Commander Sir Patrick Graham, Q.C. (1906-1993) 1943-1950
Toby Graham (b.1965) *Elected in* 2007
Sir Peter Grain 1919-1933
William Grapel (d.1888) 1870-1888
Albert Gray 1889-1906
James Hunter Gray, K.C. (d.1925) 1917-1925
Robert M.K. Gray, Q.C. (1936-1996) 1978-1996
William Howard Gray 1913-1916
Sir Allan Green, Q.C. (b.1935) *Elected in* 2004
Andrew J.D. Green, Q.C. (b.1965) *Elected in* 2001
His Hon. Barry S. Green, Q.C. (1932-2004) 1989-2004
David J.M. Green, Q.C. (b.1954) *Elected in* 2001
Henry Green, Q.C. *Elected in* 1981
D.N.K. Gregson (d.1962) 1946-1962
Lt.Col. Charles James Salkeld Green, D.S.O., M.C. (d.1962) 1904-1962
Henry David Greene, Q.C. (d.1915) 1867-1915
Greer, *see* Fairfield
Sir Henry Holman Gregory, K.C. (1864-1947) 1914-1922
Dominic Grieve, Q.C., M.P. (b.1956) *Elected in* 2009
Eric William Griffiths (d.1974) 1973-1974
Hugh Griffiths, Baron Griffiths, M.C. (b.1923) 1965-1974; *re-elected in* 1982
Islwyn Owen Griffiths, Q.C. (1924-2001) 1975-1996
Robert Griffiths, Q.C. (b.1948) *Elected in* 2009
William Russell Griffiths (d.1910) 1877-1910
James Oliff Griffits 1866-1883
Geoffrey Grimes (d.1996) 1977-1996
Charles Groom 1852-1869
Hon. Richard Cecil Grosvenor (1848-1919) 1876-1895
George Grove, Q.C. (d.1971) 1957-1971
Grusin Grusin (1925-2000) 1980-2000
Philip Guedalla (1889-1944) 1933-1944
Professor Anthony G. Guest, C.B.E., Q.C. (b.1930) *Elected in* 1966
Ivor F. Guest (b.1920) *Elected in* 1960
Gully, *see* Selby
Henry Edward Gurner (d.1915) 1883-1915
Sir Maurice Linford Gwyer, K.C. (1878-1952) 1932-1950

H
—

Sir Charles A. Haddon-Cave (b.1956) *Elected in 2004*

Charles Haigh 1876-1891

Sir Charles Hall (1843-1900) 1866-1900

Sir Charles Hall (1814-1883) 1872-1883

Sir Edward Marshall Hall, K.C. (1858-1927) 1891-1927

John A.S. Hall, D.F.C., Q.C. (d.2004) 1974-1991

Sir Hugh Imbert Periam Hallett, M.C. (1886-1967) 1940-1967

His Hon. Anthony Hallgarten, Q.C. *Elected in 1975*

Hardinge Stanley Giffard, 1ˢᵗ Earl of Halsbury (1823-1921) 1868-1886

Adrian W. Hamilton, Q.C. (b.1923) *Elected in 1978*

Eben W. Hamilton, Q.C. (b.1937) *Elected in 1977*

Joseph Arthur Hamnett (d.1928) 1916-1928

Rev. Robert F. Hannay (d.1999) 1955-1999

Sir John Dorney Harding (1809-1868) 1839-1855

John Hardwick *Original member*

Reginald C. Hare 1959-1974

Kenneth Harington (1911-2007) 1961-1966

F. Rowand Harker 1912-1930

Sir Jeremiah Le Roy Harman 1958-1975

Robert Donald Harman, Q.C. (b.1928) *Elected in 1954*

Christopher Hedley Harmer (1910-1996) 1938-1949; 1989-1996

Anthony Harmsworth 1942-1967

Joseph Charles Harper, Q.C. (b.1939) *Elected in 1991*

Paul Harriman (b.1946) *Elected in 1976*

William Lewis Harris 1922-1928

Michael H. Harrison (d.1935) 1924-1935

Henry Mark Harrod (b.1939) *Elected in 1960*

Robert W. Hart *Elected in 1977*

Walter Hart (d.1994) 1973-1994

John P.C. Hartley (b.1929) *Elected in 1989*

Richard Leslie Clifford Hartley, Q.C. (b.1932) *Elected in 1972*

Martin J. Harty (b.1952) *Elected in 1984*

John Donald Haslam (d.1985) 1968-1985

Sir Patrick Hastings, K.C. (1880-1952) 1916-1952

George F. Hatfield (d.1923) 1906-1923

John Cassie Hatton, K.C. (d.1917) 1903-1917

His Hon. Sir Mark Havelock-Allan, 5ᵗʰ Bt., Q.C. (b.1951) *Elected in 2005*

Sir Cecil Robert Havers (1889-1977) 1955-1977

Hon. Philip N. Havers, Q.C. (b.1950) *Elected in 1975*

(Robert) Michael Havers, Baron Havers, Q.C. (1923-1992) 1954-1992

His Hon. Richard Havery, Q.C. (b.1935) *Elected in 1980*

Sir Anthony Hope Hawke (1869-1941) 1910-1941

Sir Edward Anthony Hawke (1896-1983) 1918-1949; 1957-1983

Hawkins, *see* Brampton

His Hon. Richard Hawkins, Q.C. (b.1941) *Elected in 2009*

Bourchier Francis Hawksley (1851-1919) 1899-1915

Robin W.P. Hay (b.1939) *Elected in 1991*

Michael A. Hayes (b.1943) *Elected in 1998*

William Hayes (d.1869) 1855-1869

Edmund Sidney Pollock Haynes (1877-1949) 1935-1940

Sir William Goodenough Hayter, Q.C. (1792-1878) 1831-1832

Abraham Hayward (1801-1884) 1832-1841

Christopher Head (1869-1912) 1906-1912

Sir Lionel Frederick Heald, Q.C. (1897-1981) 1926-1981

John Beresford Heaton (1895-1959) 1951-1953

Anthony E.J. Heaton-Armstrong (b.1950) *Elected in 1982*

Edward J. Henry (b.1961) *Elected in 2008*

James Henry (d.1871) 1854-1871

Sir Thomas Henry (1807-1876) 1859-1876

Jesse Basil Herbert, M.C., Q.C. (1899-1972) 1962-1972

Sydney Davis Herington 1949-1980

Edward Heron-Allen (1861-1943) 1902-1943

Paul Herzog (d.1986) 1974-1986

Major Sir Thomas Hetherington, Q.C. (1926-2007) 1988-1992

Gordon Hewart, 1ˢᵗ Viscount Hewart (1870-1943) 1921-1933; 1935-1937

Herbert T. Hewett (d.1921) 1893-1921

Harry V. Higgins (d.1928) 1907-1928

Sir George Malcolm Hilbery (1883-1965) 1931-1965

G. Patrick Malcolm Hilbery (d.1987) 1968-1987

Graham S. Hill (b.1927) *Elected in 1977*

John Frederick Hill 1851-1854

Michael Hill, Q.C. (1935-2003) 1993-2003

Rupert C.S. Hill (b.1954) *Elected in 1992*

William Alfred Hill 1841-1843

His Hon. Derek Edward Hill-Smith (1922-2006) 1975-2006

Nicholas R.M. Hilliard, Q.C. (b.1959) *Elected in 1992*

Arthur Henry Hillis 1949-1953; 1963-1974

John H. Hilton, Q.C. (b.1942) *Elected in 1995*

Daniel A. Hochberg (b.1959) *Elected in 2009*

APPENDIX

Stephen A. Hockman, Q.C. (b.1947) *Elected in* 2003

His Hon. David R. Hodge, Q.C. (b.1956) *Elected in* 2006

Lieutenant Colonel J.P. Hodge 1922-1941

Edmund Dornan Hodgson (d.1895) 1871-1895

Patrick Hodgson (d.1979) 1966-1979

Richard A. Hodgson (b.1956) *Elected in* 1989

Sir John Holker, Q.C. (1828-1882) 1873-1882

Barnett Hollander (d.1973) 1957-1973

Sir Kenneth Hollings, M.C. (1918-2008) 1982-2002

Sir Anthony Hollis (1927-2003) 1992-2003

Gideon J. Hollis (b.1967) *Elected in* 2002

John George Hollway 1879-1886

Hugh Holmes, Q.C. (1840-1916) 1879-1903

Edward H. Holt 1886-1909

Richard A.A. Holt 1960-1980

Godfrey C. Honnywill 1961-1964

Henry J. Hood 1894-1900

Stephen Hood (b.1947) *Elected in* 2000

David S. Hooper (b.1948) *Elected in* 1991

Hugh Emlyn Hooson, Baron Hooson, Q.C. (b.1925) 1960-1967

G.W. Hope 1831-1833

John Hornsby (d.1985) 1973-1985

Jonathan Horsfall-Turner *Elected in* 1981

Charles P. Horsfield (b.1964) *Elected in* 2004

Peter M. Horsfield, Q.C. *Elected in* 1982

Bruce F. Houlder, Q.C. (b.1947) *Elected in* 2009

Michael N. Howard, Q.C. (b.1947) *Elected in* 2005

William McLaren Howard, Q.C. (d.1990) 1965-1990

Geoffrey Howe, Baron Howe of Aberavon, Q.C. (b.1926) *Elected in* 1983

Thomas Edward Howe 1860-1866

Sir John Walter Huddleston (1815-1890) 1850-1877

James J.S. Hudson (b.1949) *Elected in* 1988

William H. Hughes (1915-1990) 1954-1990

Hamilton John Hulse (d.1931) 1891-1931

Sir Travers Christmas Humphreys (1867-1956) 1909-1956

Travers Christmas Humphreys, Q.C. (1901-1983) 1930-1964

George Hunter 1836-1837

Robert Lewin Hunter 1914-1937

T. Mansfield Hunter (d.1925) 1907-1925

Sir Charles Huntington, 3rd Bt. (1888-1928) 1919-1925

Henry Hussey 1875-1884

William Hussey 1836-1838

Jeremy Hutchinson, Baron Hutchinson of Lullington, Q.C. (b.1915) 1958-1966

St John Hutchinson, K.C. 1909-1939

Arthur Hutton (d.1922) 1907-1922

Jeremy R.D. Hyam (b.1970) *Elected in* 2005

His Hon. Michael Hyam (1938-2004) 1985-2004

I

Frederick Andrew Inderwick, Q.C. (1836-1904) 1866-1904

Inglis, *see* Glencorse

Inskip, *see* Caldecote

Peter Irvin (b.1947) *Elected in* 1991

Derry Irvine, Baron Irvine of Lairg, Q.C. (b.1940) *Elected in* 1979

Isaacs, *see* Reading

Anthony H. Isaacs (b.1943) *Elected in* 1979

Oliver D.J. Isaacs (b.1976) *Elected in* 2002

J

Evan Stewart Maclean Jack 1948-1980

Sir Henry Mather Jackson, 2nd Bt., Q.C. (1831-1881) 1875-1881

Sir Richard Leofric Jackson (1902-1975) 1938-1940; 1940-1951

Rt.Hon. Professor Sir Robin Jacob (b.1941) *Elected in* 1987

Ernest J. Jacobson (d.1947) 1942-1947

David James 1831-1834

Edwin John James, Q.C. (1812-1882) 1843-c.1845

Henry James, Baron James of Hereford (1828-1911) 1862-1902

Sir William Milbourne James (1807-1881) 1845-1860

Nicholas F.B. Jarman, Q.C. (b.1938) *Elected in* 2002

P.D. Jeffers 1852-1854

David A. Jeffreys (b.1934) 1981-1983

Julian Jeffs, Q.C. (b. 1931) *Elected in* 1967

Edward Herbert Jessel, 2nd Baron (1904-1990) 1929-1990

S.H. Jeyes (d.1911) 1891-1911

Henry Stanhope Joel 1971-1974

Charles Bernard Johnson (d.1935) 1920-1935

Charles Plumptre Johnson (1853-1938) 1906-1913

Edward Middelton Johnson (d.1948) 1905-1948

J. Yate Johnson 1914-1922

Thomas Ian Johnson-Gilbert (1923-1998) 1991-1998

Henry Augustus Johnston (d.1928) 1883-1928

James Marsh Johnstone (d.1925) 1903-1925

J. Hampton Jones (d.1891) 1869-1891

Lt. Col. Mainwaring Jones (d.1899) 1871-1899

Colonel William Anthony Jones (d.1910) 1865-1910

Lindsay Millais Jopling (1875-1967) 1962-1967

Professor Sir Jeffrey L. Jowell, Q.C. (b.1938) *Elected in* 1988

Sir Kenneth Jupp, M.C. (1917-2004) 1963-1994

K
—

Michel Kallipetis, Q.C. (b.1941) *Elected in* 2003

Sir Seymour Edward Karminski, K.C. (1902-1974) 1938-1974

Andrew C. Kaufman (b.1948) 1990-2002

Henry M. Keary 1888-1896

Donald Keating, Q.C. (1924-1995) 1987-1995

Harry Keegan (b.1972) *Elected in* 2005

Benjamin Keen 1832-c.1840

John W. Keffer *Elected in* 1976

Virgil J. Kellogg 1923-1935

Major R.D.L. Kelly, M.C. (d.1990) 1946-1990

John Kemp (d.1924) 1900-1924

Gilbert G. Kennedy (d.1909) 1890-1909

Professor Sir Ian Kennedy (b.1941) *Elected in* 1997

William Nicholas Keogh (1817-1878) 1854-1860

Sir Duncan Mackenzie Kerly (1863-1938) 1917-1938

Sir Michael Kerr (1921-2002) 1974-2002

Gerard Le B. Kidd 1962-2002

Henry King (d.1889) *Elected in* 1847 & 1853-1889

William George King (d.1916) 1909-1916

David King-Farlow (b.1944) *Elected in* 1994

Frank Kingsford (d.1906) 1878-1906

Richard Alan Kinnersley 1939-1973

Lieutenant Colonel Claude Arthur Kirby 1920-1929

Henry G. Kirby 1870-1893

Anthony Kennedy Kisch (d.1977) 1958-1977

Dr. Paul A. Knapman (b.1944) *Elected in* 1992

His Hon. Brian J. Knight, Q.C. (b.1941) *Elected in* 1982

Edward Boards Knight 1908-1918

Sir James Lewis Knight-Bruce (1791-1866) 1839-c.1841

Charles J. Knowles, Q.C. 1833-1865

Alexander Andrew Knox (1818-1891) 1856-1881

Simon R. Kverndal, Q.C. (b.1958) *Elected in* 1998

L
—

Nigel Lambert, Q.C. (b.1949) *Elected in* 2005

John Lane 1839-1846

Robert C. Lane, C.B.E. (b.1958) *Elected in* 2009

R.O.B. Lane (d.1944) 1906-1944

Joseph David Langton (d.1918) 1915-1918

A.M. Latter 1908-1940

His Hon. Bruce Laughland, Q.C. (1931-2002) *Elected and resigned in* 1969; 1996-2002

Edward W. Laughton-Scott, Q.C. (d.1978) 1962-1978

Professor Sir Elihu Lauterpacht, C.B.E., Q.C. (b.1928) *Elected in* 1994

Nicholas Lavender, Q.C. (b.1964) *Elected in* 2008

John H. Law (d.1878) 1849-1878

Hon. Alfred Clive Lawrence (1876-1926) 1912-1926

Charles L. Lawrence 1912-1930; 1932-1935

Sir John Compton Lawrence, Q.C. (1832-1912) 1879-1885

Sir Paul Ogden Lawrence (1861-1952) 1901-1931

Sir John Laws (b.1945) *Elected in* 1993

His Hon. Michael H. Lawson, Q.C. (b.1946) *Elected in* 2004

Arnold Lawson-Walton 1937-1946; 1950-1954

Sir Frederick Horace Lawton (1911-2001) 1954-2001

Sir Frank Layfield, Q.C. (1921-2000) 1976-2000

George Pemberton Leach 1881-1904

Jeremy J.B. Leasor (b.1953) *Elected in* 1983

Peter L.O. Leaver, Q.C. (b.1944) *Elected in* 1995

Paul A. Lee (b.1946) *Elected in* 2004

Sir Thomas S. Legg, K.C.B., Q.C. (b.1935) *Elected in* 1990

Rudolph Chambers Lehmann (1856-1929) 1892-1907

Victor Lemieux (d.1979) 1974-1979

Harry Reid Lempriere 1886-1891

His Hon. Henry Cecil Leon, M.C. (1902-1976) 1959-1976

Anthony James Leonard, Q.C. (b.1956) *Elected in* 1993

Sir (Hamilton) John Leonard, Q.C. (1926-2002) 1971-2002

Anthony Lester, Baron Lester of Herne Hill, Q.C. (b.1936) 1969-1994

Sir Jeremy F. Lever, K.C.M.G., Q.C. (b.1933) *Elected in* 1969

George Herbert Lewin 1842-1853

Edward T.G. Lewis (b.1948) *Elected in* 1989

His Hon. Esyr Lewis, Q.C. (1926-2011) 1985-2011

Geoffrey M. Lewis *Elected in* 1985

Lt. Commander Sir George J.E. Lewis, 3rd Bt. (1910-1945)

James Thomas Lewis, Q.C. (b.1958) *Elected in* 2007

John H.B. Lewis, O.B.E. (b.1940) *Elected in* 1989

Hon. Trevor Lewis (d.1921) 1919-1921

W.H. Leycester (d.1925) 1913-1925

His Hon. Crawford C.D. Lindsay, Q.C. (b.1947) *Elected in* 1994

Thomas D. Lingard 1908-1924

Peter Linklater (d.1997) 1980-1997

John Vaughan, 8th Earl of Lisburne (b.1918) 1960-1968

Sir Joseph Littledale (1767-1842) *Original member*-1834

Sir Sydney Charles Thomas Littlewood (1895-1967) 1959-1967

Mark Littman, Q.C. (b. 1920) *Elected in 1973*

J.L. Litton 1868-1872

T.E. Lloyd (d.1909) 1865-1909

John Locke, Q.C. (1805-1880) 1834-1838; 1855-1880

Christopher J. Lockhart-Mummery, Q.C. (b.1947) *Elected in 1995*

Sir Frank Lockwood, Q.C. (1846-1897) 1882-1897

Lt. Colonel John Cutts Lockwood (1890-1983) 1959-1969

Oliver Lodge (d.2009) 1965-2009

Herman William Loehnis 1890-1899

David E. Long (b.1940) *Elected in 1988*

Sir Andrew Longmore, Lord Justice Longmore (b.1944) *Elected in 1992*

His Hon. Nicholas Loraine-Smith (b.1953) *Elected in 2008*

Robert Threshie Reid, 1st Earl Loreburn (1846-1923) 1869-1896

Captain C.E. Loseby, M.C. 1920-1950

Willoughby J. Loudon 1857-1899

Sir Anthony Lousada (1907-1994) 1973-1994

Dorian Lovell-Pank, Q.C. (b.1946) 1994-2010

Henry William Lovett (d.1842) 1834-1842

Lewis J. Lowdham *Original member*

William Loftus Lowndes 1831-1837

His Hon. Richard John Lowry, Q.C. (d.2001) 1968-2001

Lowther, *see* Ullswater

Samuel Lucas 1856-1866

James L. Lucena 1834-1866

Guy Lushington (d.1916) 1912-1916

Sir Herbert Lush-Wilson (1850-1941) 1906-1929

Sir Arthur Luxmoore (1876-1944) 1920-1931

Henry W. Lyall (d.1915) 1884-1915

Walter F. Lyons (d.1978) 1958-1978

M
—

Nicholas Lechmere Cunningham Macaskie, K.C. (1881-1967) 1936-1951

Sir Lynden Macassey (1876-1963) 1914-1923

D'Alton L. McCarthy, K.C. 1913-1939

Kenneth Macaulay, Q.C. (1815-1867) 1850-1858

George Buchanan McClure (1887-1955) 1932-1948

Hon. Sir Richard McCombe (b.1952) *Elected in 2006*

William Robert McConnell, Q.C. (d.1906) 1897-1906

Sir Charles Iain Robert McCullough (b.1931) 1968-c.1993

His Hon. David McEvoy, Q.C. (b.1938) 1996-2008; *re-elected in 2011*

James Macdonald (d.1873) 1842-1873

Colin McFadyean (1914-2007) 1959-1974; 1982-1983

Rt Hon Sir Andrew E. McFarlane (b.1954) *Elected in 2003*

Craig Macfarlane (1902-1969) 1955-1969

Alastair J. McGregor, Q.C. (b.1950) *Elected in 1994*

Harvey McGregor, Q.C. (b.1926) *Elected in 1977*

His Hon. John Machin (b.1941) *Elected in 2005*

Sir Malcolm McIlwraith, K.C. (d.1941) 1891-1913; 1917-1941

Theodore McKenna (d.1937) 1898-1937

Edward Mackeson (d.1898) 1867-1898

Lumsden Mackeson (d.1870) 1865-1870

Sir Francis William Maclean (1844-1913) 1882-1913

Bentley Macleod *Elected in 1846*

Nigel R.B. Macleod, Q.C. (1936-2005) 1998-2005

James McMahon 1832-1841

Sir Henry Maddocks (1871-1931) 1920-1931

Vernon Magniac 1886-1890

Hilary Magnus, Q.C. (d.1987) 1959-1987

Keith Maitland 1882-1890

John George Malcolm 1838-1842

Martin E. Mann, Q.C. (b. 1943) *Elected in 1993*

William Murray, 8th Earl of Mansfield (b.1930) 1964-1979

H.H. Marcus (d.1997) 1975-1997

Charles Marett 1864-1871

Sir William Thackcray Marriott (1834-1903) 1870-1897

George Marsden 1915-1939

Norman Stayner Marsh (1913-2008) 1962-1968

Kenneth McLean Marshall 1911-1916

Robert G. Marshall-Andrews, Q.C. (b.1944) *Elected in 2004*

Sir William Mars-Jones (1915-1999) 1963-1999

Andrew Martin, Q.C. 1968-1976

Sir Theodore Martin (1816-1909) 1865-1897

Alfred Martineau (d.1903) 1891-1903

Paul W. Matcham *Elected in 2006*

John Charles Mathew, Q.C. (b. 1927) *Elected in 1963*

Theobald Mathew (1866-1939) 1892-1927; 1930-1939

Sir Theobald Mathew, M.C. (1898-1964) 1930-1939

THE LAWYERS

Sir Charles Willie Mathews (1850-1920) 1877-1920

Harry N. Matovu (b.1964) *Elected in* 1991

Duncan H.R. Matthews, Q.C. (b.1961) *Elected in* 2003

F.C. Matthews 1868-1920

John Cyril Maude, K.C. (1901-1986) 1927-1961; 1968-1975

Robert Ormond Maugham (1823-1884) 1874-1884

(Peter) Bruce Mauleverer, Q.C. (b.1946) *Elected in* 2002

William Pryce Maunsell (1828-1920) 1854-1874

Edward H.H. Maxwell 1924-1928

Henry Stewart Maxwell-Wood (d.2011) 1971-1995; 1998-2002

Sir Anthony May (b.1940) *Elected in* 1996

Justin G. Mayall (b.1961) *Elected in* 2005

Ian Mayes, Q.C. (b.1951) *Elected in* 2004

Patrick Mayhew, Baron Mayhew of Twysden, Q.C. (b.1929) *Elected in* 1988

Joseph Maynard 1834-1838

John Christopher Medley (1902-1983) 1943-1983

Cornelius M. Medvei (b.1951) *Elected in* 1996

His Hon. James Mendl (1927-2008) 1999-2008

Charles George Merewether, Q.C. (d.1884) 1851-1884

Henry Alworth Merewether (1812-1877) 1864-1877

Herman Charles Merivale (1839-1906) 1870-1898

Henry E. Duke, 1st Baron Merrivale (1855-1939) 1905-1921

Herbert Metcalfe 1932-1934

James Mew (d.1913) 1884-1912; *Re-elected and died in* 1913

Sir Frank Cecil Meyer, 2nd Bt. (1886-1935) 1930-1935

Ronald G. Middleton, D.S.C. (d.1999) 1978-1999

Robert J. Miles, Q.C. (b.1962) *Elected in* 2003

Alfred Thomas Miller, K.C. (d.1943) 1930-1943

John Fisher Miller (d.1879) 1873-1879

Major John Francis Compton Miller (d.1992) 1943-1985; 1986-1992

Master Paul M. Miller (b.1936) *Elected in* 2003

David M.D. Mills (b.1944) *Elected in* 1979

William Primrose Mills (d.1905) 1879-1905

Sir Helenus Patrick Joseph Milmo (1908-1988) 1975-1988

David C. Milne, Q.C. (b.1945) *Elected in* 1977

Sir Frank Milton (d.1976) 1954-1976

Peter H.T. Mimpriss, C.V.O. (b.1943) *Elected in* 1990

Ernest Leslie Minty 1943-1965

Sir James William Miskin (1925-1993) 1958-1970

Paul E. Mitchell (b.1951) *Elected in* 2004

W.M. Mitchell *Elected and resigned in* 1954

Edward Alfred Mitchell-Innes, K.C. (1863-1932) 1907-1921

Hon. Sir John E. Mitting (b.1947) *Elected in* 2005

Frank R. Moat (b.1948) *Elected in* 1988

Michael J. Mockridge (1935-2006) 1987-2006

Christopher R.D. Moger, Q.C. (b.1949) *Elected in* 1990

Charles Molloy *Elected in* 1844

Sir Joseph Thomas Molony, Q.C. 1955-1974

J.W.B. Money 1850-1853

Hubert Holmes Monroe, Q.C. (d.1982) 1973-1982

William Monteith *Elected in* 1839

Andrew Moody (b.1971) *Elected in* 2009

His Hon. Peter Hopkin Morgan, Q.C. 1962-1992

Sir Ronald Peter Morison, Q.C. (1900-1976) 1955-1958

His Hon. Anthony P. Morris, Q.C. (b.1948) *Elected in* 2009

Malcolm John Morris, Q.C. 1939-1968

Rt.Hon. Sir Andrew Morritt, C.V.O. (b.1938) *Elected in* 1968

Sir John Mortimer, C.B.E., Q.C. (1923-2009) 1960-2009

Francis Arnold Moseley (d.1951) 1933-1951

John Fletcher Moulton, Baron Moulton (1844-1921) 1874-1921

Major Hon. Hugh Fletcher Moulton, M.C. (1876-1962) 1900-1962

Patrick Berkeley Moynihan, 2nd Baron Moynihan (1906-1965) 1929-1939; 1954-1965

Sir Richard David Muir (1857-1924) 1899-1924

David Mullock (d.1997) 1993-1997

Francis Stack Murphy (1807-1860) 1833-1853; 1853-1860

Nigel Murray (d.2002) 1975-2002

William Murray 1855-1880

Major John Edward Murray-Smith (d.1928) 1925-1928

Nigel Mylne, Q.C. (b.1939) 1977-1997

N
—

Sir David Napley (1915-1994) 1976-1994

Rt.Hon. Sir Brian T. Neill (b.1923) *Elected in* 1982

Patrick Neill, Baron Neill of Bladen, Q.C. (b.1926) *Elected in* 1980

James Victor Nesbitt (d.1963) 1958-1963

Wallace Nesbitt, K.C. (1858-1930) 1909-1930

David Neuberger, Baron Neuberger of Abbotsbury (b.1948) *Elected in* 2002
Clive V. Nicholls, Q.C. (b.1932) *Elected in* 1990
Colin A.A. Nicholls, Q.C. (b.1932) *Elected in* 1990
Sir Basil Nield (1903-1996) 1976-1984
James Noble 1990-1998
Hon. Gerard Eyre Noel (b.1926) *Elected in* 1951
Francis Nolan, Q.C. 1880-1895
Sir Charles Norton, M.C. (d.1974) 1963-1974
John Bruce Norton (1815-1883) 1863-1878
Thomas Norton 1847-c.1870

O
—

Peter O'Brien, 1st Baron O'Brien (1842-1914) 1888-1902
M. John O'Connell (d.1876) 1864-1876
Richard Harby Oddie 1841-c.1845
Sir James Cornelius O'Dowd (d.1903) 1854-1903
David Ogilvy 1837-c.1840
Richard Ogle 1836-1843
Hon. Sir Harry Ognall (b.1934) 1988-1996
Michael C. O'Kane (b.1969) *Elected in* 2004
Hon. David Oliver, Q.C. (b. 1949) 1985-c.1987
Sir Roland Giffard Oliver, K.C., M.C. (1882-1967) 1923-1934
William Disney Oliver (d.1884) 1847-1884
Simon M. Olswang (b.1943) *Elected in* 1998
Robert O'Maley (d.1892) 1884-1892
Sir Roger Fray Greenwood Ormrod (1911-1992) 1951-1992
Frederick K. Osborne 1831-1834
Charles Otter 1833-1837
Rt.Hon. Sir Philip Otton (b.1933) *Elected in* 1975
W. Harold S. Oulton (d.1941) 1926-1941
Sir Duncan B.W. Ouseley (b.1950) *Elected in* 2006
Sir John Owen (1925-2010) 1982-2010
His Hon. Tudor W. Owen, Q.C. (b.1951) *Elected in* 1995
David Owen-Thomas, Q.C. (1926-2007) 1984-2007

P
—

Nicholas D. Padfield, Q.C. (b.1947) *Elected in* 1993
His Hon. David Paget, Q.C. (b.1942) *Elected in* 2005
Reginald Thomas Paget, Baron Paget of Northampton, Q.C. (1908-1990) 1974-1977
Sir Richard Arthur Surtees Paget (1869-1955) 1895-1923

Martin D. Paisner, C.B.E. (b.1943) *Elected in* 2002
Bruce Palmer (b.1945) *Elected in* 2002
Dr. Roy N. Palmer (b.1944) *Elected in* 2000
Christopher H.W. Parish (b.1937) *Elected in* 1988
Rt.Hon. Sir Jonathan F. Parker (b.1937) *Elected in* 1967
Sir Thomas Parkyns, 6th Bt. (1853-1926) 1909-1926
Arthur de Clifton Parmiter (d.1917) 1905-1917
Geoffrey Vincent de Clifton Parmiter 1948-1982
Sir Edward Abbott Parry (1863-1943) 1893-1943
John Humffreys Parry (1816-1880) 1853-1880
A.F. Part 1919-1932
Nigel Spencer Knight Pascoe, Q.C. (b.1940) *Elected in* 1975
His Hon. Harold William Paton, D.S.C. (1900-1986) 1945-1954
Trevor I. Payne 1978-2000
Sir Reginald Withers Payne (1904-1980) 1965-1980
Michael A.H. Payton (b.1944) *Elected in* 2004
(Richard) Bruce Holroyd Pearce, Q.C. 1956-1966
Colin Hargreaves Pearson, Baron Pearson, K.C. (1899-1980) 1937-1980
Jasper Peck 1953-1980
Charles Peile 1876-1893
Edward F. Pellew 1877-1881
V.M.C. Pennington (d.1984) 1962-1984
Sir John Pennycuick (1899-1982) 1964-1982
Charles Spencer Perceval (1829-1889) 1864-1869
Henry Perkins 1867-1881
John Perry, Q.C. (b.1936) *Elected in* 2005
Richard D. Persse (d.1890) 1872-1890
William Comer Petheram (1835-1922) 1864-1866
Nicholas Phillips, Baron Phillips of Worth Matravers (b.1938) *Elected in* 2004
Thomas Phinn, Q.C. (d.1866) 1859-1866
Hon. Edmund Phipps (1808-1857) *Original member-c.*1840
Hubert Picarda (b.1936) 1981-1994
William Benet Pike (d.1905) 1901-1905
Gregory K. Pilkington (b.1946) *Elected in* 2002
Matthew Pintus (b.1956) *Elected in* 2003
David M. Pittaway, Q.C. (b.1955) *Elected in* 2001
His Hon. Jonathan R. Playford, Q.C. (b. 1940) *Elected in* 1975
Nigel Pleming, Q.C. (b.1946) *Elected in* 2003
Plunket, *see* Rathmore
Sir Harry Bodkin Poland, K.C. (1829-1928) 1867-1928

A. Gordon S. Pollock, Q.C. (b.1943) *Elected in* 1989

Sir George Pollock, Q.C. 1946-1966

George Frederick Pollock 1844-1853

Matthew S. Pollock (b.1964) *Elected in* 1993

Sir Reginald Ward Poole (1864-1941) 1917-1926; 1927-1941

Samuel Pope, Q.C. (1826-1901) 1885-1901

Sir Oliver Popplewell (b.1927) *Elected in* 1990

Hon. Edwin Berkeley Portman (1830-1921) 1855-1857

(Donald) Charles Potter, Q.C. (1922-2008) 1967-2008

Rt. Hon. Sir Mark H. Potter (b.1937) *Elected in* 1984

Colin Prestige (d.2004) 1970-2003

Douglas James Preston 1932-1967

Edward Preston 1836-c.1840

H.F. Previté (d.1929) 1914-1929

Leolin Price, C.B.E., Q.C. (b.1924) *Elected in* 2004

Richard Price, O.B.E., Q.C. (b.1948) *Elected in* 2007

Richard A. Price *Elected in* 1832

Arthur Robert Prideaux (d.1931) 1887-1931

Walter Prideaux (d.1889) 1845-1889

Godfrey K. Prior 1956-1966

Lt. Colonel F.E. Pritchard, K.C. 1944-1946

Albert Peter Anthony Profumo, 4th Baron Profumo of Sardinia, K.C. (1879-1940) 1938-1940

Kevin J. Prosser, Q.C. (b.1957) *Elected in* 1997

Stanley L. Prothero (b.1916) *Elected in* 1975

C.G. Prowett 1863-1873

Rt. Hon. Sir Nicholas Pumfrey (1951-2007) 2003-2007

Henry F. Purcell *Elected and resigned in* 1877

Francis J. Pym (b.1952) 1984-1998

Q

William James Chance Quarrell 1952-1953

R

Mark A. Raeside, Q.C. (b.1955) *Elected in* 2009

Frederick Herbert Ramsden (d.1950) 1899-1950

James Hildebrand Ramsden (d.1967) 1934-1967

James R.E. Rankin (b.1959) *Elected in* 1993

Captain Robert Rankin (d.1945) 1918-1945

Sir Geoffrey George Raphael (1893-1969) 1928-1963

Charles Ratcliff 1861-1884

David Robert Plunket, 1st Baron Rathmore (1838-1919) 1872-1919

Frank L. Ratto, M.C. (d.1974) 1929-1974

Alan D. Rawley, Q.C. *Elected in* 1974

Thomas Rawlinson 1854-1863

George Raymond *Original member*-1859

Hon. James Russell Rea (1902-1954) 1943-1951

Lionel F. Read, Q.C. (b.1929) *Elected in* 1984

George Edward Harold Reader 1943-1953

William Reade 1832-1836

Gerald Rufus Isaacs, 2nd Marquess of Reading (1889-1960) 1928-1939

Rufus Daniel Isaacs, 1st Marquess of Reading (1860-1935) 1905-1912

His Hon. Edward V.P. Reece (b.1936) *Elected in* 1993

Francis Bertram Reece (1888-1971) 1948-1964

Rupert V.P. Reece (b.1968) *Elected in* 2009

Alan R. Rees-Reynolds (1909-1982) 1965-1974; 1976-1982

Sir Trevor Reeve (1915-1993) 1956-1993

Reid, *see* Loreburn

Alfred George Renshaw (d.1897) 1881-1897

Arthur Henry Renshaw (d.1918) 1880-1918

John Reynolds 1981-1995

William Reynolds 1834-1836

John E. Rhodes (b.1952) 2001-2006

Robert E. Rhodes, Q.C. (b.1945) *Elected in* 2001

His Hon. Michael S. Rich, Q.C. (b.1933) *Elected in* 1990

Arthur Pierre Richards (d.1943) 1936-1943

Sir David Richards (b.1951) *Elected in* 2005

Frank Richardson (d.1917) 1904-1917

Gordon W.H. Richardson 1948-1965

Kenneth A. Richardson, Q.C. (1926-1994) 1990-1994

Cecil Guy Ridley (d.1947) 1939-1947

Hon. Sir Jasper Nicholas Ridley (1887-1951) 1912-1917

Sir Edward Ripley, 2nd Bt. (1840-1903) 1866-1903

James Herbert Robbins (d.1989) 1961-1989

Sir Denys Roberts (b.1923) 1989-2006

Geoffrey D. Roberts, Q.C. 1924-1960

Sir Owen Roberts (1835-1915) 1887-1903

W. Roberts 1832-1834

Edward George Robey (d.1983) 1946-1983

Frederic D. Robinson 1945-1961

Michael B. Robinson (b.1968) *Elected in* 2004

Vivian Robinson, Q.C. (b.1944) *Elected in* 1991

Gilbert Rodway, Q.C. (b.1937) 2004-2008

Edgar Rodwell, Q.C. 1883-1887

Benjamin Bickley Rogers (1828-1919) 1854-1856

John Rogers (d.2004) 1963-2004

Sir John Rolt, Q.C. (1804-1871) 1845-1871

Roderick Jessel Anidjar Romain (1916-2009) 1975-1986; 1989-1993

Frederick Romer 1890-1932

Ian L.R. Romer *Elected in* 1961

Mark Lemon Romer, Baron Romer (1866-1944) 1892-1928
Sir Robert Romer (1840-1918) 1889-1906
Henry Delacombe Roome 1917-c.1929
Henry G. Rooth (d.1928) 1918-1928
John Rooth (d.1930) 1923-1930
Edward Henry Rosco 1842-c.1845
Rt.Hon. Sir Christopher Rose (b.1937) *Elected in 1993*
Frank Rosenfelt (1921-2007) 1992-2000
Sir William Rose, 2nd Bt. (1846-1902) 1873-1902
(George) Ronald Rougier, Q.C. (1900-1976) 1955-1976
Sir Richard Rougier (1932-2007) 1963-2007
Malcolm D. Rowat (b.1945) *Elected in 2003*
George William Rowe 1894-1929; 1931-1935
Joshua Rozenberg (b.1950) *Elected in 1992*
John S.Y. Rubinstein (b.1951) *Elected in 1995*
Michael Bernard Rubinstein (1920-2001) 1970-2001
Sir Jack Rumbold, Q.C. (1920-2001) 1983-2001
Sir Charles Russell, 1st Bt. (1863-1928) 1896-1928
Sir Charles Ian Russell, 3rd Bt. (1918-1997) 1950-1997
Charles Ritchie Russell, Baron Russell of Killowen (1908-1986) 1939-1986
Sir Evelyn Charles Sackville Russell 1974-1985
Frank Russell, Baron Russell of Killowen (1867-1946) 1893-1946
Geoffrey Russell 1927-1955
Sir John Russell (d.1984) 1960-1974; 1978-1984
Sir Patrick Russell (1926-2002) 1994-1998
David Rutherston (d.1975) 1966-1975
Richard Calthorpe Whitmore Ryder 1878-1892

S

Norman St John Stevas, Baron St John of Fawsley (b.1929) *Elected in 1960*
Charles Thomas Salkeld-Green (d.1996) 1944-1950
Christopher Sallon, Q.C. (b.1948) *Elected in 2011*
Sir Arthur Clavell Salter, K.C. (1858-1928) 1911-1928
His Hon. John E.A. Samuels, Q.C. (b.1940) *Elected in 2008*
Major Edmund Thomas Sandars (1877-1942) 1905-1942
John Sankey, 1st Viscount Sankey (1866-1948) 1916-1946
Sir Charles Henry Sargant (1856-1942) 1889-1920
Mark Saville, Baron Saville of Newdigate (b.1936) *Elected in 2002*

D.T. Savory 1879-1903
Michael P. Sayers, Q.C. (b.1940) *Elected in 1976*
Leslie George Scarman, Baron Scarman (1911-2004) 1957-1968; 1969-1977
Ferdinand Philip Max Schiller, K.C. (d.1946) 1926-1946
Lieutenant Alfred Felix Schuster *Elected and died in 1914*
Henry James Scott, K.C. 1908-1931
Sir John Scott (1841-1904) 1899-1904
Timothy J.W. Scott, Q.C. (b.1949) *Elected in 1989*
His Hon. Conrad Seagroatt, Q.C. (b.1938) 1999-2009
Francis Seaman 1840-1879
Reginald Ethelbert Seaton 1944-1966
Harold H. Sebag-Montefiore (b.1924) *Elected in 1990*
Peter Henry Sée (d.1963) 1954-1963
Michael J. Segal (b.1937) *Elected in 2008*
James Gully, 2nd Viscount Selby (1867-1923) 1899-1916
Henry Selfe Selfe (1810-1870) 1836-1840
Sir William Lucius Selfe (1845-1924) 1900-1914
Sir Henry Wilmot Seton (1785-1848) 1835-1848
R.S. Seuffert, Q.C. 1944-1975
Guy Seward, Q.C. 1976-1999
Thomas O. Seymour (b.1952) *Elected in 1981*
Joseph Sharpe (d.1930) 1924-1930
Joseph Shaw 1899-1928
Hartley Shawcross, Baron Shawcross, K.C. (1902-2003) 1952-1966; 1989-2003
Shearer, *see* Avonside
Montague Shearman (d.1940) 1912-1940
James Sheil (d.1908) 1864-1908
Thomas Morley Shelford (1905-1986) 1957-1980
John B. Shelley, O.B.E. (b.1926) *Elected in 1982*
Thomas Shepherd 1835-1842
Thomas Shields (b.1950) 1978-1994
Sir Sidney Godolphin Shippard (1837-1902) 1894-1902
His Hon. Philip G. Shorrock (b.1956) *Elected in 2009*
John Shortt (d.1932) 1881-1892; 1896-1932
John Simon, 1st Viscount Simon (1873-1954) 1908-1939
Charles Turner Simpson (d.1902) 1850-1902
Edward Palgrave Simpson 1898-1909
Robin Simpson, Q.C. (b.1927) 1978-1996
Peter J. Singer (b.1933) *Elected in 1985*
Rt.Hon. Sir Christopher John Slade (b.1927) *Elected in 1972*
Roger Phipson Slade (1901-1969) 1958-1962
Anthony Slingsby (b.1943) 1985-1987

Gordon Slynn, Baron Slynn of Hadley, Q.C.
(1930-2009) 1969-1976
Brian Smedley, Q.C. (1934-2007) 1977-2007
Edward Arthur Last Smith 1958-1960
F.E. Smith, *see* Birkenhead
Horace W. Smith 1872-1892
J.W. Smith 1839-c.1845
His Hon. David Smout, Q.C. (1923-1987) 1982-
1987
His Hon. Alan P. Solomon 1977-1993
Thomas Smythe 1848-1855
Sir Thomas William Snagge (d.1914) 1885-1914
Ivan Edward Snell, M.C. 1926-1937
Thomas Hill Sooby (1847-1908) 1880-1908
Soskice, *see* Stow Hill
Robert Spankie 1876-1881
John Hanbury Angus Sparrow (1906-1992)
1937-1992
Francis Elmer Speed (1859-1928) 1885-1928
Sir Ernest Spencer 1913-1935
Lt. Colonel Francis Edward Weston Sproat
1935-1949
William Harold Squire (d.1924) 1899-1924
Sir Wintringham Norton Stable, M.C., K.C.
(1888-1977) 1936-1939
Henry Stack 1878-1889
Sir Edward Blanshard Stamp (1905-1984)
1965-1984
Henry Staveley-Hill 1918-1928
George Steer *Original member & re-elected* 1841
John Stenson, M.C. (d.1964) 1946-1964
Sir James Fitzjames Stephen, 1st Bt. (1829-1894)
1872-1894
Guy Stephenson 1905-1909
John Melford Stevenson 1974-1979
Rt. Hon. Sir (Aubrey) Melford Stevenson (1902-
1987) 1931-1987
Charles Edward Stewart 1889-1893
Johan Steyn, Baron Steyn (b.1932) 1991-1996
George Davey Stibbard (d.1899) 1889-1899
Hugh Stirling (d.1908) 1874-1908
Hon. Sir James Stirling (d.1974) 1951-1974
His Hon. Frank Alleyne Stockdale (d.1989)
1973-1989
James Stockdale (b.1948) 1977-1980; *re-elected
in* 2007
Evan D.R. Stone, Q.C. (b.1928) *Elected in* 1975
Sir Leonard Stone (1896-1978) 1963-1968
Frank Soskice, Baron Stow Hill, K.C. (1902-
1979) 1952-1977
Sir Douglas Straight (1844-1914) 1873-1914
James O.J. Strachan (b.1971) *Elected in* 2005
Sir Geoffrey Hugh Benbow Streatfeild, M.C.
1943-1953
Jeremy Stuart-Smith, Q.C. (b.1955) *Elected in*
1997

Julian Russell Sturgis (1848-1904) 1876-1887
Anthony James Chadwick Sumption, D.S.C.
(d.2008) 1975-2008
James H.G. Sunnocks (1925-2005) 1990-2005
Sir Michael A. Supperstone (b.1950) *Elected in*
1987
David Suratgar (b.1938) *Elected in* 2005
Andrew Sutch (b.1952) *Elected in* 2007
Richard P. Sutton, Q.C. *Elected in* 2002
Hon. Robert Manners Sutton 1881-1891
Sir Nigel H. Sweeney (b.1954) *Elected in* 2000
Colin P. Sydenham (b.1935) *Elected in* 2000
Philip J. Sykes 1948-1956
J.A. Symmons (d.1923) 1906-1923
Nicholas Joseph Synnott (d.1920) 1886-1920
Philip J. Syrett 1947-1973

T

Sir Thomas Noon Talfourd (1795-1854) *Original
member*-1854
Alick Tassell (d.1932) 1926-1932
Charles Meaburn Tatham (d.1924) 1898-1924
Christopher Kemplay Tatham (1881-1970)
1906-1970
John L. Tatham 1836-1837
Percy Tatham (d.1915) 1906-1915
Thomas Clarke Tatham (d.1914) 1866-1914
A.F. Tatlow (d.1865) 1847-1865
Simon Taube, Q.C. (b.1957) *Elected in* 2001
Sir Charles Taylor, 2nd Bt. (1817-1876) 1847-1876
J.F.K. Taylor, K.C. 1905-1927
Peter Taylor, Baron Taylor of Gosforth (1930-
1997) 1979-1997
Richard Stephens Taylor (d.1882) 1838-1882
Sir Richard Stephens Taylor (d.1928) 1895-1928
Richard Stephens Taylor (d.1950) 1912-1950
Tom Taylor (1817-1880) 1850-1880
John Marmaduke Teasdale (d.1888) 1852-1888
George Tenant *Elected in* 1838
Roger E.L. Ter Haar, Q.C. (b.1952) *Elected in*
2004
Ernest Glyn Thomas 1960-1964
Michael D. Thomas, C.M.G., Q.C. (b.1933)
Elected in 1977
Neville Thomas, Q.C. (b.1936) 1978-2008
Rt.Hon. Sir Swinton B. Thomas (b.1931) *Elected
in* 1968
His Hon. Anthony Thompson, Q.C. (b.1932)
Elected in 2009
Peter J. Thompson, O.B.E. (b.1936) *Elected in*
1986
Roger E. Thompson 1955-1958
Everard G. Thorne (d.1924) 1919-1924
H.L. Thornhill 1922-1928
Major Dick H.B. Thornton (d.1944) 1937-1944

Thomas Humphrey Tilling (1910-1991) 1949-1991

Julian Tobin (1927-1996) 1981-1996

Thomas Tomkyns (d.1832) 1831-1832

David R. Tomlinson *Elected in* 1987

Rt.Hon. Sir Stephen M. Tomlinson (b.1952) *Elected in* 2002

W. Keith Topley (b.1936) *Elected in* 1966

William Torrens McCullagh Torrens (1813-1894) 1867-1868

Harold Cuthbert Townley-Millers (d.1968) 1955-1968

Anthony J. Trace, Q.C. (b.1958) *Elected in* 2005

Samuel Smith Travers (1826-1888) 1853-1859

Andrew D.H. Trollope, Q.C. (b.1948) *Elected in* 2001

John Troutbeck 1899-1909

William S.P. Trower, Q.C. (b.1959) *Elected in* 1990

Sir Richard Tucker (b.1930) *Elected in* 1978

Sir Haydn Tudor Evans (b.1920) *Elected in* 1953

Quintin J. Tudor Evans (b.1954) *Elected in* 1991

Francis C.S. Tufton (d.2004) 1937-2004

James Stuart Tulk (d.1882) 1858-1882

Sir Stephen Tumim (1930-2003) 1976-2003

Harry K. Tunstill (d.1919) 1893-1919

Augustus Turner (d.1932) 1922-1932

Harold Horsfall Turner (d.1981) 1970-1981

His Hon. Maxwell J.H. Turner (1907-1960) 1930-1960

Michael John Turner 1965-1974

Sharon Grote Turner 1888-1902; 1909-1924

Theo Turner, K.C. 1948-1977

Richard Twiss 1845-*c.*1868

L.E.P. Tylor (d.1972) 1969-1972

U
—

James William Lowther, 1st Viscount Ullswater (1855-1949) 1877-1889

Emanuel Maguire Underdown, Q.C. (1831-1913) 1870-1879; 1889-1894

John G. Underwood (b.1939) *Elected in* 1981

Augustus Andrewes Uthwatt, Baron Uthwatt, Q.C. (1879-1949) 1937-1949

V
—

Charles Francis Vachell, K.C. 1908-1914

Hon. Edward H.B. Vaizey, M.P. (b.1968) *Elected in* 1997

Dr. Donald G. Valentine (b.1945) *Elected in* 1976

Henry M. Vane 1847-1854

Sir William van Straubenzee (1924-1999) 1986-1999

Vaughan, *see* Lisburne

John V.V. Veeder, Q.C. (b.1948) *Elected in* 2001

Frederick Villiers 1833-1839

Arthur Vincent 1915-1922

Sir John Vinelott (1923-2006) 1987-2006

Professor Werner von Simson (1908-1996) 1978-1996

Desmond Vowden, Q.C. (1921-1990) 1959-1990

Richard Henry Stackhouse Vyvyan 1869-1878

W
—

Hugh P.S. Wace (b.1948) *Elected in* 1994

Horatio Waddington (d.1867) 1846-1849

H.T. Waddy 1920-1924

Gilbert Wakefield 1932-1949

Francis Arthur John Wakeman-Long (d.1986) 1958-1986

F.P. Walesby 1840-*c.*1845

Andrew Felix Waley, Q.C. (d.1995) 1963-1995

Jacob Waley (1818-1873) 1864-1873

John H. Walford (1927-2008) 1979-2008

Richard H.H. Walford (b.1960) *Elected in* 1992

Raymond Walker (d.2009) 1979-2009

Walker-Smith, *see also* Broxbourne

Sir Jonah Walker-Smith, 2nd Bt. (b.1939) *Elected in* 1992

Thomas Wallace (d.1855) 1854-1855

Rt.Hon. Lord Justice Mark Waller (b.1941) *Elected in* 1977

John Walls 1846-1849

Dennis Walsh 1958-1960

James Walsh 1838-1841

Arthur James Walter (d.1919) 1898-1919

Bryan M. Walter (d.1984) 1962-1984

Robin Walter (b.1950) *Elected in* 1991

Robert Walters (d.1843) 1835-1837

Robert Walters (1832-1912) 1858-1912

Rt.Hon. Sir Alan Ward (b.1938) *Elected in* 2006

Arthur Samuel Ward, K.C. 1943-1950

W.R. Ward 1837-*c.*1840

Tomasz Wardynski, C.B.E. (b.1947) *Elected in* 2005

Aucher Warner, K.C. (1859-1944) 1915-1922

C.J. Warner (d.1915) 1911-1915

Ian S. Warren (b.1917) *Elected in* 1972

Sir Ronald Waterhouse, Q.C. (1926-2011) 1964-2011

His Hon. Rev. (David) Brian Watling, Q.C. (b.1935) 1981-2006

Captain Basil Watson, K.C. 1920-1933

Sir (John) Bertrand Watson (1878-1948) 1943-1948

Roderick Anthony Watson, Q.C. (d.1993) 1962-1993

W. Trevor Watson, K.C. (d.1943) 1923-1943

Laurence Watt (b.1946) *Elected in* 1997

William James Waugh, K.C. 1921-1927

Colonel Stanley Webb-Johnson (d.1965) 1952-1965

His Hon. David M. Webster, Q.C. (b.1937) *Elected in* 1982

Tom Weitzman, Q.C. (b.1959) *Elected in* 2004

Sir Mordaunt Lawson Wells (d.1885) 1866-1881

William Newland Welsby (1803-1864) 1856-1864

David G. Westcott, Q.C. (b.1957) *Elected in* 2009

His Hon. Sir David West-Russell (1921-2004) 1973-2002

Michael Mortimer Wheeler, Q.C. (1915-1992) 1961-1992

Theodore W. Whipham *Elected in* 1847

Antony C. Whitaker, O.B.E. (b.1934) *Elected in* 1994

Charles Whitby, Q.C. (1926-2003) 1970-2003

Sir Arnold W. White (d.1893) 1873-1893

Frederic White (d.1909) 1894-1909

Frederick Meadows White, Q.C. (1829-1898) 1877-1898

Henry Arnold White 1894-1904

William White 1856-1872

Charles P. Whitehead 1958-1985

(Edward Francis) Romilly Whitehead *Elected in* 1956

W. Richard L. Whittam, Q.C. (b.1959) *Elected in* 2007

James Lowry Whittle 1870-1909

Grover Wickersham (b.1949) *Elected in* 2008

David Graham Widdicombe, M.C., Q.C. 1966-2005

John Passmore Widgery, Baron Widgery (1911-1981) 1971-1981

Arthur James Wigram (d.1875) 1866-1875

Sir James Wigram (1793-1866) *Original member*-1832

Richard Wilberforce, Baron Wilberforce (1907-2003) 1931-1948

Sir Ernest Edward Wild (1869-1934) 1902-1934

William Wilkins *Elected in* 1849

Josiah Wilkinson 1878-c.1914

Leonard Rodwell Wilkinson (1868-1913) 1912-1913

Richard A. Willes 1929-1949

Henry R. Willett (d.1857) *Original member*-1857

Andrew C. Williams (b.1952) *Elected in* 1999

Charles Riddell Dingwall Williams (d.1973) 1924-1973

Ernest Edwin Williams (d.1935) 1919-1935

Geoffrey Bridgewater Williams (d.1959) 1921-1959

Sir Max Williams (b.1926) *Elected in* 1962

Montagu Stephen Williams, Q.C. (1835-1892) 1873-1892

Peter Williams 1888-1907

Romer Williams 1893-1925

W.H. Williams 1959-1980

Augustus P. Williams-Freeman (d.1906) 1894-1906

James Shaw Willis 1841-1858

Sir John Ramsay Willis (1908-1988) 1955-1988

His Hon. Roger Willis (d.1996) 1969-1996

Geoffrey D.M. Willoughby (1936-1989) 1982-1989

Sir Charles Rodger Noel Winn (1903-1972) 1949-1971

Sir John Withers (1863-1939) 1920-1930

Thomas Withers (d.1931) 1921-1931

Harry Wolton, Q.C. (b.1938) *Elected in* 2002

(Arthur) Giles Wontner *Elected in* 1975

Blanchard Allen Wontner (1839-1908) 1901-1908

John Wood (d.1905) 1878-1905

Sir John K. Wood, M.C. (b.1922) *Elected in* 1981

Hedley Stewart Maxwell Wood (d.2011) 1971-1995; 1998-2011

Robert Woodriff 1834-c.1845

Sir Raymond Woods (1882-1943) 1917-1943

Harry Woolf, Baron Woolf (b.1933) *Elected in* 1977

Charles F. Wordsworth *Elected in* 1845

Michael D.L. Worsley, Q.C. (b.1926) 1981-2009; *re-elected in* 2010

George Octavius Wray 1864-1866

J. Wright 1833-1837

F.T. Wrigley 1890-1903

David J.C. Wyld (b.1943) *Elected in* 2001

Y
—

Richard G.A. Youard 1990-2008

Younger, *see* Blanesburgh

Z
—

Ludwik Zucker (d.1985) 1975-1985

INDEX